Myself and Other Animals

Ann Danvale

Myself and Other Animals

GERALD DURRELL

**PENGUIN
VIKING**

VIKING

UK | USA | Canada | Ireland | Australia
India | New Zealand | South Africa

Viking is part of the Penguin Random House group of companies
whose addresses can be found at global.penguinrandomhouse.com.

Penguin Random House UK,
One Embassy Gardens, 8 Viaduct Gardens, London SW11 7BW

penguin.co.uk

Penguin
Random House
UK

First published 2024

001

Set in 12/14.75pt Dante MT Std
Typeset by Jouve (UK), Milton Keynes
Printed and bound in Great Britain by Clays Ltd, Elcograf S.p.A.

The authorized representative in the EEA is Penguin Random House Ireland,
Morrison Chambers, 32 Nassau Street, Dublin D02 YH68

A CIP catalogue record for this book is available from the British Library

ISBN: 978–0–241–73813–9

Penguin Random House is committed to a sustainable future
for our business, our readers and our planet. This book is made from
Forest Stewardship Council® certified paper.

MIX
Paper | Supporting
responsible forestry
FSC® C018179

Table of Contents

Foreword by Her Royal Highness
The Princess Royal, Princess Anne   ix

Preface by Lee Durrell   xi

How to Give Birth to an Autobiography   1

PART ONE: ON FAMILY: FROM INDIA TO CORFU

A Silver Spoon in His Mouth   7

Mother's Delusions of Grandeur   11

Like Being Born for the First Time   19

The Strawberry-Pink Villa   21

Tribute to My Mother   34

The World in a Wall   35

A Treasure of Spiders   42

An Omnipotent, Benign and Humorous
Greek God   50

Island Education   53

Surrounded by Miracles   64

PART TWO: ON ANIMALS: ZOOLOGICAL ADVENTURES
TO THE FOUR CORNERS OF THE EARTH

Cameroon   70

New and Rediscovered Animals   70

Table of Contents

Rainforests   72

Ground Nut Chop   74

The Hunt for the Hairy Frog   75

Some Interesting Things Which Have Happened   82

Brow-leaf Toads   85

South America   91

A Charm All of Its Own   91

The Magical Creek Lands   103

The Kitten   113

Vanished Peoples of Patagonia   120

Central America   129

Jabirus and Jaguars   129

New Zealand, Australia and Malaysia   138

Letter to Mother from New Zealand   139

Operation Takahe   146

Australian Friends   152

Great Barrier Reef   161

Dragons and Giants from the Sea   170

Mauritius & Madagascar   177

The Enchanted World   178

Miraculous Madagascar   190

Whiffling through Its Tulgey Wood   199

PART THREE: MORE BIRDS AND BEASTS:
ANIMALS I'VE KNOWN AND LOVED

The Abominable Snowman   205

Little Brown Jobs   215

Table of Contents

A Tortoise Called Melville   219

The Art of Birdwatching   224

Dogs in My Life   228

An Explorer in Lilliput   237

Panda Politics   240

PART FOUR: ON THE ARK: NOTES ON CONSERVATION

First Job   245

Student Keeper   256

'Who do you know that is stinking rich . . .'   259

A Zoo in My Luggage   263

A Zoo that is More than a Zoo   275

A Zoo of My Own   282

Letter to J. F. Lipscomb   288

A Successful Marriage   290

Return to the Wild   300

The Princess and the Zoo   312

Extinct and Vanishing Animals   317

Time Capsule   330

Message from Durrell Wildlife Conservation Trust   332

Acknowledgements   333

Sources   335

List of Illustrations   337

BUCKINGHAM PALACE

Twenty-five years ago I wrote a foreword for a collection of the best of Gerald Durrell's writings, and I am equally delighted to do so again today. To celebrate his life and times in his centenary year, 2025, this new book brings together some much-loved pieces as well as unpublished memoires.

Gerald Durrell was a remarkable man, not only for his incomparable way with words, which move his readers from laughter to tears, from despair to joy with respect to nature, but also for the fact that he took effective action to make the world a better place for all living beings and the wild places they inhabit. He established a unique zoo and a charitable trust with a single purpose in mind: to save species from extinction and make people aware of the importance of doing so.

The work of Durrell Wildlife Conservation Trust has gone from strength to strength in the thirty years since its Founder passed away and will no doubt continue to do so, saving species and restoring their habitats, training conservationists, collaborating with local communities and reconnecting people

ix

with nature. For Gerry's work is not finished yet. As Sir David Attenborough said, 'The world needs Durrell.'

I would add that the world will continue to need Durrell for the future. I hope your children and grandchildren will become part of that vital work.

Anne

Preface
by Lee Durrell

In the one hundred years since Gerald Durrell was born, much has happened from the human perspective. Life expectancy has been prolonged from less than forty years to more than seventy. Medicine has progressed from antibiotics to gene editing, and technology from television to smartphones and AI. World literacy has risen from 32 per cent to 86 per cent, and extreme poverty dropped from 60 per cent to 9 per cent. This sounds like a wonderful time to be a human being.

The global population, however, has mushroomed from about 2 billion to just under 8 billion. Feeding those 8 billion has destroyed 90 per cent of the world's forests and accounts for 70 per cent of the world's freshwater consumption. Humans and their livestock outweigh all the wild mammals of land and sea by a staggering factor of seventeen.

Currently, species are disappearing at least a hundred, possibly a thousand or more, times faster than the 'normal' rate of extinction. Half of the species of vertebrates and insects are in population decline, as are nearly half of plant species. Decline obviously precedes extinction, but while it is happening, it disrupts the balance of animal and plant communities, which in turn disturbs the broader workings of ecosystems, such as soil production, nutrient recycling, plant pollination, air and water purification and climate stabilization, to name just a few of the functions on which all living beings, including humans, rely.

If the 10 million or so other species with which we share the planet have a perspective, it would no doubt be one of pessimism.

This rapid and substantial loss of biodiversity is unlike the previous mass extinctions on Earth, which were triggered by 'natural' phenomena such as volcanic eruption and meteorite impact. The ensuing climate change resulted in the disappearance of species over thousands, even millions of years. Today's loss, however, is caused by us alone: by our profligate use of the planet's resources to serve our own interests, with its many dangerous side-effects, including habitat destruction, over-exploitation, pollution, climate change and extinction.

There is no excuse now for not knowing that humans and other species are intricately and inextricably linked, and that what happens to one species has consequences for the others. When Gerald Durrell started writing, few people understood this, and even fewer were willing to accept some sort of responsibility to try and put things right. Gerry sounded the alarm more than half a century ago when he wrote, 'The world is as delicate and as complicated as a spider's web, and like a spider's web, if you touch one thread, you send shudders running through all the other threads that make up the web. But we're not just touching the web, we're tearing great holes in it . . .'

Gerry's books were hugely popular and immensely influential, and their impact on environmental awareness, lifestyle choices, education and nature writing in the twentieth and twenty-first centuries cannot be overstated.

His classic work *My Family and Other Animals* still gives rise to comments such as 'it helped me learn to read', 'it made me love reading' and 'it awakened in me a love of nature'. For many young people this book was what led them to their careers in science and conservation.

As a writer, Gerry will be remembered for his lyrical prose, his sense of humour and his extraordinary empathy with the natural world, particularly animals. This last is fundamental to how he will be remembered as a conservationist – he championed *all* animals, not just the charismatic, large, fierce or pretty creatures, but also the obscure, the small, the drab, the ones he nicknamed the 'the little brown jobs' or sometimes 'the little ones of God'. He knew that all species are components of ecosystems which make our planet tick. He believed that we, the human animal, had no right to drive any other species to extinction.

But Gerry did not just talk and write about conservation – he actually did it, he lived and breathed it. His mission was simply stated – *to save species from extinction*. That mission lives on through the work of the charity he set up more than sixty years ago, now called Durrell Wildlife Conservation Trust. The results of the trust's efforts to date are impressive: we have helped over one hundred species recover from the brink of extinction.

Durrell Conservation Academy, based at Jersey Zoo, has trained more than 7,000 conservation practitioners from more than two-thirds of the world's countries in the complex aspects of conservation. The academy was one of Gerry's proudest achievements. Even in the earliest days of Jersey Zoo he would say that rare animals should be bred for conservation purposes in their countries of origin, but lamented the lack of expertise in captive breeding. He dreamed of bringing together people from all over the world to work with our staff at the zoo, learn how to care for and breed our animals and then return to their own countries to put their new knowledge and skills into practice. Our first student arrived in 1978, and by 1984 the 'mini-university for conservation' was in full swing, officially opened by HRH Princess Anne, who had been our Royal Patron for twelve years.

I recall a particularly emotional moment with Gerry soon after the academy's official opening. We were playing croquet on the lawn with a dozen conservationist hopefuls from a dozen different countries. Gerry burst into tears, saying that he hadn't believed his dream would come true, and yet here he was, surrounded by his students who'd come from all corners of the earth to learn how to save their own precious animals, plants and wild places.

What do the next one hundred years hold for our planet? Gerry often said that so-called human progress moves at the speed of an Exocet missile, whereas conservation moves at the pace of a donkey and cart. In recent years there have been some amazingly positive breakthroughs in how we use the planet's resources and in environmental awareness, such as the switch to renewable energy and the desire to 'reduce, reuse, recycle', but are these enough to forestall the existential threats of mass extinction and climate change?

In a hundred years, dare we hope 'that there will be fireflies and glow-worms at night to guide you and butterflies in hedges and forests to greet you . . . that your dawns will have an orchestra of birdsong and that the sound of their wings and the opalescence of their colouring will dazzle you . . . that there will still be the extraordinary varieties of creatures sharing the land of the planet with you to enchant you and enrich your lives as they have done for us . . . '?

Gerald Durrell did. He ended this prose poem he wrote nearly four decades ago with optimism: 'We hope that you will be grateful for having been born into such a magical world.'

How to Give Birth to an Autobiography

When you set out to write your autobiography, it has, as I have discovered, a very salutary effect on diminishing one's self-esteem.

Full of enthusiasm, you have sharpened up your goose quill (metaphorically speaking), the inkwell is brimming, the capacious sandbox is ready to dry each precious sheet of parchment, but then you are suddenly overcome with terrible doubts, the chief one being that, while you know that you are the most interesting person in the world, will everyone else share your view?

A disturbing thought.

There cannot be, you say smugly to yourself, anyone in the English-speaking world who is so uncouth and illiterate as to not share your views of yourself. Comforted with this tarradiddle, you announce your intention to your friends. They immediately laugh and say that you have written over thirty books, most of which have been more or less autobiographical, so what is there left to say?

I explain, rather tartly, that when you have travelled as much as I have and met such an extraordinary variety of *Homo sapiens* and other astonishing creatures, there is always plenty more to say. When you have spent, for example, six months in a country collecting live animals and you sit down to write a book about it, it is not the paucity of material that alarms you, but the sheer bulk of it. You spend an enormous amount of time dissecting and selecting this rich material, busy as a jackdaw in a jewellery box. You choose one memory and polish it into a paragraph, but the moment it is – as it were – planted, it in turn produces a hundred side shoots, a hundred more roots suddenly giving way to myriad experiences you had forgotten. If I had used all the material from just one of my trips, each book would have been approximately 800,000 words long and still have left me with a huge pile of notes and anecdotes.

I have always said I dislike writing, which I suppose is not strictly true. What I do not enjoy is the self-inflicted discipline of writing. What I do enjoy is the juxtaposition of words or the amalgamation of sentences to create an effect. I suspect that people who are addicted to crossword puzzles get the same satisfaction when they see a word slot neatly into place. I think painters get the same feeling when they shade one colour into another and find it true and pleasing. I think sculptors get it when they release a beautiful body trapped in a slab of stone. However, the crossword addict, the painter and the sculptor are different from the writer. The crossword addict has private fulfilment, and the painter has the satisfaction of seeing admiring guests at his exhibitions, as does the sculptor. However, the author is a lonely soul, like an albatross. He desires connection with the reader but does not know if his carefully structured sentences truly portray (as in my case) the furry intimacy of a bird-eating spider, the throbbing crucible of incandescent colour that is a hummingbird. He does not know if what he thinks is funny is merely funny to him but not to a thousand other people. He has the black looming shadow always over his shoulder, the knowledge that he can write 50,000 words and no one will read them or, if they do, understand what he is trying to say.

Take diaries, for example. I have, in my youth, floundered through so many political and scientific diaries that one begins to almost feel an antipathy to the English language. A friend of my brother's kept a diary from the age of seven to the time of her death and I cannot imagine anything more introspective or boring. I admit that I have, on occasion, kept diaries but they were more like simple logbooks. I find that if I keep a detailed diary, when I come to write a book I simply copy the diary down instead of using it as an aide-mémoire, which is what you should do when writing.

Fortunately, I have been blessed with a very retentive memory and so these jottings, though somewhat haphazard, do represent my past life.

It was George III who, when presented with a complimentary copy by the author of Gibbon's *Decline and Fall of the Roman Empire*, said, 'Another damn, great, thick book. Scribble, scribble, scribble, Mr. Gibbon, huh?'

I hope that these scribbles will amuse.

PART ONE

On Family

From India to Corfu

'The child is mad, snails in his pockets!'

Lawrence Durrell, c. 1931

In India, I saw, heard and felt and smelt (zoo) with a great intensity. The colours stirred me as they were illuminated by the sunshine. Back in England of course I experienced the same sensations, but they were bland, subdued, the difference between eating a curry and a blanc-mange. When I got to Corfu the sun injected me and all my senses came to full life again. Corfu town – sea smell – olive groves – sun smell.

– Fragment from unpublished autobiography

My childhood in Corfu shaped my life and even today I can recall Win-ters when the winds made the sun-blistered shutters chatter like teeth, when Spring spread a Persian carpet of flowers among the olives, and when Summers were endlessly blue, chorused by the zither of cicadas. If I had the craft of Merlin, I would give every child the gift of my childhood.

– 'My Favourite Photograph', *Sunday Express*, 1993

A Silver Spoon in His Mouth

I was born in Jamshedpur, India, on 7 January 1925. My diminutive mother swelled up to an unwonted degree while she was pregnant and went into hiding because she was so ashamed of her enormous size. She said she was infuriated by my father because he suggested that what she needed to do was to get out and about, and go down to the club, the centre at which all the Great White Raj used to congregate. She said to him, 'How can I possibly go out looking like this? I look like an elephant.' Whereupon my father suggested that she wore a howdah, and she didn't speak to him for two days. Unlike other ladies, who have a craving for asparagus or tonnes of coal, she had a craving for champagne and drank it in inordinate quantities. I am sure that this is the reason that I have, throughout my life, always had a strong penchant for alcohol.

Mother said that the birth was very simple. I slipped out of her like an otter into a pool. The great number of people employed by my father, and our enormous household staff, clustered round to congratulate, and my mother said that the curious thing was that, although everybody congratulated her on the births of my brothers and my sister, on this particular occasion they said, 'Ah, he is born with a silver spoon in his mouth.' Looking back at my life, I see that they were quite right, because I have had a charmed life.

My first really coherent thoughts were at the age of two. That was a time when, I think, my senses of smell, hearing, touch and taste developed. My ayah refused to wake me up unless it was to the gramophone, because otherwise I could be grumpy and morose and she couldn't do anything with me. The gramophone was a wind-up one, and, although it was very scratchy, like a lot of mice in a tin box, it was wonderful to my ears, and I would wake up with a beaming smile on my face, which made my ayah heave a sigh of relief.

At that time, I used to be dressed in little shorts and a tunic made out of tussore and I can remember how delicious this silky material felt on my body as my ayah dressed me. I can also remember the wonderful taste of my favourite breakfast, which was rice boiled in buffalo milk, with sugar.

My sense of colour, I think, came from watching everybody around me who was dressed so beautifully, so subtly and yet so flamboyantly. I remember going for a walk one day with my ayah, who was wearing a snow-white sari. We were walking along a laterite road, and I noticed how marvellous the white was against that extraordinary, almost blood-red soil. At one point during our walk, we met some friends of hers and again I was astonished by colours. The man, wearing a turban, was dressed all in white with a green cummerbund, but his wife – as gaudy as any bird – was wearing a magenta sari. I was riveted by it, and it has remained one of my favourite colours.

I left my ayah (bent on a long gossip) and wandered to the edge of the road, where there was a shallow ditch in which were two slugs. To me they looked enormous, but they were probably only three or four inches long. They were gently sliding over each other in what looked like a dance. They were a pale coffee colour with black, ridged stripes. They were glutinous and beautiful. I watched them for some time until my ayah suddenly discovered I had escaped her and she came and told me I must not touch slugs as they were dirty. I could not understand that she should think such beautiful, shiny creatures could be dirty, and throughout my life I have met so many people who think things are disgusting or dirty or dangerous when they are nothing of the sort but miraculous pieces of creation.

There was a little local zoo, and once having been there, nothing could keep me away. In fact, it drove my ayah to despair because twice a day she had to take me for a walk, and when asked where I wanted to go, I would say 'Zoo!', loudly and belligerently. My ayah was forced to complain to my mother that there was no other place that I wanted to go for my walks. If I was not taken to the zoo, my screams of frustration could be heard to the top of Mount Everest and as far south as Australia. They had, in minuscule cages, a leopard, a tiger and a small group of monkeys. I remember the lovely black freckles on the leopard's skin and the tiger, as he walked to and fro, looking like a rippling golden sea. It was the strong scent of these big cats that lingers in my memory. Probably the cages were never cleaned out and certainly, if I saw the zoo today, I would be the first one to have it closed down. But to me as a child it was a magic place, and it instilled in me my deep interest in and love of animals.

As Gerry discovered his five senses and the richness of life they revealed, he also became aware of death and loss. His father, Lawrence Durrell Sr, a well-known and respected civil engineer in India, died of a brain haemorrhage when Gerry was three years old. Gerry's mother, Louisa Durrell, was heartbroken and gave in to the urgings of family and friends to 'go home to England'. Their first two abodes were in the suburbs of London, the third and fourth in Bournemouth – Berridge House and Dixie Lodge.

Mother's Delusions of Grandeur

Needless to say, Mother's delusions of grandeur could not be confined. She decided – on the advice of some friends – to move to Bournemouth, that salubrious seaside resort stuffed with genteel ladies eking out modest pensions while trying to keep up appearances, and decaying members of Her Majesty's Forces, straight-backed, heavily moustached, who spent most of their remaining years writing indignant letters to *The Times* or the local paper, the *Echo*.

Here, Mother discovered what can only be described as a mini-mansion, Berridge House, lurking in some four acres of grounds, which included an orchard, a pine wood, a lawn on which one could play two games of tennis simultaneously, and a herbaceous border slightly wider than the Nile and home to nearly every known weed, with the exception of Mandrake.

The house itself had gigantic attics fit for a coven of witches, a cellar which Dracula would have envied and, in between, a parquet-floored ballroom running the length and width of the house, a huge kitchen and dining room and enough bedrooms to give succour to at least twenty people. When asked by someone if it was not a trifle large for a widowed lady and one small boy, she answered – rather vaguely – that it had to have room for her children's friends (Margo at Malvern, Leslie at Dulwich and Larry at a crammer's). The fact that they could have brought every pupil from each of their schools and still left a number of rooms empty passed unnoticed.

But, incarcerated in this gigantic house with only a small

boy as company, Mother took to mourning the death of my father in earnest with the aid of Demon Drink. Needless to say, I was unaware of this. To me, the vast, overgrown garden was a world to explore and delight in. To have an orchard where you picked the pink-cheeked apples and felt the sharp juice trickle down your chin, plucked ripe, sun-warmed apricots from a tree that sprawled across the sunny flank of the house – fruit golden as honey, soft as velvet – all this was, to me, bliss.

Mother, rather unsteadily, fought to get the herbaceous border to look like the pictures on the seed packets and gave me cooking lessons in the unwieldy kitchen, full of archaic culinary clobber. But, idyllic as it was to me, it could not last. So Miss Burroughs entered our lives. She had a face which disappointment had crumpled, and embedded in it were two eyes, grey and sharp as flints.

Mother departed to a nursing home to have what was, in those days, called a nervous breakdown, and I and Miss Burroughs, in the huge echoing house, made our awkward acquaintance. I don't think she had ever had to deal with a small boy before and so to begin with was terrified that I might disappear. A regime of door locking was instituted, as if I were a dangerous prisoner. I was locked in the kitchen, the drawing room and the dining room, but the worst was that she banished Simon from my bedroom, saying that dogs were full of germs, and locked me in at night so that by morning my bladder was bursting and I dared not wet the bed for fear of some terrible retribution.

Another thing was that Miss Burroughs's cooking left nearly everything to be desired. She is the only person I have ever met who put sago in the gruel she called soup so that it was like drinking frog spawn. Gone were the delicious curries Mother used to concoct, gone the steaming bowls of rice like elongated pearls, chutneys like liquid amber filled with delicious fruit, gone the wonderful Indian sweets like jalebi cooked in sugar.

If the weather was bad, I was confined to the ballroom, where Simon and I would invent our own games.

Sometimes, miraculously, he would become a pride of lions and I a lone Christian in an arena. As I prepared to strangle him, he would behave in the most un-lionlike way, slobbering over me with his crooning endearments. At other times, I would change into a dog and follow him round the ballroom on all fours, panting when he panted, scratching when he scratched and flinging myself down in abandoned attitudes as he did.

Although basically a coward, he would hunt imaginary tigers or elephants with me with great skill and cunning and, when our prey (my teddy bear) was captured, we would sing a rapturous duet together. I tried, without success, to teach him the Charleston, but he could waltz fairly successfully on his hind legs if I held his front paws in an iron grip.

Although the house and grounds of Dixie Lodge were not nearly as extensive as those of Berridge House, it was a pleasanter place and the garden contained a number of very climbable trees and groups of shrubs, which were home to all sorts of strange insects. So I settled down there quite happily under the raucous and benign influence of Lottie, our Swiss maid. But then Mother did something so terrible that I was bereft of words. She enrolled me in the local school, and not a pleasant kindergarten like The Birches, where you sang and made things out of plasticine and drew pictures. This was a real school where they expected you to learn things like algebra and mathematics and history and – what was anathema to me above all else – sports. It was run on the lines of most schools in those days, where your scholastic achievements did not matter so very much as long as you were a good sportsman. As both my scholastic achievements and my interest in sports were nil, I was, not unnaturally, somewhat of a dullard. In cricket, for example, a slow game whose rules I could never master, I spent a lot of time watching the activities of the bees in the clover, with the result that I missed several potential catches. Football was even worse for my only achievement in this field was to kick with unerring accuracy the ball straight into our own goal. The only part of the curriculum which would appeal to me was the one and a half hours per week given over to natural history, and this was taken by the gym mistress, Miss Allard, a tall blonde lady with protuberant blue eyes. As soon as she realized my genuine interest in natural history, she went out of her way to take a lot of trouble with me, and therefore she became my heroine.

Among the acquaintances that we made was one Alan Thomas, who ran the magnificent Commins Bookshop. He and Larry struck up an immediate friendship and it was practically every evening that Alan used to come round to have a meal with us and drink and sing to the piano. Not long after I had joined the unhappy ranks of Witchwood Boys, Alan spotted the headmaster browsing in his shop. He went up to him and said, 'Oh, I believe you have the son of some friends of mine at school.'

'Oh?' said the headmaster. 'What's the name?'

'Durrell, Gerald Durrell,' Alan replied.

'The most ignorant boy in the school,' snapped the headmaster, and stalked out of the shop.

We had to do a lot in gym, which meant climbing up ladders and sliding down ropes, all to no purpose as far as I could see, and then once a week a torture so monstrous that even today I shudder at the thought of it. There was a tiled room in which there was a small swimming pool, and we were stripped and ranged shiveringly along the edge. Then each one of us had a huge canvas belt fitted round their waist which allowed them to be lowered into the water, like a frozen bouquet garni, and instructions as to what to do with their arms and legs were shouted at them. I, of course, like many of the other pupils, did not learn how to swim.

There was amongst us a very unpleasant boy who, if he saw anyone struggling, would try to rattle them further and then report their poor performance to the master or mistress in charge of whatever punitive manoeuvre we were supposed to be undertaking. Thus, quite innocent people had to go up to see the headmaster, the ultimate in threats. One day this boy had been particularly obnoxious to me and I forget exactly how things turned out but I saw an opportunity to get my own back and seized it, whereupon his wails of distress had to be heard to be believed, and I was immediately told that I would have to go up to see the headmaster within the half hour. I went up the broad staircase into the upper part of the house and tapped timidly on the door of the great man's sanctum. He told me to come in and then gave me a lecture on bullying and how I would never get on in life if I persisted in this sort of attitude. Then he made me take down my trousers and bend over a chair. He delivered six hearty, stinging slaps to my backside and then said he hoped he wouldn't have occasion to see me up in his study again.

It was fortunate that this had happened at the end of the day. I was flushed with embarrassment, mortification and rage. Nobody had ever lifted a finger to me, however bad my misdemeanour might have been. I half ran, half walked back home, the tears streaming down my face. I burst into the house and told the whole story to my horrified mother. I was shaking like a leaf with indignation and the unpleasantness of the whole thing. Mother wrapped me up in a blanket, put me by the fire and made me an eggnog.

'Don't you worry,' she said. 'That's the last time you'll be going to that school.'

She then sat down and wrote to the headmaster saying she had no intention of keeping her son at a school where the children were flogged for misdemeanours. Larry, arriving home in the midst of this, said he thought Mother was making far too great a fuss.

'Nonsense,' said Mother, 'the boy was terribly upset, and you would have been too, if you'd been flogged.'

'You can't call a few slaps on the bum a flogging,' said Larry. 'You're talking about it as though he had been brutalized by a cat o' nine tails.'

'Nevertheless,' said Mother, 'he is not going to go back.'

The only part of Witchwood that I regretted leaving was the natural history courses with Miss Allard, and I asked Mother whether we could invite Miss Allard to tea. She said of course we could and wrote to Miss Allard, who came up and partook of scones and cream and sponge cake and hot tea with us. I showed her, with great pride, my white mice, my wigged canary and my collection of stones which I added to every time we went for a walk on the beach, and she was visibly impressed by all this. She said to Mother that she had tried to prevent the happening that had so distressed me for she knew the other little boy was a very unpleasant bully, but unfortunately she couldn't do much about it.

On my recovery, Mother decided that I needed a present of some sort to expunge the episode from my mind, so we got on one of the clanking trams and went down to the pet shop.

Mother said that I could choose a dog for myself. There was a whole litter of curly-headed black puppies in the window, and I stood for a long time contemplating them and wondering which one I should buy. At length I decided on the outcast runt of the litter, and he turned out to be one of the bravest and loveliest dogs that I have ever had. Roger grew rapidly into something resembling a small Airedale covered with the sort of curls you found on a poodle. He was very intelligent and soon mastered several tricks such as dying for his king and country and 'credit and paid for'. This was a rather useful trick, actually. What you did was to put two pieces of food on the ground and tell him that one was paid for and the other one was on credit. He could eat the one that was paid for, but he then had to wait until you told him that the one on credit could be eaten.

With Roger the garden became an even more exciting place, for there were two of us to have adventures within it. But then Lottie's husband grew desperately ill in Brighton, I think with some form of cancer, and so, reluctantly, Lottie had to leave us in order to attend to his sick-bed. Thus we got back to square one. Lonely evenings, where Mother had only me for company, as Larry was busy trying to earn a living in London and could only come down for weekends. So loneliness, of course, edged Mother closer and closer to the Demon Drink. Larry, recognizing the pitfalls that lay ahead, decided that decisive action must be taken.

The Durrell family missed India – the colours, the warmth, the exuberance. Louisa had lived there all her life, and her children, Larry, Leslie, Margo and Gerry, felt little affinity with England, which Larry referred to as 'Pudding Island'. In the seven years since they had left India, the first three children had nearly grown – Larry a budding writer, Leslie obsessed with firearms, Margo bored with school. Gerry was ten and fascinated by animals. Driven by the English weather (and possibly Louisa's looming penury) and urged by a friend of Larry who sang the praises of the Greek island of Corfu, they departed England in 1935, Corfu-bound.

Like Being Born for the First Time

It was an overnight run and so, very early in the morning, we were up on deck, straining our eyes to see our new destination, our new home. We rounded the north end of the island with great slabs of rock and tottering bookcase-like cliffs, on top of which grew vast quantities of broom. As the ship went into the main grand bay of Corfu, the sun was gilding the sea with a dozen different colours, and we saw the great eiderdowns of green-grey olives with, here and there, clusters of cypress trees like black pencils, and when the ship had dropped anchor and silence more or less prevailed we could hear some wonderful creaky singing of cicadas. We had arrived at a place that was to be of enormous influence on all of us and me in particular. It was like being allowed back into Paradise.

It's hard to describe the impact Corfu had on us, after the rather sedate lives we had been leading in England. It was as though our English world had been depicted in pastels, whereas as soon as we got to the Mediterranean everything was painted in oils of the most vivid colours. And then of course there was the light. In England the light was always muted, diffuse, always seen through a sort of veil, even when it wasn't raining. In Corfu the light was so intense, so brilliant that it brought out every minute detail of landscape, trees, creatures, the sea and the rocks. This brilliant light, of course, heightened not only the colours but also the scents of flowers, trees, the sea and the very earth of which the island was constructed.

Our arrival in Corfu was like being born for the first time and we all of us felt this in different ways.

The Strawberry-Pink Villa

The villa was small and square, standing in its tiny garden with an air of pink-faced determination. Its shutters had been faded by the sun to a delicate creamy green, cracked and bubbled in places. The garden, surrounded by tall fuchsia hedges, had flower beds worked in complicated geometrical patterns, marked with smooth white stones. The white cobbled paths, scarcely as wide as a rake's head, wound laboriously round beds hardly larger than a big straw hat, beds in the shape of stars, half-moons, triangles, and circles, all overgrown with a shaggy tangle of flowers run wild. Roses dropped petals that seemed as big and smooth as saucers, flame red, moon white, glossy, and unwrinkled; marigolds like broods of shaggy suns stood watching their parent's progress through the sky. In the low growth the pansies pushed their velvety, innocent faces through the leaves, and the violets drooped sorrowfully under their heart-shaped leaves. The bougainvillæa that sprawled luxuriously over the tiny front balcony was hung, as though for a carnival, with its lantern-shaped magenta flowers. In the darkness of the fuchsia hedge a thousand ballerina-like blooms quivered expectantly. The warm air was thick with the scent of a hundred dying flowers, and full of the gentle, soothing whisper and murmur of insects. As soon as we saw it, we wanted to live there; it was as though the villa had been standing there waiting for our arrival. We felt we had come home.

Having lumbered so unexpectedly into our lives, Spiro now took over complete control of our affairs. It was better, he explained, for him to do things, as everyone knew him, and he would make sure we were not swindled.

'Donts you worrys yourselfs about anythings, Mrs Durrells,' he had scowled; 'leaves everythings to me.'

So he would take us shopping, and after an hour's sweating and roaring he would get the price of an article reduced by perhaps two drachmas. This was approximately a penny; it was not the cash, but the principle of the thing, he explained. The fact that he was Greek and adored bargaining was, of course, another reason. It was Spiro who, on discovering that our money had not yet arrived from England, subsidized us, and took it upon himself to go and speak severely to the bank manager about his lack of organization. That it was not the poor manager's fault did not deter him in the least. It was Spiro who paid our hotel bill, who organized a car to carry our luggage to the villa, and who drove us out there himself, his car piled high with groceries that he had purchased for us.

That he knew everyone on the island, and that they all knew him, we soon discovered was no idle boast. Wherever his car stopped, half a dozen voices would shout out his name, and hands would beckon him to sit at the little tables under the trees and drink coffee. Policemen, peasants, and priests waved and smiled as he passed; fishermen, grocers, and café owners greeted him like a brother. 'Ah, Spiro!' they would say, and smile at him affectionately as though he were a naughty but lovable child. They respected his honesty and his belligerence, and above all they adored his typically Greek scorn and fearlessness when dealing with any form of governmental red tape. On arrival, two of our cases containing linen and other things had been confiscated by the customs on the curious grounds that they were merchandise. So, when we moved out to the strawberry-pink villa and the problem of bed linen arose, Mother told Spiro about our cases languishing in the customs, and asked his advice.

'Gollys, Mrs Durrells,' he bellowed, his huge face flushing red with wrath; 'whys you never tells me befores? Thems bastards in the customs. I'll take you down theres tomorrows and fix thems: I knows thems alls, and they knows me. Leaves everythings to me – I'll fix thems.'

The following morning he drove Mother down to the customs shed. We all accompanied them, for we did not want to miss the fun. Spiro rolled into the customs house like an angry bear.

'Wheres these peoples things?' he inquired of the plump little customs man.

'You mean their boxes of merchandise?' asked the customs official in his best English.

'Whats you thinks I means?'

'They are here,' admitted the official cautiously.

'We've comes to takes thems,' scowled Spiro; 'gets thems ready.' He turned and stalked out of the shed to find someone to help carry the luggage, and when he returned he saw that the customs man had taken the keys from Mother and was just lifting the lid of one of the cases. Spiro, with a grunt of wrath, surged forward and slammed the lid down on the unfortunate man's fingers.

'Whats fors you open it, you sonofabitch?' he asked, glaring.

The customs official, waving his pinched hand about, protested wildly that it was his duty to examine the contents.

'Dutys?' said Spiro with fine scorn. 'Whats you means, dutys? Is it your dutys to attacks innocent foreigners, eh? Treats thems like smugglers, eh? Thats whats yous calls dutys?'

Spiro paused for a moment, breathing deeply; then he picked

up a large suitcase in each great hand and walked towards the door. He paused and turned to fire his parting shot.

'I knows you, Christaki, sos donts you go talkings about dutys to me. I remembers when you was fined twelve thousand drachmas for dynamitings fish. I won't have any criminal talkings to me abouts dutys.'

We rode back from the customs in triumph, all our luggage intact and unexamined.

'Thems bastards thinks they owns the islands,' was Spiro's comment. He seemed quite unaware of the fact that he was acting as though he did.

Once Spiro had taken charge he stuck to us like a burr. Within a few hours he had changed from a taxi driver to our champion, and within a week he was our guide, philosopher, and friend. He became so much a member of the family that very soon there was scarcely a thing we did, or planned to do, in which he was not involved in some way. He was always there, bull-voiced and scowling, arranging things we wanted done, telling us how much to pay for things, keeping a watchful eye on us all and reporting to Mother anything he thought she should know. Like a great, brown, ugly angel he watched over us as tenderly as though we were slightly weak-minded children. Mother he frankly adored, and he would sing her praises in a loud voice wherever we happened to be, to her acute embarrassment.

'You oughts to be carefuls whats you do,' he would tell us, screwing up his face earnestly; 'we donts wants to worrys your mothers.'

'Whatever for, Spiro?' Larry would protest in well-simulated astonishment. 'She's never done anything for us . . . why should we consider her?'

'Gollys, Master Lorrys, donts jokes like that,' Spiro would say in anguish.

'He's quite right, Spiro,' Leslie would say very seriously; 'she's really not much good as a mother, you know.'

'Donts says that, donts says that,' Spiro would roar. 'Honest to Gods, if I hads a mother likes yours I'd gos down every mornings and kisses her feets.'

So we were installed in the villa, and we each settled down and adapted ourselves to our surroundings in our respective ways. Margo, merely by donning a microscopic swim suit and sun-bathing in the olive groves, had collected an ardent band of handsome peasant youths who appeared like magic from an apparently deserted landscape whenever a bee flew too near her or her deck chair needed moving. Mother felt forced to point out that she thought this sun-bathing was rather unwise.

'After all, dear, that costume doesn't cover an awful lot, does it?' she pointed out.

'Oh, Mother, don't be so old-fashioned,' Margo said impatiently. 'After all, you only die once.'

This remark was as baffling as it was true, and successfully silenced Mother.

It had taken three husky peasant boys half an hour's sweating and panting to get Larry's trunks into the villa, while Larry bustled round them, directing operations. One of the trunks was so big it had to be hoisted in through the window. Once they were installed, Larry spent a happy day unpacking them, and the room was so full of books that it was almost impossible to get in or out. Having constructed battlements of books round the outer perimeter, Larry would spend the whole day in there with his typewriter, only emerging dreamily for meals. On the second morning he appeared in a highly irritable frame of mind, for a peasant had tethered his donkey just over the hedge. At regular intervals the beast would throw out its head and let forth a prolonged and lugubrious bray.

'I ask you! Isn't it laughable that future generations should be deprived of my work simply because some horny-handed idiot has tied that stinking beast of burden near my window?' Larry asked.

'Yes, dear,' said Mother, 'why don't you move it if it disturbs you?'

'My dear Mother, I can't be expected to spend my time chasing donkeys about the olive groves. I threw a pamphlet on Theosophy at it; what more do you expect me to do?'

'The poor thing's tied up. You can't expect it to untie itself,' said Margo.

'There should be a law against parking those loathsome beasts anywhere near a house. Can't one of you go and move it?'

'Why should we? It's not disturbing us,' said Leslie.

'That's the trouble with this family,' said Larry bitterly; 'no give and take, no consideration for others.'

'You don't have much consideration for others,' said Margo.

'It's all your fault, Mother,' said Larry austerely; 'you shouldn't have brought us up to be so selfish.'

'I like that!' exclaimed Mother. 'I never did anything of the sort!'

'Well, we didn't get as selfish as this without some guidance,' said Larry.

In the end, Mother and I unhitched the donkey and moved it farther down the hill. Leslie meanwhile had unpacked his revolvers and startled us all with an apparently endless series of explosions while he fired at an old tin can from his bedroom window. After a particularly deafening morning, Larry erupted from his room and said he could not be expected to work if the villa was going to be rocked to its foundations every five minutes. Leslie, aggrieved, said that he had to practise. Larry said it didn't sound like practice, but more like the Indian Mutiny.

Mother, whose nerves had also been somewhat frayed by the reports, suggested that Leslie practise with an empty revolver. Leslie spent half an hour explaining why this was impossible. At length he reluctantly took his tin farther away from the house where the noise was slightly muffled but just as unexpected.

In between keeping a watchful eye on us all, Mother was settling down in her own way. The house was redolent with the scent of herbs and the sharp tang of garlic and onions, and the kitchen was full of a bubbling selection of pots, among which she moved, spectacles askew, muttering to herself. On the table was a tottering pile of books which she consulted from time to time. When she could drag herself away from the kitchen, she would drift happily about the garden, reluctantly pruning and cutting, enthusiastically weeding and planting.

For myself, the garden held sufficient interest; together Roger and I learned some surprising things. Roger, for example, found that it was unwise to smell hornets, that the peasant dogs ran screaming if he glanced at them through the gate, and that the chickens that leaped suddenly from the fuchsia hedge, squawking wildly as they fled, were unlawful prey, however desirable.

This doll's-house garden was a magic land, a forest of flowers through which roamed creatures I had never seen before. Among the thick, silky petals of each rose bloom lived tiny, crablike spiders that scuttled sideways when disturbed. Their small, translucent bodies were coloured to match the flowers they inhabited: pink, ivory, wine red, or buttery yellow. On the rose stems, encrusted with green flies, lady-birds moved like newly painted toys; lady-birds pale red with large black spots; lady-birds apple red with brown spots; lady-birds orange with grey-and-black freckles. Rotund and amiable, they prowled and fed among the anæmic flocks of greenfly. Carpenter bees, like furry, electric-blue bears, zigzagged among the flowers, growling fatly and busily. Humming bird hawk-moths, sleek and neat, whipped up and down the paths with a fussy efficiency, pausing occasionally on speed-misty wings to lower a long, slender proboscis into a bloom. Among the white cobbles large black ants staggered and gesticulated in groups round strange trophies: a dead caterpillar, a piece of rose petal or a dried grass-head fat with seeds. As an accompaniment to all this activity there came from the olive groves outside the fuchsia hedge the incessant shimmering cries of the cicadas. If the curious, blurring heat haze produced a sound, it would be exactly the strange, chiming cries of these insects.

At first I was so bewildered by this profusion of life on our very doorstep that I could only move about the garden in a daze, watching now this creature, now that, constantly having my attention distracted by the flights of brilliant butterflies that drifted over the hedge. Gradually, as I became more used to the bustle of insect life among the flowers, I found I could concentrate more. I would spend hours squatting on my heels or lying on my stomach watching the private lives of the creatures around me, while Roger sat nearby, a look of resignation on his face. In this way I learned a lot of fascinating things.

I found that the little crab spiders could change colour just as successfully as any chameleon. Take a spider from a wine-red rose, where he had been sitting like a bead of coral, and place him in the depths of a cool white rose. If he stayed there – and most of them did – you would see his colour gradually ebb away, as though the change had given him anæmia, until, some two days later, he would be crouching among the white petals like a pearl.

I discovered that in the dry leaves under the fuchsia hedge lived another type of spider, a fierce little huntsman with the cunning and ferocity of a tiger. He would stalk about his continent of leaves, eyes glistening in the sun, pausing now and then to raise himself up on his hairy legs to peer about. If he saw a fly settle to enjoy a sun-bath he would freeze; then, as slowly as a leaf growing, he would move forward, impercept-ibly, edging nearer and nearer, pausing occasionally to fasten his life-line of silk to the surface of the leaves. Then, when close enough, the huntsman would pause, his legs shift minutely as he got a good purchase, and then he would leap, legs spread out in a hairy embrace, straight onto the dreaming fly. Never did I see one of these little spiders miss its kill, once it had man-oeuvred into the right position.

All these discoveries filled me with a tremendous delight, so that they had to be shared, and I would burst suddenly into the house and startle the family with the news that the strange, spiky black caterpillars on the roses were not caterpillars at all, but the young of lady-birds, or with the equally astonishing news that lacewing flies laid eggs on stilts. This last miracle I was lucky enough to witness. I found a lacewing fly on the roses and watched her as she climbed about the leaves, admiring her beautiful, fragile wings like green glass, and her enormous liquid golden eyes. Presently she stopped on the surface of a rose leaf and lowered the tip of her abdomen. She remained like that for a moment and then raised her tail, and from it, to my astonishment, rose a slender thread, like a pale hair. Then, on the very tip of this stalk, appeared the egg. The female had a rest, and then repeated the performance until the surface of the rose leaf looked as though it were covered with a forest of tiny club moss. The laying over, the female rippled her antennæ briefly and flew off in a mist of green gauze wings.

Perhaps the most exciting discovery I made in this multicol-oured Lilliput to which I had access was an earwig's nest. I had long wanted to find one and had searched everywhere without success, so the joy of stumbling upon one unexpectedly was overwhelming, like suddenly being given a wonderful present. I moved a piece of bark and there beneath it was the nursery, a small hollow in the earth that the insect must have burrowed out for herself. She squatted in the middle of it, shielding underneath her a few white eggs. She crouched over them like a hen and did not move when the flood of sunlight struck her as I lifted the bark. I could not count the eggs, but there did not seem to be many, so I presumed that she had not yet laid her full complement. Tenderly I replaced her lid of bark.

From that moment I guarded the nest jealously. I erected a protecting wall of rocks round it, and as an additional precaution I wrote out a notice in red ink and stuck it on a pole nearby as a warning to the family. The notice read: 'BEWAR – EARWIG NEST – QUIAT PLESE.' It was only remarkable in that the two correctly spelled words were biological ones. Every hour or so I would subject the mother earwig to ten minutes' close scrutiny. I did not dare examine her more often for fear she might desert her nest. Eventually the pile of eggs beneath her grew, and she seemed to have become accustomed to my lifting off her bark roof. I even decided that she had begun to recognize me, from the friendly way she waggled her antennæ.

To my acute disappointment, after all my efforts and constant sentry duty, the babies hatched out during the night. I felt that, after all I had done, the female might have held up the hatching until I was there to witness it. However, there they were, a fine brood of young earwigs, minute, frail, looking as though they had been carved out of ivory. They moved gently under their mother's body, walking between her legs, the more venturesome even climbing onto her pincers. It was a heart-warming sight. The next day the nursery was empty: my wonderful family had scattered over the garden. I saw one of the babies some time later; he was bigger, of course, browner and stronger, but I recognized him immediately. He was curled up in a maze of rose petals, having a sleep, and when I disturbed him he merely raised his pincers irritably over his back. I would have liked to think that it was a salute, a cheerful greeting, but honesty compelled me to admit that it was nothing more than an earwig's warning to a potential enemy. Still, I excused him. After all, he had been very young when I last saw him.

I came to know the plump peasant girls who passed the garden every morning and evening. Riding side-saddle on their slouching, drooping-eared donkeys, they were shrill and colourful as parrots, and their chatter and laughter echoed among the olive trees. In the mornings they would smile and shout greetings as their donkeys pattered past, and in the evenings they would lean over the fuchsia hedge, balancing precariously on their steeds' backs, and, smiling, hold out gifts for me – a bunch of amber grapes still sun-warmed, some figs black as tar striped with pink where they had burst their seams with ripeness, or a giant watermelon with an inside like pink ice. As the days passed, I came gradually to understand them. What had at first been a confused babble became a series of recognizable separate sounds. Then, suddenly, these took on meaning, and slowly and haltingly I started to use them myself; then I took my newly acquired words and strung them into ungrammatical and stumbling sentences. Our neighbours were delighted, as though I had conferred some delicate compliment by trying to learn their language. They would lean over the hedge, their faces screwed up with concentration, as I groped my way through a greeting or a simple remark, and when I had successfully concluded they would beam at me, nodding and smiling, and clap their hands. By degrees I learned their names, who was related to whom, which were married and which hoped to be, and other details. I learned where their little cottages were among the olive groves, and should Roger and I chance to pass that way the entire family, vociferous and pleased, would tumble out to greet us, to bring a chair, so that I might sit under their vine and eat some fruit with them.

Gradually the magic of the island settled over us as gently and clingingly as pollen. Each day had a tranquillity, a timelessness, about it, so that you wished it would never end. But then the dark skin of night would peel off and there would be a fresh day waiting for us, glossy and colourful as a child's transfer and with the same tinge of unreality.

Of all the characters in Gerry's world in Corfu, three stand out as having had a huge influence on his later life. Louisa, of course, as his mother, had played a starring role since he was born. Larry, as the eldest of the Durrell offspring, became a father figure, notwithstanding the lampooning he constantly receives in the book. It was Larry who urged Gerry to write and who was one of his greatest literary champions. Gerry's mentor, Dr Theodore Stephanides, opened the boy's eyes to science, poetry and humour, possessing the 'wide-spectrum mind' Gerry forever venerated in others.

Tribute to My Mother

I should like to pay a special tribute to my mother, to whom *My Family and Other Animals* is dedicated. Like a gentle, enthusiastic, and understanding Noah, she has steered her vessel full of strange progeny through the stormy seas of life with great skill, always faced with the possibility of mutiny, always surrounded by the dangerous shoals of overdraft and extravagance, never being sure that her navigation would be approved by the crew, but certain that she would be blamed for anything that went wrong. That she survived the voyage is a miracle, but survive it she did, and, moreover, with her reason more or less intact. As my brother Larry rightly points out, we can be proud of the way we have brought her up; she is a credit to us. That she has reached that happy Nirvana where nothing shocks or startles is exemplified by the fact that one weekend recently, when all alone in the house, she was treated to the sudden arrival of a series of crates containing two pelicans, a scarlet ibis, a vulture, and eight monkeys. A lesser mortal might have quailed at such a contingency, but not Mother. On Monday morning I found her in the garage being pursued round and round by an irate pelican which she was trying to feed with sardines from a tin.

'I'm glad you've come, dear,' she panted; 'this pelican is a little difficult to handle.'

When I asked her how she knew the animals belonged to me, she replied, 'Well, of course I knew they were yours, dear; who else would send pelicans to me?'

Which goes to show how well she knows at least one of her family.

The World in a Wall

The crumbling wall that surrounded the sunken garden alongside the house was a rich hunting ground for me. It was an
ancient brick wall that had been plastered over, but now this
outer skin was green with moss, bulging and sagging with the
damp of many winters. The whole surface was an intricate
map of cracks, some several inches wide, others as fine as hairs.
Here and there large pieces had dropped off and revealed the
rows of rose-pink bricks lying beneath like ribs. There was a
whole landscape on this wall if you peered closely enough to
see it; the roofs of a hundred tiny toadstools, red, yellow, and
brown, showed in patches like villages on the damper portions;
mountains of bottlegreen moss grew in tuffets so symmetrical
that they might have been planted and trimmed; forests of
small ferns sprouted from cracks in the shady places, drooping
languidly like little green fountains. The top of the wall was a
desert land, too dry for anything except a few rust-red mosses
to live in it, too hot for anything except sun-bathing by the
dragon-flies. At the base of the wall grew a mass of plants –
cyclamen, crocus, asphodel – thrusting their leaves among the
piles of broken and chipped roof-tiles that lay there. This whole
strip was guarded by a labyrinth of blackberry hung, in season,
with fruit that was plump and juicy and black as ebony.

The inhabitants of the wall were a mixed lot, and they were
divided into day and night workers, the hunters and the hunted.
At night the hunters were the toads that lived among the bram-
bles, and the geckos, pale, translucent, with bulging eyes, that

lived in the cracks higher up the wall. Their prey was the population of stupid, absent-minded crane-flies that zoomed and barged their way among the leaves; moths of all sizes and shapes, moths striped, tessellated, checked, spotted, and blotched, that fluttered in soft clouds along the withered plaster; the beetles, rotund and neatly clad as business men, hurrying with portly efficiency about their night's work. When the last glow-worm had dragged his frosty emerald lantern to bed over the hills of moss, and the sun rose, the wall was taken over by the next set of inhabitants. Here it was more difficult to differentiate between the prey and the predators, for everything seemed to feed indiscriminately off everything else. Thus the hunting wasps searched out caterpillars and spiders; the spiders hunted for flies; the dragon-flies, big, brittle and hunting-pink, fed off the spiders and the flies; and the swift, lithe, and multicoloured wall lizards fed off everything.

But the shyest and most self-effacing of the wall community were the most dangerous; you hardly ever saw one unless you looked for it, and yet there must have been several hundred living in the cracks of the wall. Slide a knife-blade carefully under a piece of the loose plaster and lever it gently away from the brick, and there, crouching beneath it, would be a little black scorpion an inch long, looking as though he were made out of polished chocolate. They were weird-looking little things, with their flattened, oval bodies, their neat, crooked legs, and enormous crablike claws, bulbous and neatly jointed as armour, and the tail like a string of brown beads ending in a sting like a rose-thorn. The scorpion would lie there quite quietly as you examined him, only raising his tail in an almost apologetic gesture of warning if you breathed too hard on him. If you kept him in the sun too long he would simply turn his back on you and walk away, and then slide slowly but firmly under another section of plaster.

I grew very fond of these scorpions. I found them to be pleasant, unassuming creatures with, on the whole, the most charming habits. Provided you did nothing silly or clumsy (like putting your hand on one) the scorpions treated you with respect, their one desire being to get away and hide as quickly as possible. They must have found me rather a trial, for I was always ripping sections of the plaster away so that I could watch them, or capturing them and making them walk about in jam jars so that I could see the way their feet moved. By means of my sudden and unexpected assaults on the wall I discovered quite a bit about the scorpions. I found that they would eat bluebottles (though how they caught them was a mystery I never solved), grasshoppers, moths, and lacewing flies. Several times I found one of them eating another, a habit I found most distressing in a creature otherwise so impeccable.

By crouching under the wall at night with a torch, I managed to catch some brief glimpses of the scorpions' wonderful courtship dances. I saw them standing, claws clasped, their bodies raised to the skies, their tails lovingly entwined; I saw them waltzing slowly in circles among the moss cushions, claw in claw. But my view of these performances was all too short, for almost as soon as I switched on the torch the partners would stop, pause for a moment, and then, seeing that I was not going to extinguish the light, would turn round and walk firmly away, claw in claw, side by side. They were definitely beasts that believed in keeping themselves to themselves. If I could have kept a colony in captivity I would probably have been able to see the whole of the courtship, but the family had forbidden scorpions in the house, despite my arguments in favour of them.

Then one day I found a fat female scorpion in the wall, wearing what at first glance appeared to be a pale fawn fur coat.

Closer inspection proved that this strange garment was made up of a mass of tiny babies clinging to the mother's back. I was enraptured by this family, and I made up my mind to smuggle them into the house and up to my bedroom so that I might keep them and watch them grow up. With infinite care I manoeuvred the mother and family into a match-box, and then hurried to the villa. It was rather unfortunate that just as I entered the door lunch should be served; however, I placed the match-box carefully on the mantelpiece in the drawing-room, so that the scorpions should get plenty of air, and made my way to the dining-room and joined the family for the meal. Dawdling over my food, feeding Roger surreptitiously under the table, and listening to the family arguing, I completely forgot about my exciting new captures. At last Larry, having finished, fetched the cigarettes from the drawing-room, and lying back in his chair he put one in his mouth and picked up the match-box he had brought. Oblivious of my impending doom I watched him interestedly as, still talking glibly, he opened the match-box.

Now I maintain to this day that the female scorpion meant no harm. She was agitated and a trifle annoyed at being shut up in a match-box for so long, and so she seized the first opportunity to escape. She hoisted herself out of the box with great rapidity, her babies clinging on desperately, and scuttled onto the back of Larry's hand. There, not quite certain what to do next, she paused, her sting curved up at the ready. Larry, feeling the movement of her claws, glanced down to see what it was, and from that moment things got increasingly confused.

He uttered a roar of fright that made Lugaretzia, our Greek maid, drop a plate and brought Roger out from beneath the table, barking wildly. With a flick of his hand he sent the unfortunate scorpion flying down the table, and she landed midway between Margo and Leslie, scattering babies like confetti as she thumped onto the cloth. Thoroughly enraged at this treatment, the creature sped towards Leslie, her sting quivering with emotion. Leslie leaped to his feet, overturning his chair, and flicked out desperately with his napkin, sending the scorpion rolling across the cloth towards Margo, who promptly let out a scream that any railway engine would have been proud to produce. Mother, completely bewildered by this sudden and rapid change from peace to chaos, put on her glasses and peered down the table to see what was causing the pandemonium, and at that moment Margo, in a vain attempt to stop the scorpion's advance, hurled a glass of water at it. The shower missed the animal completely, but successfully drenched Mother, who, not being able to stand cold water, promptly lost her breath and sat gasping at the end of the table, unable even to protest. The scorpion had now gone to ground under Leslie's plate, while her babies swarmed wildly all over the table. Roger, mystified by the panic, but determined to do his share, ran round and round the room, barking hysterically.

'It's that bloody boy again . . .' bellowed Larry.

'Look out! Look out! They're coming!' screamed Margo.

'All we need is a book,' roared Leslie; 'don't panic, hit 'em with a book.'

'What on earth's the matter with you all?' Mother kept imploring, mopping her glasses.

'It's that bloody boy . . . he'll kill the lot of us . . . Look at the table . . . knee-deep in scorpions . . .'

'Quick . . . quick . . . do something . . . Look out, look out!'

'Stop screeching and get a book, for God's sake . . . You're worse than the dog . . . Shut up, Roger . . .'

'By the grace of God I wasn't bitten . . .'

'Look out . . . there's another one . . . Quick . . . quick . . .'

'Oh, shut up and get me a book or something . . .'

'But how did the scorpions get on the table, dear?'

'That bloody boy . . . Every match-box in the house is a death-trap . . .'

'Look out, it's coming towards me . . . Quick, quick, do something . . .'

'Hit it with your knife . . . your knife . . . Go on, hit it . . .'

Since no one had bothered to explain things to him, Roger was under the mistaken impression that the family were being attacked, and that it was his duty to defend them. As Lugaretzia was the only stranger in the room, he came to the logical conclusion that she must be the responsible party, so he bit her in the ankle. This did not help matters very much.

By the time a certain amount of order had been restored, all the baby scorpions had hidden themselves under various plates and bits of cutlery. Eventually, after impassioned pleas on my part, backed up by Mother, Leslie's suggestion that the whole lot be slaughtered was quashed. While the family, still simmering with rage and fright, retired to the drawing-room, I spent half an hour rounding up the babies, picking them up in a tea-spoon, and returning them to their mother's back. Then I carried them outside on a saucer and, with the utmost reluctance, released them on the garden wall. Roger and I went and spent the afternoon on the hillside, for I felt it would be prudent to allow the family to have a siesta before seeing them again.

The results of this incident were numerous. Larry developed a phobia about match-boxes and opened them with the utmost caution, a handkerchief wrapped round his hand. Lugaretzia limped round the house, her ankle enveloped in yards of bandage, for weeks after the bite had healed, and came round every morning, with the tea, to show us how the scabs were getting on. But, from my point of view, the worst repercussion of the whole affair was that Mother decided I was running wild again, and that it was high time I received a little more education.

A Treasure of Spiders

A tiny green grasshopper with a long, melancholy face sat twitching his hind legs nervously. A fragile snail sat on a moss sprig, meditating and waiting for the evening dew. A plump scarlet mite, the size of a match-head, struggled like a tubby huntsman through the forest of moss. It was a microscopic world, full of fascinating life. As I watched the mite making his slow progress I noticed a curious thing. Here and there on the green plush surface of the moss were scattered faint circular marks, each the size of a shilling. So faint were they that it was only from certain angles they were noticeable at all. They reminded me of a full moon seen behind thick clouds, a faint circle that seemed to shift and change. I wondered idly what could have made them. They were too irregular, too scattered to be the prints of some beast, and what was it that would walk up an almost vertical bank in such a haphazard manner? Besides, they were not like imprints. I prodded the edge of one of these circles with a piece of grass. It remained unmoved. I began to think the mark was caused by some curious way in which the moss grew.

I probed again, more vigorously, and suddenly my stomach gave a clutch of tremendous excitement. It was as though my grass-stalk had found a hidden spring, for the whole circle lifted up like a trapdoor. As I stared, I saw to my amazement that it was in fact a trapdoor, lined with silk, and with a neatly bevelled edge that fitted snugly into the mouth of the silk-lined shaft it concealed. The edge of the door was fastened to the lip of the tunnel by a small flap of silk that acted as a hinge. I gazed at this magnificent piece of workmanship and wondered what on earth could have made it. Peering down the silken tunnel, I could see nothing; I poked my grass-stalk down, but there was no response.

For a long time I sat staring at this fantastic home, trying to decide what sort of beast had made it. I thought that it might be a wasp of some sort, but had never heard of a wasp that fitted its nest with secret doors. I felt that I must get to the bottom of this problem immediately. I would go down and ask George if he knew what this mysterious beast was. Calling Roger, who was busily trying to uproot an olive tree, I set off at a brisk trot.

I arrived at George's villa out of breath, bursting with suppressed excitement, gave a perfunctory knock at the door, and dashed in. Only then did I realize he had company. Seated in a chair near him was a figure which, at first glance, I decided must be George's brother, for he also wore a beard. He was, however, in contrast to George, immaculately dressed in a grey flannel suit with waistcoat, a spotless white shirt, a tasteful but sombre tie, and large, solid, highly polished boots. I paused on the threshold, embarrassed, while George surveyed me sardonically.

'Good evening,' he greeted me. 'From the joyful speed of your entry I take it that you have not come for a little extra tuition.'

I apologized for the intrusion, and then told George about the curious nests I had found.

'Thank heavens you're here, Theodore,' he said to his bearded companion. 'I shall now be able to hand the problem over to expert hands.'

'Hardly an expert . . .' mumbled the man called Theodore, deprecatingly.

'Gerry, this is Doctor Theodore Stephanides,' said George. 'He is an expert on practically everything you care to mention. And what you don't mention, he does. He, like you, is an eccentric nature-lover. Theodore, this is Gerry Durrell.'

I said how do you do, politely, but to my surprise the bearded man rose to his feet, stepped briskly across the room and held out a large white hand.

'Very pleased to meet you,' he said, apparently addressing his beard, and gave me a quick, shy glance from twinkling blue eyes.

I shook his hand and said I was very pleased to meet him, too.

Then we stood in awkward silence, while George watched us, grinning.

'Well, Theodore,' he said at last, 'and what d'you think produced these strange secret passages?'

Theodore clasped his hands behind his back, lifted himself on his toes several times, his boots squeaking protestingly, and gravely considered the floor.

'Well . . . er . . .' he said, his words coming slowly and meticulously, 'it sounds to me as though they might be the burrows of the trapdoor spider . . . er . . . it is a species which is quite common here in Corfu . . . that is to say, when I say common, I suppose I have found some thirty or . . . er . . . forty specimens during the time I have been here.'

'Ah,' said George, 'trapdoor spiders, eh?'

'Yes,' said Theodore. 'I feel that it's more than probable that that is what they are. However, I may be mistaken.'

He rose and fell on his toes, squeaking gently, and then he shot me a keen glance.

'Perhaps, if they are not too far away, we could go and verify it,' he suggested tentatively. 'I mean to say, if you have nothing better to do, and it's not too far . . .' His voice trailed away on a faintly interrogative note.

I said that they were only just up the hill, not really far.

'Um,' said Theodore.

'Don't let him drag you about all over the place, Theodore,' said George. 'You don't want to be galloped about the countryside.'

'No, no, not at all,' said Theodore. 'I was just about to leave, and I can easily walk that way back. It is quite a simple matter for me to . . . er . . . cut down through the olive groves and reach Canoni.'

He picked up a neat grey Homburg and placed it squarely on his head. At the door he held out his hand and shook George's briefly.

'Thank you for a delightful tea,' he said, and stumped gravely off along the path by my side.

As we walked along I studied him covertly. He had a straight, well-shaped nose; a humorous mouth lurking in the ash-blond beard; straight, rather bushy eyebrows under which his eyes, keen but with a twinkle in them and laughter-wrinkles at the corners, surveyed the world. He strode along energetically, humming to himself. When we came to a ditch full of stagnant water he stopped for a moment and stared down into it, his beard bristling.

'Um,' he said conversationally, '*Daphnia magna*.'

He rasped at his beard with his thumb, and then set off down the path again.

'Unfortunately,' he said to me, 'I was coming out to see some people . . . er . . . friends of mine, and so I did not bring my collecting bag with me. It is a pity, for that ditch might have contained something.'

When we branched off the fairly smooth path we had been travelling along and started up the stony goat-track, I expected some sort of protest, but Theodore strode behind me with unabated vigour, still humming. At length we came to the gloomy olive grove, and I led Theodore to the bank and pointed out the mysterious trapdoor.

He peered down at it, his eyes narrowed.

'Ah-ha,' he said, 'yes . . . um . . . yes.'

He produced from his waistcoat pocket a tiny penknife, opened it, inserted the point of the blade delicately under the little door, and flipped it back.

'Um, yes,' he repeated; '*cteniza.*'

He peered down the tunnel, blew down it and then let the trapdoor fall into place again.

'Yes, they are the burrows of the trapdoor spiders,' he said, 'but this one does not appear to be inhabited. Generally, the creature will hold on to the . . . er . . . trapdoor . . . with her legs, or rather, her claws, and she holds on with such tenacity that you have to be careful or you will damage the door, trying to force it open. Um . . . yes . . . these are the burrows of the females, of course. The male makes a similar burrow, but it is only about half the size.'

I remarked that it was the most curious structure I had seen.

'Ah-ha! yes,' said Theodore, 'they are certainly very curious. A thing that always puzzles me is how the female knows when the male is approaching.'

I must have looked blank, for he teetered on his toes, shot me a quick look and went on: 'The spider, of course, waits inside its burrow until some insect – a fly or a grasshopper, or something similar – chances to walk past. They can judge, it seems, whether the insect is close enough to be caught. If it is, the spider . . . er . . . pops out of its hole and catches the creature. Now when the male comes in search of the female he must walk over the moss to the trapdoor, and I have often wondered why it is that he is not . . . er . . . devoured by the female in mistake. It is possible, of course, that his footsteps sound different. Or he may make some sort of . . . you know . . . some sort of sound which the female recognizes.'

We walked down the hill in silence. When we reached the place where the paths forked I said that I must leave him.

'Ah, well, I'll say good-bye,' he said, staring at his boots. 'I have enjoyed meeting you.'

We stood in silence for a moment. Theodore was afflicted with the acute embarrassment that always seemed to overwhelm him when greeting or saying good-bye to someone. He stared hard at his boots for a moment longer, and then he held out his hand and shook mine gravely.

'Good-bye,' he said. 'I . . . er . . . I expect we shall meet again.'

He turned and stumped off down the hill, swinging his stick, staring about him with observant eyes. I watched him out of sight and then walked slowly in the direction of the villa. I was at once confused and amazed by Theodore. First, since he was obviously a scientist of considerable repute (and I could have told this by his beard), he was to me a person of great importance. In fact he was the only person I had met until now who seemed to share my enthusiasm for zoology. Secondly, I was extremely flattered to find that he treated me and talked to me exactly as though I were his own age. I liked him for this, as I was not talked down to by my family, and I took rather a poor view of any outsider who tried to do so. But Theodore not only talked to me as though I were grown up, but also as though I were as knowledgeable as he.

The facts he told me about the trapdoor spider haunted me:

the idea of the creature crouching in its silken tunnel, holding the door closed with its hooked claws, listening to the movement of the insects on the moss above. What, I wondered, did things sound like to a trapdoor spider? I could imagine that a snail would trail over the door with a noise like sticking-plaster being slowly torn off. A centipede would sound like a troop of cavalry. A fly would patter in brisk spurts, followed by a pause while it washed its hands – a dull rasping sound like a knife-grinder at work. The larger beetles, I decided, would sound like steam-rollers, while the smaller ones, the lady-birds and others, would probably purr over the moss like clockwork motor cars. Fascinated by this thought, I made my way back home through the darkening fields, to tell the family of my new discovery and of my meeting with Theodore. I hoped to see him again, for there were many things I wanted to ask him, but I felt it would be unlikely that he would have very much time to spare for me. I was mistaken, however, for two days later Leslie came back from an excursion into the town and handed me a small parcel.

'Met that bearded johnny,' he said laconically; 'you know, that scientist bloke. Said this was for you.'

Incredulously I stared at the parcel. Surely it couldn't be for me? There must be some mistake, for a great scientist would hardly bother to send me parcels. I turned it over, and there, written on it in neat, spidery writing, was my name. I tore off the paper as quickly as I could. Inside was a small box and a letter.

My dear Gerry Durrell,

I wondered, after our conversation the other day, if it might not assist your investigations of the local natural history to have some form of magnifying instrument. I am therefore sending you this pocket microscope, in the hope that it will be of some use to you. It is, of course, not of very high magnification, but you will find it sufficient for field work.

With best wishes,
Yours sincerely,
Theo. Stephanides

P.S. If you have nothing better to do on Thursday, perhaps you would care to come to tea, and I could then show you some of my microscope slides.

An Omnipotent, Benign and Humorous Greek God

Written just after Theo's death in 1983,
at the age of eighty-seven.

I had known Theodore for over 40 years. When I was ten years old, he strolled into my life, tweed-suited, trilby-hatted, his walking stick with its tiny net on the end, his bag of tubes and bottles slung on his hip, his beard twinkling in the sun, as a sort of walking, hirsute encyclopaedia. The effect of Theodore's erudition on a budding naturalist was enormous. To me, just starting to explore and learn about the world I lived in, to have Theodore as a guide, philosopher and friend was one of the most important things that has happened to me in my life. Not many young naturalists have the privilege of having their footsteps guided by a sort of omnipotent, benign and humorous Greek god. Theodore had all the very best qualities of the early Victorian naturalists, an insatiable interest in the world he inhabited and the ability to illuminate any topic with his observations and thoughts. His wide interests are, I think, summed up by the fact that (in this day and age) he was a man who had a microscopic water crustacean named after him, as well as a crater on the moon.

Such an immense fund of knowledge could lead some people to become boring, but Theodore was never this, for he larded his immense scientific knowledge with a puckish sense of humour. An example of this was in the epilogue of a book he wrote, called 'Island Trails', where he describes how all his notebooks, manuscripts and specimens were destroyed by the German and Italian bombing of Corfu. This must have been a great blow to him, but he then goes on to say: 'The manuscript of my magnum opus, *A Survey of the Freshwater Biology of Corfu and of Certain Other Regions of Greece*, was saved by a happy chance and was published in 1948 by the Hellenic Institute of Freshwater Biology. I have never heard of it becoming a best seller in spite of the fact that it contains, among other good things, a suggestive account of the sexual aberrations of the water-flea *Cyclops bicuspidatus* Claus var. *lubbocki* Brady. Any reader, however, who might wish to go further into this matter, will find a copy of the above monograph in the library of the Entomostraca Section of the British Museum.'

I can only sum up my feeling for him by saying that if I had the power of magic, I would confer two gifts on every child – the enchanted childhood that I had on the island of Corfu, and to be guided and befriended by Theodore Stephanides.

Gerry had a succession of tutors, but it seemed that none was spectacularly successful in drilling into him the elements of an education typical of the times. Nevertheless, the boy learned a lot from them, and from pursuing his natural curiosity. Gerry had, shall we say, a creative interpretation of education.

The first piece, a script for radio read by Gerry in 1952, was his first effort at revealing the memories of his magical childhood in a public forum, and it led him to write My Family and Other Animals three years later. The second piece indicates the great degree to which Gerry was self-taught as a boy. For example, he loved doing dissections of the dead creatures he would come across on his rambles and bring back to the villa, much to the disgust of the family after several days of warm weather.

Island Education

The idea that your school days are the happiest days of your life is one of those beliefs that is firmly held by nearly everyone over the age of twenty, and, a schoolboy of my acquaintance assures me, it is entirely erroneous. However, I cannot speak from personal experience, because, strictly speaking, I never went to school. Lest I be mistaken for one of those people who still have to sign their names with a cross let me hasten to explain: I spent what is called my 'formative years' running riot on a Greek island, while no less than four tutors tried assiduously to educate me. Though their methods were, perhaps, unorthodox, I can in all honesty say those were the happiest days of my life.

Some time before the war my family decided that the climate of England left much to be desired, and so we streamed across Europe like a flock of migrating swallows, to spend six months on a remote Greek island, where, we were assured, the sun shone all the year round. Such is the charm of the place that at the end of the six months we had given up trying to pretend that we were going to come back to England, and so we happily settled down and stayed five years. During the six months' 'holiday' period my mother had worried little about my education, and I had been allowed to run riot among the olive groves and vineyards. But, as soon as the six months were up and we had decided to stay, the family with one accord, and in spite of my strenuous objections, decided that I must be educated. In consequence my mother engaged the services of a friend of my brother's, who had retired to this remote spot to write a novel that was going to shake the world. Most of my brother's friends at that time were busily engaged in writing either poems or novels that were going to shake the world, or else painting pictures that were going to make Rembrandt look like a pavement artist of the more haphazard variety. Thomas Johnson reluctantly left his unfinished masterpiece and started on the job of teaching me, being obviously of the wise opinion that a few pounds in the pocket was worth any masterpiece on the desk.

He was an incredibly tall and thin individual, with a fine pointed brown beard so necessary to the intellectual who is going to accomplish anything. He had a grave deep voice that he liked the sound of, and I found it surprising and flattering that he treated me as a grown up. He was an expert fencer and was, at that time, busily engaged in learning some of the local peasant dances, for which he had a passion. He would practice fencing stance, or else complicated dance steps, while waiting for me to finish my sums, a thing that I found disconcerting to say the least, and to which I will always attribute my inability to do mathematics. Place a sum before my eyes and it immediately conjures up a vision of Thomas's lanky body swaying and jerking round our small sitting room with all the angular grace of a skeleton, while he accompanied himself with a melodious humming. Occasionally the humming would stop abruptly, a steely look would come into his eyes and he would throw himself into the attitude of defence, waving an imaginary foil at an imaginary enemy. He would fight his adversary across the room, skilfully avoiding the furniture, and eventually kill him with a brilliant thrust through the heart in the corner. Through all this I would be watching him open-mouthed, the exercise of sums lying forgotten in front of me.

His teaching was rather hampered at first by lack of books, but, nothing daunted, he taught me French from a large and battered copy of Rabelais, English from various books in his library which ranged from Oscar Wilde to Gibbon, and Geography from the maps in the back of a Pears' encyclopaedia. Among other things, he taught me how to swim, how to inhale smoke without coughing, and the Facts of Life. This latter information he imparted in such a pedantic and scientific manner that it was fully a week before the full realisation of what he had been saying dawned on me, but as I had for some time been keeping a large menagerie of pets, I needed no initiating into these mysteries. It was Thomas who taught me the delights of what he called outdoor lessons. He would arrive, some mornings, clad in his enormous straw hat with a frayed brim, carrying over his arm a towel. We would make our way down through the olive groves, along the white dusty road, and then down the cliff face, following a narrow goat track, until we came to a tiny, secluded bay, with a half moon-shaped beach, white as snow. The water in this little bay was so clear and placid that it was hard to believe, looking at it from the top of the cliff, that there was any water there at all. We would strip beneath the olive trees and then plunge into the blood-warm sea, and spend an interesting hour investigating the private lives of hermit crabs, or seeing who could dive the deepest to retrieve the coloured shells that littered the seabed. After a while it would suddenly occur to Thomas that all this, though very entertaining, could hardly be called education in the strictest sense of the word, so he would assume a fierce expression and strike out for the shore. Here we would lie on the beach and cover ourselves with hot sand, and Thomas would begin the lesson. He would ask the questions and I would do my best to give the right answers. Gradually, however, the combination of sea air and hot sun would prove too much, and the pause between each question would become longer and longer, until I could see that slumber had overtaken him. Then I would steal silently away and spend an enjoyable and instructive half hour in the olive groves, chasing the butterflies or frightening the innocent Trap-door Spiders out of their wits by pushing grass stalks down their tunnels. When Thomas at last woke up and found me, he would be very contrite and explain that that particular day had been in the nature of a holiday, and that, to make up for it, we would 'get down to it' on the morrow.

When, eventually, urgent affairs called Thomas away from the island I was left tutorless. I cannot say that this caused me any undue anxiety, but I was however genuinely alarmed when I heard that yet another acquaintance of my brother's was coming out from England to take Thomas's place. He turned out to be a tall, good-looking young man, with an aptitude for rowing and swimming. Lest this be held against him let me hastily add that there were other, finer sides to his character. He was, for example, writing a book that would, on publication, shake the literary world. This I found quite natural: indeed, if I had been presented at that time with a tutor who was *not* writing a book to shake the literary world, I would have considered him a charlatan.

Michel did his best to give me a Public School education, which, in the absence of a public school, was difficult. He carved me a cricket bat out of wood and tried to teach me to keep a straight bat. This experiment was abandoned when he received the ball in the pit of his stomach one hot afternoon. He did, however, teach me to ride bareback on one of the scraggy local ponies, and I enjoyed this immensely. I liked Michel very much, and for some time I believed him to be infallible. But then, to my disgust, I discovered my idol had feet of clay. He happened to see me one day when I was running like a hare, hotly and blasphemously pursued by a peasant whose chickens I and my dog had been chasing, and Michel thought it was a heaven-sent opportunity to give me a little homily: he explained firmly and kindly that in life one meets all sorts of Situations, and makes all sorts of Mistakes, but one simply could not Run Away from them. One had to be Brave. One had to Face Things. With a brave heart one would always Win Through. He then suggested that I should be brave and go and apologise to the peasant for chasing his hens. Rather impressed by all these platitudes I went down to the peasant's farm and, from a safe distance, I apologised. The peasant was charming and gave me a bunch of grapes, so my opinion of Michel went up considerably, and for several days my family had doubts as to my sanity, for I went around fearlessly admitting such faults as that it was I who had left the matchbox full of scorpions on the desk, it was I who had forgotten to clean the bath, and that it was entirely my fault that the dog was sick on the sofa because I had given him too many cakes to eat. For days I went about with a Brave Heart. Then came the crash. I idly wondered if Michel would show the same magnificent braveness he had advocated for me if he was faced with some danger. I decided to experiment. It was Michel's custom to swim every morning in the bay below the villa, and so I followed him down that morning and sat dumbly on the sand while he did his exercises and plunged in. I let him get a good distance from shore before yelling out a bloodcurdling screech. 'Shark!' I yelled frantically. 'A shark behind you!'

With interest I waited to see if he would turn to face this unpleasant situation in the same fearless manner he had spoken of, but to my surprise he started to swim to shore at an incredible speed. Every time he started to slow down, I would yell,

'Look out, it's coming!', to give him another chance to turn and face it, but he would merely accelerate even more. He arrived on shore dripping and panting, with his face an unhealthy cheese colour. I gazed at his cowering form with contempt: so this was the man who had told me to face unpleasant situations with a brave heart. And what could be more unpleasant than a shark whose arrival he had greeted with such a cowardly retreat? When I informed him, with ill-concealed disgust, that there was in reality no shark, and that I had just been testing him, I had to beat a fairly rapid retreat myself. Later that day I went down with my dog and chased the peasant's chickens again, and this time I didn't apologise to the man. My faith in Michel had evaporated.

When Michel left us I was once more without a tutor, but my mother was determined that, until we found a new one, I would at least keep my French under control. So she made arrangements for me to go every morning to the house of the Belgian Consul in the town. The Belgian Consul's house was situated in a maze of narrow, smelly alleyways that made up the Jewish quarter of the town. It was a fascinating area, full of little street stalls piled high with gaily coloured cloth, or shining piles of sweetmeats, or ornaments of beaten silver. The cobbled alleys were so narrow that you had to flatten yourself against the walls of the houses to let the donkeys stagger past with their great loads of vegetables. Right in the centre of this rich and colourful section of the town, in a tall and rickety building, lived the Consul. He was a sweet little man whose most striking attribute was a magnificent three-pointed beard. He was always dressed in the most immaculate clothes, black cutaway coat, striped trousers, fawn-coloured spats over shining shoes, and a large and glittering top hat. One could see him at any hour of the day, dressed like this, picking his way down the dirty narrow alleyways, stepping daintily among the puddles, or, with a magnificently courteous gesture, drawing himself back against the wall to allow a donkey to pass, and tapping it coyly on the rump with his Malacca cane.

The first morning I arrived he had decided to test me to see how much French I knew, so he sat me down at a table in his tiny living room and asked me to read a page out of Le Petit Larousse. To read a page out of an English dictionary is bad enough, but to do the same with a French one is, I contend, almost an impossibility. As I struggled down the page the Consul stood looking out the window, his hands clasped behind him. Suddenly he stiffened and uttered a supressed exclamation. I thought that he was shocked by my French accent, but it was apparently nothing to do with me, for he fled across the room to a cupboard and pulled out a powerful-looking air rifle which he proceeded to load frantically, dropping pellets all over the floor in his excitement. Then he took careful aim at something out of the window and, after a moment's awful suspense, he fired. Then he laid down the gun, and turning towards me I was surprised to see there were tears in his eyes. He took out an enormous silk handkerchief and blew his nose violently. 'Ah!' he intoned dolefully. 'Ze poor poor leetle thing. But we must to work. Continuez wis your reading.' For the rest of the morning I toyed with the idea that the Consul had committed a murder before my very eyes, or at least was carrying out some sort of blood feud with a neighbouring householder. It was quite some time, however, before I discovered the real reason for the Consul's sudden dashes to the window with a loaded gun.

In the Jewish quarter, as elsewhere in the town, the cats were allowed to breed unchecked, and there were, quite literally, hundreds of them. They belonged to no one, so no one looked after them or bothered to feed them, and in consequence most of them were in a frightful state. Some were so thin, and covered in so many suppurating sores, that it was astonishing that they managed to live at all. Now the Belgian Consul was a cat-lover: he possessed a large, well-fed Persian to prove it. So the sight of all these starving, sore-ridden cats walking about the rooftops opposite his windows was too much for his sensitive nature. 'I cannot feed zem all,' he would explain, 'so I try and make them happiness by shooting them. They are better so, but it makes me feel so sad.' Indeed he was performing a very humane service, as anyone who has seen those cats could testify. So my French lessons were continually being interrupted while the Consul leaped to the window to send yet another cat to a happier hunting ground. After the sharp report of the gun there would be a moment's silence, in respect for the dead, and then the Consul would blow his nose violently, sigh deeply, and we would plunge once more into the intricacies of French verbs.

For some strange reason the Consul was under the impression that my mother could speak French, and would never lose an opportunity of engaging her in conversation. If she had the good fortune to see his top hat bobbing through the crowd towards her, she would hastily take refuge in the nearest shop, and nervously purchase a number of things she had no use for, until the danger was past, but occasionally the Consul would appear suddenly out of an alleyway and catch Mother by surprise. He would advance with a broad smile that displayed all his gold fillings, twirling his cane skilfully. With an aristocratic gesture he would sweep off his top hat and bow almost double in front of my mother, while clasping one of her reluctantly offered hands and pressing it passionately into his beard. Then he would break into a flood of French, gesturing elegantly with his hat and stick, and apparently unaware of the blank and uncomprehending expression on my parent's face. When he had to pause for breath he would interject an enquiring 'n'est-ce pas?', and this was my mother's cue. Summoning all her courage she would display her complete mastery over the French language by saying 'er . . . er . . . oui, oui . . . quite.' This procedure seemed to satisfy the French Consul, and I am quite sure that he never suspected that these were the only French words my mother knew. But these conversations were a nerve-wracking ordeal for my parent, and the mere sight of a top hat would send her tearing away down the street at a ladylike walk that was dangerously near a gallop.

I had got halfway through the 'E's in Larousse with the Consul when my mother discovered another tutor for me, and so we parted company, and he was left in peace to fire out his drawing room window at the local cats.

My new tutor was a small, humped-backed man with enormous liquid hazel eyes. He had Polish, French and English in his ancestry, and could speak seven languages with an annoying ease. He was extremely interested in birds, a thing I strongly approved of, and at the top of his house he had a large attic room which was devoted to aviculture. Here there were goldfinches, canaries, greenfinches, bullfinches, thrushes, the rare Blue Rock Thrush from the Albanian mountains, and a host of other birds. The chorus of their songs deafened you when you entered the room. As soon as my tutor found that I shared his interest in birds, we spent many happy hours up in his birdroom, tending his charges, feeding and watering, and arguing as to when the next nest of eggs was due to hatch out. During this I was forced to speak in French, in order to lend some sort of educational aspect to the affair. The same applied when we visited the local bird market to see what specimens there were there.

I had not long been with my new tutor when I noticed a curious side to his character. If, during the course of a lesson, you asked him a question on some totally unrelated subject, his eyes would glow happily and he would wander off on a trail of thoughts that would occupy at least half an hour. It was during these little excursions into reminiscence that he sometimes told me a story about his past life, and these were generally rather extraordinary. For example, the time he had strangled a bulldog in Hyde Park, and another time when he had been attacked by bandits in Turkey and had killed twenty-five of them with a clasp knife and driven off the rest. These stories I found quite believable, and I could not understand why they were greeted with hoots of derisive laughter when I related them at home as examples of my tutor's bravery and courage. Gradually however the stories got so wild and improbable that even I had difficulty in believing him. But one day he happened to tell me something that I found quite plausible: he informed me that he had once been the champion wrestler of France, and went on to describe how he had thrown all his opponents from the ring with skilful flicks of his wrist. All his opponents were, of course, much bigger than he was. I decided that the fact that wrestling had not so far been numbered among my accomplishments was a regrettable oversight. That afternoon my tutor came to our house for tea, and in front of a large crowd of people I begged that he teach me the finer points of wrestling. The unfortunate man could do nothing else. He explained that the idea was to rush in and grab your opponent by the waist and endeavour to throw him to the ground. Having grasped this essential first principle I proceeded to demonstrate: I rushed at him, grasped him firmly round the waist, squeezed as hard as I could to prevent his escape, and with a dextrous twist flung him into the nearest chair. The poor man got up, and his face was pale as death. On visiting the doctor the next day he discovered that I had cracked two ribs and badly bruised the rest. For some weeks he had to go about with his ribs strapped up, and a martyred look on his face. He refused to discuss wrestling with me again, to my disappointment, or show me any more tricks. But he did tell me a long story of how he won several times at Brooklands at a speed that would have made John Cobb quite envious. He was quite safe in his racing reminiscences, for there were no racing cars on the island. However, just in case one turned up, he hastily told me that he had never driven again after his dreadful crash of 1921.

Eventually, as always happens, my mother decided that although the island was lovely, I would do better if we returned to England, and so ended our Corfu sojourn in 1939. For myself I found the educational system here was, to say the least, uninteresting, and the tutors I had did not measure up to what I thought a tutor ought to be. None of them were writing books to shake the literary world, none of them kept birds in the attic, and none of them suggested that we should take our books down to the beach for an outdoor lesson. I suppose they knew best, but of one thing I am certain: I will remember those who taught me and what they taught me during my island education, long after the memory of the other and more orthodox education has faded away.

Surrounded by Miracles

I think it was by doing primitive dissections that I first started appreciating the complex and fantastic structure in which I dwelt – my body – and most of it functioning without any apparent direction from me, its owner or temporary inhabitant. I was unaware how my kidneys functioned. I gave them no orders and yet they continued to do their duty. If I put out my hand to pick something up, I was aware that my brain had given my hand instructions to perform this task, yet I was not even on speaking terms with my kidneys. Did a hedgehog, I wondered, give instructions to the web of muscles so that he rolled into a spiky ball when danger hove into view, or did it happen automatically? (I longed to dissect a cow or a horse, but I knew that the intricacies of smuggling so large a corpse into my bedroom would surely lead to detection and my experiments being brought to an end.)

Then there was the amazing difference between various creatures. The difference between the musculature and bone structure of a bat and a bird, for example. After all, although they were bird and mammal, they both flew and so you would expect their internal organs to be the same. Then there was the difference between a lizard, a snake and a tortoise. The snake with its long meandering necklace of ribs that functioned like feet, the lizard with its ribs like a cage and four feet to support, and the tortoise with its skeleton welded into the dome of its shell, leaving only the legs, neck and head free to protrude. All this was fascinating enough, but when you got to the insects who, for the most part, wore their protective armour outside, the mind boggled at the shapes they had assumed and the incredible architecture and articulation of their body parts. Then, of course, there were the transformations as startling and bizarre as anything a stage magician could produce. The dragonfly larvae, like some strange steam shovels in the pond's depths, who, when the time was right, would crawl up a leaf or twig and split open like strange sandwiches, and from their uncouth interiors would emerge the adults, hawk-eyed, wings glittering like a thousand church windows, and with a quick-ness and manoeuvrability that no man-made flying machine could match.

Then the cicadas, who had been lurking so long in the dun-geon of the earth, would emerge like so many grass-green hunchbacks. Again, like the dragonfly larvae, they would split their skins and emerge, bodies brown as nuts, wings a laby-rinth of transparent scales, and they would fly away to the olive groves, there to make the blue days of summer vibrate with their zithering song.

Then the tadpoles, like chocolate fishes, who would grow legs in instalments and, when thus equipped, hop busily on to the land.

Leaf to bud, caterpillar to butterfly, tadpole to toad or frog, I was surrounded by miracles. I was surrounded by magic as though Merlin has passed through and casually touched the island with his wand.

Sometimes the blue summer sky would entertain a host of grey cumulus clouds like pouter pigeons, who would come to irrigate the island with great drops of warm rain the size of marbles. Then Margo and I would put on our swimming cos-tumes and go walking in the rain. The peasants thought we were quite mad.

'You will catch cold and die,' they would shout. 'Go home.'

'The rain is lovely,' Margo would reply, 'warm as a bath.'

As no tiny peasant house boasted more than two rooms, one of which was the kitchen, talk of bathrooms was rather superfluous. It was as futile as trying to describe an elephant to an Inuit.

Now the ditches and ponds filled and Theodore and I would prowl among them, as alert as fishing herons. I was seeking the terrapin, the frog or toad or snake to add to my menagerie, while Theo, his little net with a bottle on the end, would seek the smaller fauna, some almost invisible to the eye.

'Ah ha!' he would exclaim when, having swept his net through the water, he lifted the little bottle to his eye. 'Now this is – er, um – most interesting. I haven't seen one of these since I was in Epir . . .'

'Look Theo,' I would say, lifting a baby ladder snake towards him.

'Um – er – yes,' Theo would reply, 'pretty thing.'

An adult calling a snake a pretty thing was music to my ears.

I had few books to guide and explain, so Theodore was for me a sort of walking bookcase.

PART TWO

On Animals

Zoological Adventures to the Four Corners of the Earth

'The man is mad, crawling around snake-infested jungles!'

Lawrence Durrell, c. 1952

A world without birds, without forests, without animals of every shape and size, would be one that I, personally, would not care to live in . . .

– Menagerie Manor

When you travel about the world in search of animals, you do not follow the well-worn trail of the tourist. You do not check in at the local Hilton. You do not have ice in your drinks, nor get your shoes polished. Your abode is more like to be a mud hut, or bamboo dwelling with none of the refinements of hot and cold running water, but with a multitude of fascinating creatures from scorpions and snakes to snails and spiders sharing the hospitality with you. I am not saying that you do not grab at the luxuries when you can get them, but by sticking to the tourist trails you are less likely to meet fascinating animals, both human and otherwise.

– Fragment from unpublished autobiography

That animals are an essential part of Gerry's life – he cannot exist without them, be they common or yet to be discovered – is the theme of Part Two. His deep emotional relationship to animals and the spectacular natural habitats in which they live is palpable, demonstrating the phenomenon of 'nature-connectedness' long before it was recognized in the modern sense. Some say his accounts of animals are anthropomorphic. It is true that he uses human descriptors in writing about animals, but he never sentimentalizes the animals 'as human'. His inimitable imagery is his way of bringing readers closer to animals than ever before.

Cameroon

New and Rediscovered Animals

It was Cuvier, at the beginning of the nineteenth century, who made the rather pretentious and unwise statement that now all large creatures on the planet had been discovered and described. Since his day, of course, a host of creatures, ranging from pygmy hogs to white rhinos, Komodo dragons to coelacanths, have turned up to confound him. Usually, the local people were aware of the animal, but it was not known to European science. Pygmy people, for example, knew all about the okapi long before Johnson 'discovered' it. In many cases, it is lack of observation that keeps a creature a secret from science for so long.

I remember being on a live animal collecting trip in Cameroon, and I had the fruits of my labours, some 250 specimens of fourteen different species, housed in a large marquee on the riverbank. The local District Officer asked if he might come and see them, so I welcomed him with warm beer and showed him round. He was absolutely dumbfounded. He told me that he had worked for twenty-five years in West Africa and he had never seen any of these creatures. Where, he asked, had I found them? I told him that I had caught a good number of them in the tiny strip of forest at the end of his garden. I think he thought I was making fun of him, as our relationship remained somewhat cool from that moment onwards.

However, I was rather neatly hoist by my own petard for, on

that particular expedition, I had quartered miles of forest searching for the nesting site of the rare Bald Rock Crow (*Picathartes oreas*) with no success. Returning a year later, I made my base camp in the same village and the hunters told me with pride that they had found the nest site of the bird I wanted so badly. To my embarrassment and chagrin, they led me to a rock face approximately two hundred yards from where, the year previously, I had made my base camp. *Picathartes* build swallow-like mud nests and I could see this nest site was an old one. So while I had blundered about the forest looking for the 'elusive' bird, it had been happily nesting almost in my tent.

I cannot understand why scientists on the whole look scornfully at the idea of some large unknown animal lurking in a lake or in the sea or on land. They don't believe it until they have a specimen – preferably dead – in their hands. I believe everything is possible. With delighted anticipation, I await the discovery of a sea serpent or, better still, an Abominable Snowman and, if he proves too close to us in appearance for comfort, what do we do with him? Put him in a cage or send him to university?

Rainforests

Rainforests are one of the most complex, beautiful and important of the many ecosystems of this planet. They are also ones that, primarily out of greed, we are destroying with the savage, unthinking ferocity of a troop of drunken apes in an art gallery. But whereas pictures can be repainted, tropical rainforests can't be recreated, and at the rate we are destroying them this bodes ill for the future of the planet, for these vast forests are climate controllers, desert preventers and huge storehouses of as yet untapped natural resources. The bounty we have already received from them in the shape of everything from timber and spices to medicines is staggering, and there is obviously an enormous amount still to be discovered if we do not destroy this treasure trove.

I remember vividly the first time I entered a tropical rainforest. I spent a whole day bewildered and enchanted by all the sights, sounds and scents. The leafmould alone contained hundreds of insects I had never seen or heard of before. Roll over any rotting log and I found a world as bizarre as anything thought up by science fiction. Each hollow tree was an apartment block containing anything from snakes to bats, from owls to flying mice. Every forest stream was an orchestra of frogs, a ballet of tiny fish, and from the canopy high above came the constant rain of fruit, twigs and pirouetting blossoms thrown down by that great army of creatures – mammals, birds, reptiles and insects – that inhabit this high, sunlit, flower-scented realm. I did not know where to look next. Every leaf, flower, liana; every insect, frog, fish or bird was a lifetime's study in itself, and I knew that there was another hidden, secretive army of creatures that would emerge at night to take over. As any naturalist knows, there is nothing like a tropical rainforest for replacing arrogance with awe.

Ground Nut Chop

My favourite recipe is Ground Nut Chop, which I learned to prepare on many occasions when I went on expedition to West Africa. The recipe is as follows:

You take a chicken big enough for the number of people you wish to serve, cut it into serving pieces and use the carcase to make a stock. In this stock you put one or two cans or bottles of peanut butter and in this mixture you simmer the chicken until it is tender. At the last moment, add either a tin of coconut cream or else a pint of double cream. This is served on rice, to be accompanied by what the West Africans, in pidgin English, used to call 'Small Small Tings'. They can be as numerous as you like – chopped bananas; chopped mandarins; fried, desiccated coconut; roasted peanuts; chutney and so on – in fact a really good Ground Nut Chop should look very exotic, with all the small plates around the main dish of feed. You will find this extremely filling and, for those of you on a diet, very fattening. You can accompany it with wine, but probably the best thing is beer.

When I was out hunting animals, this used to be the main dish at least three or four times a week in the evening, because you got back, after a hard day in the forest, extremely hungry.

The Hunt for the Hairy Frog

Our base camp in the Cameroons was in a clearing on the banks of the Cross River, at the edge of the forest. Here we erected a huge marquee, and in this we lived, together with our specimens. As the news of our arrival spread hunters from all parts came to our camp clearing, bringing animals to sell to us. Sometimes the capture would be in a basket, sometimes wrapped in leaves or tied on the end of a stick, or, occasionally, it would arrive wrapped up in its owner's loin cloth, and the hunter would stand there naked and unembarrassed while he bargained fiercely with us over the price. The animals these hunters brought were, for the most part, the more common forest creatures: we soon found that if you wanted the rarities you had to go into the forest and get them yourself. Naturally, it was the rarities we *did* want, such things as the White Mongoose, that rare primate the Angwantibo, the Booming Squirrel, and last but not least the fabulous Hairy Frog.

Now, in the great forests of Africa, seeing any animals at all is quite an achievement and to capture them amounts almost to a miracle. You can walk for hours, sometimes days, in the cool twilight interior of the forest, and not see anything more exciting than a few butterflies, or an occasional bird. Every bush does *not* harbour a writhing mass of deadly snakes, or a brace of hungry leopards . . . many's the time I've wished this popular misconception of the jungle was true. You have to use a variety of methods to capture your animals, and a great deal of patience, for sometimes it's weeks or months before you're successful.

All the hunters that we interviewed knew the animals we wanted, and where they were to be found. They knew them all, that is, except the one we wanted most . . . the Hairy Frog. They had never even heard of such a thing: frogs, certainly, but frogs with *hairs*! . . . well, the looks they gave me left me in no doubt as to what they were thinking. With the air of one humouring a child they would suggest that perhaps what I meant was a water rat. No, I did not mean a water rat. A frog with hair on its legs was what I wanted, and nothing else would please me. So the hunters, while very enthusiastic in helping me catch the other animals, would not bother to search for the Hairy Frog, for they were convinced that it did not exist, and so to look for it would be a waste of time In view of the fact that not one of them had ever seen it, I decided to concentrate on catching the other animals we wanted, and keep hoping that the Hairy Frog would be discovered in the course of my hunting.

By now we had got nearly all the specimens we wanted, and the collection in our marquee would have turned any naturalist green with envy. There were Chimpanzees, Moustached Monkeys, Baboons, the rare and beautiful Golden Cat, and the priceless Angwantibos. Boxes of snakes and frogs and crocodiles, and tortoises by the score. There were owls and vultures, sunbirds and kingfishers. Only two important items were missing; one was the Booming Squirrel, and the other, of course, was the elusive Hairy Frog. I had questioned dozens of hunters, but none of them knew this frog; I had searched in ponds, streams, and in rivers, and in every place that could possibly harbour the animal, but with no success. I caught green frogs, yellow frogs, and frogs with pink spots, frogs that looked like bits of leaf, and others that looked like sticks, but I couldn't find a frog with hair. So, being unsuccessful in the lowlands, I decided to travel a hundred miles or so up country from the base camp, up into the mountains where the forest gives way to a shaggy, rolling mountain grassland. What little forest there is in this area is confined to narrow strips bordering the streams in the valleys, so this made hunting slightly easier, for you are more or less on the same level as your quarry. These small areas of forest, I found, were full of Booming Squirrels, and their capture was a simple matter. They spent their days in the tree-tops, but in the early morning and evening they would come down to the ground, and venture out into the grass to feed, hopping cautiously between the tufts of grass. We concealed ourselves under the trees early one morning, and as soon as the squirrels had gone out into the grass, we advanced on them, driving them further and further away from the forest, until at last they went to earth in tussocks of grass or hollow stumps. Then we dug them out, and they were pushed into sacks, chattering and biting with indignation, and carried back to camp. The Booming Squirrel gets its name from its curious cry, a resounding thrumming noise like the last vibrations of a giant gong, which it generally utters in the early morning. They are big, handsome animals, with grey and reddish upper parts, a yellow underside, and a great black and white striped tail, which flicks up and down like a flag as they scamper through the branches.

After catching these squirrels I asked the local hunters what other kinds of animals were found in the grassland, and in particular, of course, I asked about the Hairy Frog, though by then I had given up all hope of ever catching one. To my delight and astonishment, instead of treating me as though I was mad as the lowland tribes had done, these hunters agreed that there was a frog with hairs, and, what's more, they knew where to find it. Apparently they were to be seen in the fast running streams in the valleys. On hearing this my delight was so great that I insisted on going out at once to look for them, so, armed with torches, we spent the rest of that night getting thoroughly soaked in a local stream, and, of course, we caught nothing. This went on for a week: night after night the hunters and I would wade up and down these icy watercourses, turning over rocks and peering into holes, shouting to make ourselves heard above the roar of the waterfalls. I had just decided that we were going to be unsuccessful once again, when I caught sight of my first Hairy Frog.

He was perched on a rock at the edge of a deep pool, a great, fat, beautiful, chocolate-coloured frog, big enough to cover a saucer, and his legs and sides were covered with a thick pelt of hair. I knew that if he jumped into those dark waters there was no chance of catching him, so I flung myself forward and grabbed him by one hind leg. But I had overlooked this frog's defensive armoury: his claws. In the fleshy toes of each hind foot this remarkable amphibian has a set of long white claws, which are retractile, like a cat's. As this frog kicked out with his free leg the claws appeared from their sheaths and, sharp as razors, slashed through the skin and flesh of my hand, and, to my shame . . . I let him go! He plopped into the deep pool, leaving me lying on my stomach in the cold waters, nursing my bleeding hand. You can imagine my feelings; to have a Hairy Frog actually in my hand, and then to let it escape. I was sure that I wouldn't get that sort of chance again, but I was wrong, for a little later on that night we caught five Hairy Frogs, a female and four males, and all these males had their hair fully developed. Now, this so-called hair is not really hair at all, but consists of elongated filaments of skin, which grow on the frog's fat thighs and along the sides of its belly. The reason for this curious adornment is obscure, but it's thought that these filaments act as a sort of additional breathing apparatus, like gills, enabling the frog to extract a certain amount of air from the water while it's actually submerged.

There are a great number of extraordinary amphibians in the world, but I think pride of place must go to this one: after all, a frog with a hairy covering to its legs, and claws like a cat, is not the sort of thing one finds every day. I don't think they would be called beautiful by ordinary standards, but to me they had a charm that was all their own. Their great mouth was spread in a perpetual grin under their pop eyes, and they would squat on their hairy haunches and gaze up at me with a trustful, slightly imbecile expression from the depth of their box.

On the journey back from the mountains to base camp these frogs caused me endless worry. In the highlands it's cool and dry, but as you reach the lowland forests it's like entering a Turkish bath. The Hairy Frogs objected to this climate in no uncertain manner, and to prevent them dying I had to stop my lorry load of animals every few miles, and sink the frogs' box into a stream so they would stay cool and moist. Luckily, streams are plentiful in the Cameroons, and you are never very far from water. It was only in this way that I got them back to base camp alive. But on arrival I found that they had rubbed their noses on the woodwork of their boxes, and this was a great danger, for their noses are one of the most delicate parts of their anatomy, and when they get rubbed like this a fungus-like disease is liable to develop and kill the frogs. So a special box was made for them, lined with soft cloth and padding of cottonwool and in this they travelled safely back to England.

By now our collection numbered one hundred and fifty

mammals, birds and reptiles. Our marquee was bulging with cages, and there was hardly room for us to live in it as well. To keep this collection alive and well called for hard and continuous work from early morning until late at night, and both my companion and myself were confined to camp, for we could not spare the time for any more hunting trips into the forest. Collecting is not just a matter of sticking an animal into a cage and throwing it a bit of food now and then. Firstly, your design of cage has to be right, or the animal won't thrive, and in some cases (as with the Hairy Frogs) you have to pad the inside of the cage so that the animal does not get bruised or bumped. Then there's the feeding problem . . . it's worse than new babies. You can't feed them on just anything; fruit that's a bit over-ripe will cause havoc with the stomachs of the more delicate kind of monkey or antelope. Other creatures have a very restricted diet in the wild state, it may be crabs, or termites, or some wild fruit or other. With these animals you have a very difficult job for you have to teach them to eat a substitute food, a food that can be obtained in England. Then, of course, you have the babies: well, they have to be bottle-fed, kept warm, and given unceasing attention if you want them to live. The cages with these animals in were always kept round our beds, so that we could feed the babies in the middle of the night without too much trouble. At one time we had eight young animals at once, ranging from monkeys to antelope, and the noise at one o'clock in the morning when they were fed had to be heard to be believed. All these were problems you had to deal with, as well as the daily routines of cleaning the cages, cutting up food, housing new arrivals, and so on. New arrivals always seemed to appear just when we had run out of boxwood, or lost the hammer, and then we would have to rush around and make some sort of temporary cage out of sticks and rope, until a fresh supply of boxwood arrived, or the hammer was found, and we could deal with the housing shortage.

When the time came for us to leave, it took three large lorries and a van to move the collection two hundred miles down to the coast, and it was a nerve-wracking journey. We travelled at night, as it was cooler for the animals, and snatched what sleep we could in the lorries, but as each bump or jolt left us wondering if some specimen had been killed or hurt, we could not get really good rest. By morning, when it was time to unload and feed the animals, we were bordering on a nervous breakdown wondering what dreadful things had happened among the cages during the night. Once onboard ship things were slightly easier, but we still had to face the long voyage home, with all its attendant difficulties of change of climate, rationing of fresh fruit, and so on.

But, in spite of these difficulties and hardships, I would not have missed those months in the Cameroons for anything. You soon forget the trials and worries, and then you only remember the pleasant things: the cool green interior of the forest, criss-crossed with sparkling streams; the monkeys in the evening, on their way down to drink, crashing through the tree-tops with a sound like great breakers on a rocky shore; the red earth road winding through the trees, and on the drooping telegraph wires alongside it, the Pygmy Kingfishers, small as sparrows, sitting glinting in the sun like opals.

Some Interesting Things Which Have Happened

Gerry's letter to Louisa from the second expedition
to Cameroon in 1949. The town of
Victoria is now Limbé.

April 16
c/o Barclays Bank, Victoria

Dear Mother, just a short note to let you know of some
interesting things which have happened since I last wrote.
Firstly, a thing which will shock you to the core, I was bitten
by a snake. It happened like this: just after I wrote my last
letter, when I was still in Bafut, one evening I was sitting
sipping my tea, when Pious appeared to say that a man had
brought a snake. I went out and found he had brought it in a
calabash. I asked him what kind it was, and he said it was the
kind that go for ground, meaning the harmless blind burrowing snake. I tipped the thing out on the ground to have a look
at it. Sure enough it looked exactly like a burrowing snake, so I
picked it up behind the head. As I was looking at it I noticed
that it had a very well formed pair of eyes. Instead of dropping
it I said, 'look, Pious, this has got eyes'. As I said it the bloody
thing turned its head slightly and dug a fang into the ball of
my right thumb. I dropped it at once and started to squeeze
my thumb, while rushing into the house. Luckily P. has been
well drilled, and within three seconds I had a tie round the

82

base of my thumb, and the P. of Potash to hand. Then I had to steel myself and slash open the wound with a razor blade to rub the potash in. In the meantime a messenger had been sent hot foot to call the driver of the Fon's kitcar to take me into Bamenda to the doctor. While I paced up and down the room drinking French Brandy and noting my second-by-second symptoms Pious packed a bag, cut sandwiches, poured out brandy and generally kept his head. At last the driver arrived, and then of course the bloody kitcar would not start. I stood at the top of the steps, my hand rolled up in yards of brightly coloured tie, shouting abuse at the fifty odd people who were pushing the car up and down. By this time my thumb was very swollen and painful, and the glands in my armpits also. At last the car was started and off we went. The first stop was at the Basle Mission, my nearest neighbours, about five miles down the road. They had no serum, but tied two bandages round my arm so tightly that my hand went quite blue, and I had delightful thoughts of gangrene. Then we shot off to Bamenda, doing the sixteen miles there in about thirty minutes dead. I decanted myself somewhat unsteadily at the doctor's house about three quarters of an hour after I had been bitten. The doc. was very good, rushed me inside and proceeded, with medical relish, to give me five injections of serum: two in the thumb, one in the wrist, and two in my arm. These were extremely painful, and made me feel quite sick and dizzy. When he had finished the doc. gave me a large whisky which I made short work of. Then I had a hot bath and was packed off to bed, only being allowed a light supper. I slept like a log, and the next morning the swelling in my hand had gone down a lot, and there was no pain at all. In about four days I could use the hand alright, although it ached a lot if I used it too much. However, it is quite o.k. now.

Just before leaving Bafut and rejoining Ken at Mamfe I got the rarest specimen I could get up there. A half-grown Golden Cat. This is about five times as large as a domestic cat, a rich tawny-gold, with a white belly covered with black spots. Its eyes are a lovely blue-green colour. We had a wonderful job getting it out of the bag it was brought in and into a cage. London Zoo have not had this species for about fifty years, so we are very proud of it.

Our job at the moment is to try and catch a hippo in the Mamfe river. We went down to see a large herd about two miles downstream yesterday, and got a wonderful view of them, getting within about fifty yards. They looked simply lovely, but the old bull had a dirty look in his eye, so we kept our distance. On the way back (we were in a very unsafe canoe) we paused for a swim in the shallows, just near some rapids. This was very nice, and grandfather Smith nearly got carried over the waterfall by the current, but luckily got wedged into a small gap, and was saved by six husky canoe men. When we continued on our way, not a hundred yards further on, we met a large crocodile about six foot long floating downstream to our bathing place. Smith, of course, blamed me: There You Are, You See, We Might Have Been Killed, Or Had Our Leg Bitten Off, Or Our Arms. He got quite excited and nearly overturned the banana-shaped craft.

Well, mum, that's all for the moment. Will write again soon, and may have news of a Hippo capture, I hope. Give my love to everyone.

Much love, Gerry

Brow-leaf Toads

I have always liked toads, for I have found them to be quiet, well-behaved creatures with a charm of their own; they have not the wildly excitable and rather oafish character of the frog, nor his gulping and moist appearance. But, until I met these two, I had always imagined that all toads were pretty much the same, and that having met one you had met them all as far as personality was concerned, though they might differ much in colour and appearance. But I very soon found out that these two amphibians had personalities so striking that they might almost have been mammals.

These creatures are called Brow-leaf Toads, because the curious cream-coloured marking on the back is, in shape and colour, exactly like a dead and withered leaf. If the toad crouches down on the floor of the forest it merges into its background perfectly. Hence its English title; its scientific title is 'Eyebrow Toad', which in Latin sounds even more apt: *Bufo superciliaris*, for the Brow-leaf, on first acquaintance, gives the impression of being overwhelmingly supercilious. Above its large eyes the skin is hitched up into two little points, so that the creature has its eyebrows raised at the world in a markedly sardonic manner. The immensely wide mouth adds to this impression of aristocratic conceit by drooping gently at the corners, thus giving the toad a faintly sneering expression that can only be achieved by one other animal that I know of, the camel. Add to this the slow, swaggering walk, and the fact that the creature squats down every two or three steps and gazes at you with a sort of pitying disdain, and you begin to feel that superciliousness could not go much farther.

My two Brow-leafs squatted side by side on a bed of fresh grass in the bottom of the basket and gazed up at me with expressions of withering scorn. I tipped the basket on its side, and they waddled out on to the floor with all the indignation and dignity of a couple of Lord Mayors who had been accidentally locked in a public lavatory. They walked about three feet across the floor and then, apparently exhausted by this effort, squatted down, gulping gently. They surveyed me very fixedly for some ten minutes with what appeared to be ever-increasing disgust. Then one of them wandered away and eventually crouched down by the leg of the table, evidently under the mistaken impression that it was the trunk of a tree. The other continued to stare at me, and after mature reflection he summed up his opinion of my worth by being sick, bringing up the semi-digested corpses of a grasshopper and two moths. Then he gave me a pained and reproachful look and joined his friend under the table.

As I had no suitable cage ready for them, the Brow-leafs spent the first few days locked in my bedroom, wandering slowly and meditatively about the floor, or squatting in a trance-like state under my bed, and affording me untold amusement by their actions. I discovered, after a few hours' acquaintance with my plump roommates, that I had sadly misjudged them, for they were not the arrogant, conceited creatures they pretended to be. They were actually shy and easily embarrassed beasts, completely lacking in self-confidence; I suspect that they suffered from deep and ineradicable inferiority complexes and that their insufferable air of superiority was merely a pose to hide from the world the hideous truth, that they had no faith in their fat selves. I discovered this quite by accident the night of their arrival. I was making notes on their coloration, while the toads squatted on the floor at my feet, looking as though they were composing their own entries for Burke's Peerage. Wanting to examine their hindquarters more closely, I bent down and picked up one of them between finger and thumb, holding him under the armpits, so that he dangled in the air in a most undignified manner. He uttered a loud indignant belch at this treatment and kicked out with his fat hind legs, but my grip was too strong for him and he just had to dangle there until I had finished my examination of his lower regions. Eventually, when I replaced him on the ground next to his companion, he was a different toad altogether. Gone was his aristocratic expression: he was a deflated and humble amphibian. He crouched down, blinking his great eyes nervously, while a sad and timid expression spread over his face. He looked almost as if he was going to cry. This transformation was so sudden and complete that it was astonishing, and I felt absurdly guilty at having been the cause of his ignominy. In order to even things up a bit, I picked up the other one and let him dangle for a while, and he, too, lost his self-confidence and became timid and embarrassed when I replaced him on the floor. They sat there looking so dejected and miserable that it was ludicrous, and my unmannerly laughter proved too much for their sensitive natures, for they waddled rapidly away and hid under the table for the next half-hour. But now that I had learnt their secret I could deflate them at will when they became too haughty: all I had to do was to rap them gently on the nose with my finger, and they would crouch down guiltily, looking as though they were about to blush, and gaze at me with pleading eyes.

I built a nice large cage for my Brow-leafs, and they settled down in it quite happily; however, to keep them healthy, I allowed them to have a walk in the garden every day. When the collection increased, I found that there was too much work to be done for me to be able to stand around patiently while my two blue-blooded aristocrats took the air; I had to cut down on their walks, much to their annoyance. Then, one day, I found a guardian for them in whose hands I could safely leave them while I got on with my work. This guardian was none other than Pavlova the Patas monkey.

Pavlova was extremely tame and gentle, and she took an intense interest in everything that went on around her. The first time I put the Brow-leafs out for a walk near her she was quite captivated by them and stood up on her hind legs, craning her neck to get a better view as they walked sedately across the compound. Going back ten minutes later to see how the toads were getting on, I found that they had both wandered close to the spot where Pavlova was tied. She was squatting between them, stroking them gently with her hands, and uttering loud purring cries of astonishment and pleasure. The toads had the most ridiculously self-satisfied expressions on their faces, and they were sitting there unmoving, apparently flattered and soothed by her caresses.

Every day after that I would put the toads out near to the place where Pavlova was tied, and she would watch them wandering about. She would give occasional cries of amazement at the sight of them, or else stroke them gently until they lay there in a semi-hypnotized condition. If ever they wandered too far away and were in danger of disappearing into the thick undergrowth at the edge of the compound, Pavlova would get very excited and call me with shrill screams to let me know that her charges were escaping, and I would hurry down and bring them back to her. One day she called me when the toads had wandered too far afield, but I did not

hear her, and when I went down some time later Pavlova was
dancing hysterically at the end of her string, screaming furi-
ously, and the Brow-leafs were nowhere to be seen. I undid the
monkey's leash, and she at once led me towards the thick
bushes at the edge of the compound, and within a very short
time she had found the runaways and had fallen on them with
loud purring cries of joy.

Pavlova really got terribly fond of these fat toads, and it was
quite touching to see how eagerly she greeted them in the
morning, gently stroking and patting them, and how worried
she got when they wandered too far away. A thing that she
found very difficult to understand was why the toads were not
clad in fur, as another monkey would be. She would touch
their smooth skins with her fingers, endeavouring to part the
nonexistent fur, a worried expression on her little black face;
occasionally she would bend down and lick their backs in a
thoughtful sort of way. Eventually she ceased to worry over
their baldness, and treated them with the same gentleness and
affection she would have displayed towards offspring of her
own. The toads, in their own curious way, seemed to become
quite fond of her as well, though she sometimes upset their
dignity, which annoyed them. I remember one morning I had
just given them both a bath, which they thoroughly enjoyed,
and on walking across the compound they got various bits of
stick and dirt stuck to their wet tummies. This worried Pavlova, for she liked her protégés to be clean and neat. I found her
sitting in the sunshine, her feet resting on the back of one
Brow-leaf as though he were a footstool, while the other one
dangled in the most undignified fashion from her hand. As he
slowly revolved in midair, Pavlova solemnly picked all the bits
of rubbish from his tummy, talking to him all the time in a

series of squeaks and trills. When she had finished with him she put him on the ground, where he sat looking very crestfallen, while his partner was hoisted up into the air and forced to undergo the same indignity. The poor Brow-leafs had no chance of being superior and pompous when Pavlova was around.

South America

A Charm All of Its Own

Though South America, from a zoologist's point of view, is lacking in the large, flamboyant forms of life that the Old World has to offer, yet it possesses many species that are unique and found nowhere else. The habitats that it offers to its fauna are tremendously varied, ranging from desert to tropical forest, from open pampa land to cold mountain upland. This variety of terrain provides homes for a fantastic assortment of creatures, from the smallest monkeys and birds in the world to the largest rodent, from six-foot-long Iguanas to tree frogs the size of your little fingernail. Having made several trips to different parts of South America to study and catch alive some of these creatures, I find that this fauna has for me a charm all of its own.

South American monkeys are the real story-book monkeys, for they can hang by their tails, unlike those in other parts of the world where the tail is used merely as an organ of balance. Not all of the New World monkeys have this gift, but those that have – the Spider, Woolly, Howler and Capuchin – are so deft and skilful that, watching them, you soon become convinced that it is not a tail but another arm they possess. The Spider Monkey is perhaps the most proficient in the use of its tail. It is a charming, angular creature with a small pert face, and a lanky grace of movement that has to be seen to be believed. The tail always strikes me as being a thing with a life of its own, for it twines and twists, grasps and pulls like a snake, without, it seems, any direction from its owner. I remember watching a large male once sitting upright in the fork of a tree, wearing a solemn and meditative expression on his face, while around him his tail moved like a compass needle, grasping delicately at the twigs and pulling them to within reach of his mouth. The skill of the tail, combined with the apparently absent-minded attitude of the owner, gave the whole performance a ludicrous appearance. In captivity I have seen a Spider Monkey use its tail to drag things towards its cage, sitting upright against the bars with an innocent expression on its face as though disclaiming any responsibility for the action of its rear appendage.

The Howler Monkeys are perhaps one of the most publicised of the New World primates. In some respects they deserve to be, for they are one of the most beautifully coloured mammals, with their black, sullen faces and their thick coats of auburn hair. I once saw a small party of these monkeys moving in their deliberate, rather hunch-backed way, through the trees, with the light of the setting sun falling on them, and they were an unforgettably lovely sight. Their coats gleamed as though on fire, changing from fox-red to almost a wine colour as they moved. Strangely enough, the most publicised thing about Red Howlers is not their colour but their voices. When the spirit moves them, they sing in a powerful, if untuneful chorus, a sound that is commonly heard in the South American forest even at night. This chorus has been described as frightening, awe-inspiring and incredible by various naturalists, and has been compared to the majestic roaring of lions on the plains of Africa. I have heard it on numerous occasions and, I regret to say, found it neither awe-inspiring nor majestic. If I had not known that it was produced by monkeys, I would have said that some careless person had locked a pack of hungry wolves in an empty swimming pool.

The other two species of primates that have prehensile tails are the Woolly Monkey and the Capuchin. The Woolly Monkey is one of the most charming of simians, looking, even when adult, like a curious baby with large dark eyes, a smooth black face and clad in a coat of dense, soft, grey-brown fur. The Capuchin is probably one of the best known of the South American monkeys, for, being intelligent and hardy, it was for many years – until more sophisticated amusements appeared – the main assistant of the organ-grinder. Perched on the organ, clad in a coat and hat, it would solemnly hold out a hut for the pennies of those music lovers who passed by.

It is a curious thing that the New World, unlike Africa and Asia, has produced no ground-dwelling monkeys, nothing to compare to the baboon or the macaques. All the primates live exclusively in trees, but if they are conservative in habits they are certainly not so in appearance, for this Continent has produced some of the most weirdly decorated monkeys in the world. There are the Sakis with shaggy fur and thick, stumpy unprehensile tails, the males of which have their faces decked out in a mask of short, stiff white fur that makes them look as though they had just dipped their heads into a bowl of icing sugar. Then there are the Red Uacaris, that have completely bald heads and faces. As the skin is bright red, they resemble elderly men, clad in shabby brown fur coats, who are just recovering from an acute attack of scarlet fever with its attendant depression. Then, among the Marmosets and Tamarins, the tiny leprechaun-like inhabitants of the tropical forest, you find the Red-handed Tamarin, a squirrel-size beast, coal-black all over, but wearing what appears to be rather smart socks and gloves of a dashing golden yellow; and the Emperor Tamarin, which is decked out with an enormous Kaiser moustache, in white, which is almost the size of its owner. Among the Marmosets you get long white ear tufts, white eyebrow markings, and even one species that has a shock of white hair like some ancient and respected man of letters.

The Douracouli is more sober in appearance, contenting itself with looking rather like an owl. Strictly nocturnal, it is a dainty, delicate little animal that possesses an astonishingly varied vocabulary, even for a monkey. As they hunt, a troop of them carry on an incessant conversation of trills, twitters, gasps, squeaks and purrs, interspersed with a noise like somebody rubbing a wet thumb along a balloon and, in moments of panic, a harsh scream. Apart from this comprehensive language, Douracoulis have other curious habits. I have seen them sit facing one another on a branch, clasping each other's front paws and purring gently for sometimes as long as half an hour. At other times they would sit like this and then suddenly clasp each other passionately while pressing their mouths together like two humans kissing, a most unusual action in a monkey. Both their actions and their language would make a rewarding study for a naturalist.

A group of creatures that has developed many extraordinary forms in South America are the Edentates, the family that includes anteaters, armadillos and the sloths.

Paraguay is the home of the Three-banded Armadillo, one of the daintiest and most curious looking of the family. It is one of the few species capable of rolling itself into a complete ball, like a woodlouse, a trick that offers it a perfect protection from all but the most powerful animals. The hardness of the shell can be judged by the fact that in Paraguay little boys frequently use it as a football, a process that must be acutely uncomfortable to the creature but which does not appear to harm it in any way. They walk very daintily, taking tiny little steps and on the front feet using only the large centre claw, on the tip of which they walk like a ballet dancer. To see their curved shells moving through the undergrowth, with the tiny legs tip-toeing underneath, makes them look like some strange mechanical toy. They are difficult to establish in captivity, as, if the floor of their cage is not of the right softness, they develop a form of ulcer on their feet, and they are finicky about their food as well. But I eventually found they could be kept very successfully on raw brain, raw mincemeat, mashed banana, milk and a vitamin product – a mixture that looked like a bad street accident, but one which these peculiar little creatures seemed to relish.

On the whole, armadillos seem to be very silent creatures, although they are said in moments of extreme panic to utter a scream like a miniature pig. Of the many I have kept, the only sounds I heard them make were tiny grunting noises at the sight of their food, and in the case of the Three-banded Armadillo a subdued hiss when rolling up into a ball, but it was difficult to establish whether this was due to the action of the closing shell or was produced by the animal itself.

The sloths are very much maligned creatures. For years they have been portrayed as animals so lethargic that they could scarcely summon up sufficient energy to get out of the way of an enemy, and as creatures who spend a blissfully lazy existence hanging in some tropical tree. On the whole, they are slow-moving and meditative animals, but one has only to try to catch an excited sloth among the branches of a large tree, and the idea that they are incapable of speed is dispelled.

Unlike the sloths, the anteaters are found both on the ground and in trees. There is the Giant Anteater – a terrestrial species; the smaller Tamandua which is equally at home on the ground or up in trees, possessing a strong prehensile tail; and lastly the Pigmy or Silky Anteater which is strictly arboreal. The Giant is a very large beast: a fully grown specimen may measure five to six feet from the tip of its long nose to the end of its tail and stand three feet at the shoulder. The Tamandua, on the other hand, is only about the size of a small dog, whereas the Silky Anteater is a minute six-inch long creature, from which sticks a tiny pink snout. It has an odd habit of sitting on its hind legs with its tail twisted round a branch and its forelegs raised up above its head. It sits as still as a Guardsman until you touch it or the branch on which it is perched, when the animal will fall forward and chop at you with the sharp claws on its forelegs, which can inflict a nasty wound on the back of your hand. It is not nearly as active as the other two species of anteater, being more slow-moving and sloth-like in its actions.

As everywhere else in the world, rodents are widely spread in South America, and are found in a variety of shapes and sizes, ranging from the Chinchilla with its beautiful, soft fur, high in the Andes, to the little Soldier Rat in the forest of Guiana, whose coarse fur is intermixed with flat, pliable spines. The best known of the South American rodents is the Capybara which has achieved fame only because it is the largest rodent in the world. They are enormous, superior-looking creatures and possess a high degree of personality and intelligence in comparison to other types of rodents found there. It is fortunate that they are strict vegetarians and have adapted themselves to aquatic life along riverbanks, for, should they have taken a liking to the amenities offered by civilised communities and have been able to adapt themselves, as the Brown Rat has done, the damage they could do could be frightful. I have seen a fully grown Capybara gnaw through a half-inch plank in approximately twenty-eight minutes, wearing throughout an expression of acute boredom.

One of the most charming South American rodents is the Tree Porcupine with its long naked prehensile tail, its neat covering of black and white spines and its great bulbous nose and tiny sad eyes. They are definitely the comedians of the forests they inhabit, indulging in a number of ridiculous antics which I have never seen practiced by any other animals. They will sit solemnly, for example, on a branch and juggle with a mango seed, pretending to drop it and retrieving it at the last moment, and each time looking faintly astonished at their success. A pair I had in captivity used to indulge in what I can only describe as shadow-boxing, standing up on their hind legs on a branch, facing each other, holding tight with their tails, and sparring with their front feet, never touching one another and never varying their expression of slightly bemused good humour.

The Opossums are another curious group, and one which you would not expect to find in South America, for they carry their young in pouches. They are, in fact, the only marsupials found outside the Australian region. They range in size from ones as small as a mouse to others the size of a cat. The young, as in all marsupials, are born in a very unfinished condition, and they then make their way up into the mother's pouch where they fix themselves firmly to her teats and stay there to complete their development. In Guiana I met several hunters who, though extremely knowledgeable about animals, were unaware of the Opossum's habits, and, when I explained the process to them, flatly refused to believe that any creature could, as they put it, be born before their time. No amount of argument on my part could convince them, and when I was eventually brought a female Opossum with a bulging pouch I felt it was an ideal opportunity to convert the disbelievers. Having once again delivered my lecture on the breeding habits of marsupials, I turned the female on her back, and with my thumbs opened her pouch to display the half-formed youngsters inside, like a row of tiny, quivering pink sausages in a furry can. The hunters were astounded, and I was rather pleased with the result of my demonstration. I was soon deflated, however, for one of the hunters turned to me and said that what was really puzzling them was how I had manged to split the mother open so neatly with such a casual gesture. After that I gave up attempting to give my hunters natural history lectures.

South America, of course, is immensely rich in reptiles, and particularly so in frogs which appear to have gone out of their way to produce the most extraordinary habits in both breeding and in the care of their young. The pride of place must go to the Pipa or Surinam Toad who, it seems, tries to emulate the Opossum. I must admit that even to the most ardent amphibian lover, this creature leaves a lot to be desired, looking rather as though it had been run over by a very heavy lorry and was partially decomposed. However, when you witness its fevered sex life you forget its unprepossessing appearance.

During the breeding season the skin on the back of the Pipa Toad becomes thickened, spongy and pitted. During mating, the female releases eggs, which are manoeuvred onto her back and then pressed into her spongy skin by the male's rhumba-like movements. Here they adhere, half-buried in the spongy skin, each one in its individual pocket. The half of the egg that protrudes hardens like a little cap. The entire metamorphosis from egg to the completed toad takes place in these pockets, and when the tiny toads are ready to appear, the half of the shell that projects about the mother's back becomes softened and is pushed back like a manhole cover, and the minute speck of life moves free of its mother's rubbery skin. I was lucky enough to witness the hatching of these baby toads on a collecting trip to British Guiana. They chose to come into the world in the middle of the night in the mid-Atlantic, and as well as myself there was an audience of sailors who sat crouched round the kerosene tin in which I kept them, watching with awed interest the struggles of each baby toad to emerge from its cell.

The frogs, not to be outdone by the toads, have produced an extraordinary member of their own, the Paradoxical Frog. This is quite an ordinary-looking amphibian and, like most people with a past, displays no sign of it on its rather vacuous face. The amazing thing about this frog is its early childhood. The tadpoles, having hatched from the spawn, proceed to grow apace until they reach nightmare proportions, nearly six inches long and with bodies the size of a large hen's egg. As if this wasn't enough, when the fore legs and hind legs appear, instead of growing larger as any self-respecting froglet does, the Paradoxical Frog proceeds to shrink, so that the final result of a gargantuan tadpole is a perfectly normal-looking adult.

Among the reptiles are, naturally, the much-maligned Boa Constrictor and Anaconda, the former being one of the most handsome snakes in the world, with its beautiful Persian carpet-like patterning of pink, grey, black, silver and brown. Why these unfortunate reptiles should have acquired such an undeserved reputation for ferocity I can't imagine, unless it is because explorers of South America were short of exciting incidents to keep their readers on their toes, but in fact you would have to go a long way before finding a snake with a more amiable disposition than the average Boa Constrictor, or one that was as retiring as the Anaconda. The aboriginal people of Guiana used at one time to keep the Anaconda in their huts in lieu of cats, for they dealt with the average rat more speedily and successfully than a cat could, and, when lying draped along the beams, were more decorative. The Anaconda, however large, is only too eager to get out of your way and would not dream of deliberately attacking you, unless it was cornered and being irritated.

When you come to examine the bird life that inhabits South America you are bewildered by the variety of shapes and sizes, and by the incredible combination of colours that some of them display. Here you have everything, from the sober black and white ecclesiastical garb of the Andean Condor, the largest flying bird in the world, with a wingspan of nine feet, down to the Hummingbirds the size of a Bumblebee, that looks as though they have been powdered with crushed jewels. For weird adornment you have the Umbrella Bird with its round wig of feathers on the head, and the long, pendulous feathered 'handle' hanging from its breast; and the species of Bell Bird with three long, slender horns, one in the centre of its forehead, and two dropping from the sides of its beak like the moustaches of a Mandarin.

From an ornithologist's point of view, the most interesting species of bird is the Hoatzin, locally known by the uncomplimentary term of Stinking Anna. Here we have a bird that in its early stages resembles the prehistoric Archaeopteryx. It is a brown and white bird the size of a pigeon, with a tattered-looking crest. It lives in the thorn bushes overhanging the creeks in tropical forests. Owing to several physical peculiarities, it is gradually losing its power of flight, but it is in the young Hoatzin that you see the most remarkable features. As soon as they are hatched, and before they have got their feathers, they are extremely active and can scramble about the branches of trees, using for this purpose a 'thumb' on the wing which is elongated and furnished with a sharp claw. Should they be frightened by an enemy, they simply drop from the tree straight into the water where they can swim and dive with all the skill of a frog. Gradually, during its development, this extraordinary 'thumb' grows shorter until in the adult bird it is almost normal, but a young Hoatzin crawling round the branches of a thorn tree, or diving into the stream below, is the nearest approach we shall see to the ancestor of all birds that swam and climbed on earth millions of years ago. Even the adult birds as you watch them hopping heavily through the thorn branches, or taking short ungainly flights, raising and lowering their crests as they land, have something vaguely reptilian about them.

South America, in many respects neglected, when it comes to the point of producing extraordinary forms of animal life, can more than hold its own with any other part of the world.

Gerry's love affair with South America began in British Guiana, now known as Guyana. The following account of his crisscrossing the creek lands of that extraordinary country is noteworthy for revealing his empathy for animals. Normally, Gerry would let nature take its course, but here he 'interferes' with the natural process of predation, clearly overcome by solicitude for the prey.

The Magical Creek Lands

British Guiana, lying in the northern part of South America, is probably one of the most beautiful places in the world, with its thick tropical forest, its rolling savannah land, its jagged mountain ranges and giant foaming waterfalls. To me, however, one of the most lovely parts of Guiana is the creek lands. This is a strip of coastal territory that runs from Georgetown to the Venezuelan border; here a thousand forest rivers and streams have made their way down towards the sea, and on reaching the flat land have spread out into a million creeks and tiny tributaries that glimmer and glitter like a flood of quicksilver. The lushness and variety of the vegetation is extraordinary, and its beauty has turned the place into an incredible fairyland.

In 1950 I was in British Guiana collecting wild animals for zoos in England, and during my six months there I visited the savannah lands to the north, the tropical forest and, of course, the creek lands, in pursuit of the strange creatures living there. I had chosen a tiny village near a place called Santa Rosa as my headquarters in the creek lands, and to reach it required a two-day journey. First, by launch down the Essequibo River and then through the wider creeks until we reached the place where the launch could go no farther, for the water was too shallow and too choked with vegetation. Here we took to dugout canoes, paddled by the quiet and charming indigenous people who were our hosts, and leaving the broad main creek we plunged into a maze of tiny waterways on one of the most beautiful journeys I can remember.

Some of the creeks along which we travelled were only about ten feet wide, and the surface of the water was completely hidden under a thick layer of great creamy water-lilies, their petals delicately tinted pink, and a small fern-like water-plant that raised, just above the surface of the water, on a slender stem, a tiny magenta flower. The banks of the creek were thickly covered with undergrowth and great trees, gnarled and bent, leant over the waters to form a tunnel; their branches were festooned with long streamers of greenish-grey Spanish moss and clumps of bright pink-and-yellow orchids. With the water so thickly covered with vegetation, you had the impression when sitting in the bows of the canoe that you were travelling smoothly and silently over a flower-studded green lawn that undulated gently in the wake of your craft. Great black woodpeckers, with scarlet crests and whitish beaks, cackled loudly as they flipped from tree to tree, hammering away at the rotten bark, and from the reeds and plants along the edges of the creek there would be a sudden explosion of colour as we disturbed a marsh bird which flew vertically into the air, with its hunting-pink breast flashing like a sudden light in the sky.

The village, I discovered, was situated on an area of high ground which was virtually an island, for it was completely surrounded by a chess-board of creeks. The little native hut that was to be my headquarters was some distance away from the village and placed in the most lovely surroundings. On the edge of a tiny valley an acre or so in extent, it was perched amongst some great trees which stood round it like a group of very old men, with long grey beards of Spanish moss. During the winter rains the surrounding creeks had overflowed so that the valley was now drowned under some six feet of water out of which stuck a number of large trees, their reflections shimmering in the sherry-coloured water. The rim of the valley had grown a fringe of reeds and great patches of lilies. Sitting in the doorway of the hut, one had a perfect view of this miniature lake and its surroundings.

Along one side of the valley some previous owner of the hut had planted a few mango and guava trees, and while I was there the fruit ripened and attracted a great number of creatures. The tree-porcupines were generally the first on the scene. They lumbered out of the undergrowth, looking like portly and slightly inebriated old men, their great bulbous noses whiffling to and fro, while their tiny and rather sad little eyes, that always seemed full of unshed tears, peered about them hopefully. They climbed up into the mango trees very skilfully, winding their long, prehensile tails round the branches to prevent themselves from falling, their black-and-white spines rattling among the leaves. They then made their way along to a comfortable spot on a branch, anchored themselves firmly with a couple of twists of the tail, then sat up on their hind legs, and plucked off a fruit. Holding it in their front paws, they turned it round and round while their large buck teeth got to work on the flesh. When they had finished a mango they sometimes began playing a rather odd game with the big seed. Sitting there they looked round in a vague and rather helpless manner while juggling the seed from paw to paw as though not quite certain what to do with it, and occasionally pretending to drop it and recovering it at the last moment. After about five minutes of this they tossed the seed down to the ground below and shuffled about the tree in search of more fruit.

Sometimes when one porcupine met another face to face on a branch, they both anchored themselves with their tails, sat up on their hind legs and indulged in the most ridiculous boxing match, ducking, and slapping with their front paws, feinting and lunging, giving left hooks, uppercuts and body blows, but never once making contact. Throughout this performance (which lasted perhaps for a quarter of an hour) their expression never changed from one of bewildered and benign interest. Then, as though prompted by an invisible signal, they went down on all fours and scrambled away to different parts of the tree. I could never discover the purpose of these boxing bouts nor identify the winner, but they afforded me an immense amount of amusement.

Naturally these animals made only sporadic appearances; there were, however, two creatures which were in constant evidence in the waters of the drowned valley. One was a young cayman, the South American alligator, about four feet long. He was a very handsome reptile with black-and-white skin as knobbly and convoluted as a walnut, a dragon's fringe on his tail, and large eyes of golden-green flecked with amber. He was the only cayman to live in this little stretch of water. I could never understand why no others had joined him, for the creeks and waterways, only a hundred feet or so away, were alive with them. None the less this little cayman lived in solitary state in the pool outside my hut and spent the day swimming round and round with a rather proprietary air. The other creature always to be seen was a jacana, probably one of the strangest birds in South America. In size and appearance it is not unlike the English moorhen, but its neat body is perched on long slender legs which end in a bunch of enormously elongated toes. It is with the aid of these long toes and the even distribution of weight they give that the jacana manages to walk across water, using the water-lily leaves and other water-plants as its pathways. It has thus earned its name of lily-trotter.

The jacana disliked the cayman, while the cayman had formed the impression that Nature had placed the jacana in his pool to add a little variety to his diet. He was, however, a young and inexperienced reptile, and at first his attempts to stalk and capture the bird were ridiculously obvious. The jacana would come mincing out of the undergrowth, where it used to spend much of its time, and walk out across the water, stepping delicately from one lily leaf to the next, its long toes spreading out like spiders and the leaves dipping gently under its weight. The cayman, on spotting it, immediately submerged until only his eyes showed above water. No ripple disturbed the surface, yet his head seemed to glide along until he got nearer and nearer to the bird. The jacana, always pecking busily among the water-plants in search of worms and snails and tiny fish, rarely noticed the cayman's approach and would probably have fallen an easy victim if it had not been for one thing. As soon as the cayman was within ten or twelve feet he would become so excited that instead of submerging and taking the bird from underneath he would suddenly start to wag his tail vigorously and shoot along the surface of the water like a speedboat, making such large splashes that not even the most dim-witted bird could have been taken unawares; and the jacana would fly up into the air with a shrill cry of alarm, wildly flapping its buttercup-yellow wings.

For a long time it did not occur to me to wonder why the bird should spend a greater part of the day in the reed-bed at one end of the lake. But on investigating this patch of reed I soon discovered the reason, for there on the boggy ground I found a mat neatly made of weed on which lay four round creamy eggs heavily blotched with chocolate and silver. The bird must have been sitting for some time, for only a couple of days later I found the nest empty and a few hours after that the jacana leading out her brood for its first walk into the world.

She emerged from the reed-bed, trotted out on to the lily leaves, then paused and looked back. Out of the reeds her four babies appeared, with the look of outsize bumble-bees, in their golden-and-black fluff, while their long slender legs and toes seemed as fragile as spider-webs. They walked in single file behind their mother, always a lily leaf behind, and they waited patiently for their mother to test everything before moving forward. They could all cluster on one of the great plate-like leaves, and they were so tiny and light that it scarcely dipped beneath their weight. Once the cayman had seen them, of course, he redoubled his efforts, but the jacana was a very careful mother. She kept her brood near the edge of the lake, and if the cayman showed any signs of approaching, the babies immediately dived off the lily leaves and vanished into the water, to reappear mysteriously on dry land a moment later.

The cayman tried every method he knew, drifting as close as possible without giving a sign, concealing himself by plunging under a mat of waterweeds and then surfacing so that the weeds almost covered eyes and nose. There he lay patiently, sometimes even moving very close inshore, presumably in the hope of catching the jacanas before they ventured out too far. For a week he tried each of these methods in turn, and only once did he come anywhere near success. On this particular day he had spent the hot noon hours lying, fully visible, in the very centre of the lake, revolving slowly round and round so that he could keep an eye on what was happening on the shore. In the late afternoon he drifted over to the fringe of lilies and weeds and managed to catch a small frog that had been sunning itself in the centre of a lily. Fortified by this, he swam over to a floating raft of green weeds, studded with tiny flowers, and dived right under it. It was only after half an hour of fruitless search in other parts of the little lake that I realized he must be concealed under the weeds. I trained my field-glasses on them, and although the entire patch was no larger than a door, it took me at least ten minutes to spot him. He was almost exactly in the centre and as he had risen to the surface a frond of weed had become draped between his eyes; on the top of this was a small cluster of pink flowers. He looked somewhat roguish with this weed on his head, as though he were wearing a vivid Easter bonnet, but it served to conceal him remarkably well. Another half an hour passed before the jacanas appeared and the drama began.

The mother, as usual, emerged suddenly from the reed-bed, and stepping daintily on to the lily leaves paused and called her brood, who pattered out after her like a row of quaint clockwork toys and then stood patiently clustered on a lily leaf, awaiting instructions. Slowly the mother led them out into the lake, feeding as they went. She would poise herself on one leaf and, bending over, catch another in her beak, which she would pull and twist until it was sufficiently out of the water to expose the underside. A host of tiny worms and leeches, snails and small crustaceans, generally clung to it. The babies clustered round and pecked vigorously, picking off all this small fry until the underside of the leaf was clean, whereupon they all moved off to another.

Quite early in the proceedings I realized that the female was leading her brood straight towards the patch of weeds beneath which the cayman was hiding, and I remembered then that this particular area was one of her favourite hunting-grounds. I had watched her standing on the lily pads, pulling out the delicate, fern-like weed in large tangled pieces and draping it across a convenient lily flower so that her babies could work over it for the mass of microscopic life it contained. I felt sure that, having successfully managed to evade the cayman so far, she would notice him on this occasion, but although she paused frequently to look about her, she continued to lead her brood towards the reptile's hiding place.

I was now in a predicament. I was determined that the cayman was not going to eat either the female jacana or her brood if I could help it, but I was not quite sure what to do. The bird was quite used to human noises and took no notice of them whatever, so there was no point in clapping my hands. Nor was there any way of getting close to her, for this scene was being enacted on the other side of the lake, and it would have taken me ten minutes to work my way round, by which time it would be too late, for already she was within twenty feet of the cayman. It was useless to shout, too far to throw stones, so I could only sit there with my eyes glued to my field-glasses, swearing that if the cayman so much as touched a feather of my jacana family I would hunt him out and slaughter him. And then I suddenly remembered the shotgun.

It was, of course, too far for me to shoot at the cayman: the shot would have spread out so much by the time it reached the other side of the lake that only a few pellets would hit him, whereas I might easily kill the birds I was trying to protect. It occurred to me, however, that as far as I knew the jacana had never heard a gun, and a shot fired into the air might therefore frighten her into taking her brood to safety. I dashed into the hut and found the gun, and then spent an agonizing minute or two trying to remember where I had put the cartridges. At last I had it loaded and hurried out to my vantage-point again. Holding the gun under my arm, its barrels pointing into the soft earth at my feet, I held the field-glasses up in my other hand and peered across the lake to see if I was in time.

The jacana had just reached the edge of the lilies nearest the weed patch. Her babies were clustered on a leaf just behind and to one side of her. As I looked she bent forward, grabbed a large trailing section of weed and pulled it on to the lily leaves, and at that moment the cayman, only about four feet away, rose suddenly from his nest of flowers and weeds and, still wearing his ridiculous bonnet, charged forward. At the same moment I let off both barrels of the shotgun, and the roar echoed round the lake.

Whether it was my action that saved the jacana or her own quick-wittedness I do not know, but she rose from the leaf with extraordinary speed just as the cayman's jaws closed and cut the leaf in half. She swooped over his head, he leapt half out of the water in an effort to grab her (I could hear the clop of his jaws) and she flew off unhurt but screaming wildly.

The attack had been so sudden that she had apparently given no orders to her brood, who had meanwhile been crouching on the lily leaf. Now, hearing her call, they were galvanized into action, and as they dived over-board the cayman swept towards them. By the time he reached the spot, they were under water, so he dived too and gradually the ripples died away and the surface of the water became calm. I watched anxiously while the female jacana, calling in agitation, flew round and round the lake. Presently she disappeared into the reed-bed and I saw her no more that day. Nor did I see the cayman for that matter. I had a horrible feeling that he had succeeded in catching all those tiny bundles of fluff as they swam desperately under water, and I spent the evening planning revenge.

The next morning I went round to the reed-bed, and there to my delight I found the jacana, and with her three rather subdued-looking babies. I searched for the fourth one, but as he was nowhere to be seen it was obvious that the cayman had been at any rate partially successful. To my consternation the jacana, instead of being frightened off by her experience of the previous day, proceeded once more to lead her brood out to the water-lilies, and for the rest of the day I watched her with my heart in my mouth. Though there was no sign of the cayman, I spent several nerve-wracking hours, and by evening I decided I could stand it no longer. I went to the village and borrowed a tiny canoe which two people kindly carried down to the little lake for me. As soon as it was dark I armed myself with a powerful torch and a long stick with a slip-knot of rope on the end, and set off on my search for the cayman. Though the lake was so small, an hour passed before I spotted him, lying on the surface near some lilies. As the torch-beam caught him, his great eyes gleamed like rubies. With infinite caution I edged closer and closer until I could gently lower the noose and pull it carefully over his head, while he lay there quietly, blinded or mesmerized by the light. Then I jerked the noose tight and hauled his thrashing and wriggling body on board, his jaws snapping and his throat swelling as he gave vent to loud harsh barks of rage. I tied him up in a sack and the next day took him five miles deep into the creeks and let him go. He never managed to find his way back, and for the rest of my stay in the little hut by the drowned valley I could sit and enjoy the sight of my lily-trotter family pottering happily over the lake in search of food, without suffering any anxiety every time a breeze ruffled the surface of the rich tawny water.

The Kitten

The news had spread through the village that there had arrived a mad gringo who was willing to pay good money for live animals, and the first trickle of specimens started. The first arrival was a local man carrying, on the end of a length of string, a coral snake striped in yellow, black and scarlet, like a particularly revolting old school tie. Unfortunately, in his enthusiasm, the man had tied the string too tightly about the reptile's neck, and so it was very dead.

I had better luck with the next offering. A man arrived clasping a large straw hat tenderly to his bosom. After a polite exchange of greetings I asked to see what he had so carefully secured in his hat. He held it out, beaming hopefully at me, and then looking into the depths of the hat I saw reclining at the bottom, with a dewy-eyed expression on its face, the most delightful kitten. It was a baby Geoffroy's cat, a small species of wild cat which is getting increasingly rare in South America. Its basic colouring was a pale fawny yellow, and it was dappled all over with neat, dark brown spots. It regarded me with large bluey-green eyes from the interior of the hat, as if pleading to be picked up. I should have known better. In my experience it is always the most innocent-looking creatures that can cause you the worst damage. However, misled by its seraphic expression, I reached out my hand and tried to grasp it by the scruff of the neck. The next moment I had a bad bite through the ball of my thumb and twelve deep red grooves across the back of my hand. As I withdrew my hand, cursing, the kitten resumed its innocent pose, apparently waiting to see what other little game I had in store for it. While I sucked my hand like a half-starved vampire, I bargained with the man and eventually purchased my antagonist. Then I tipped it, hissing and snarling like a miniature jaguar, out of the hat and into a box full of straw. There I left it for an hour or so to settle down. I felt that its capture and subsequent transportation in a straw hat might be mainly responsible for its fear and consequent bad temper, for the creature was only about two weeks old, as far as I could judge.

When I thought it had settled down and would be willing to accept my overtures of friendship, I removed the lid of the box and peered in hopefully. I missed losing my left eye by approximately three millimetres. I wiped the blood from my cheek thoughtfully; obviously my latest specimen was not going to be easy. Wrapping my hand in a piece of sacking I placed a saucer of raw egg and minced meat in one corner of the box, and a bowl of milk in the other, and then left the kitten to its own devices. The next morning neither of the two offerings of food had been touched. With a premonition that this was going to hurt me more than the kitten, I filled one of my feeding-bottles with warm milk, wrapped my hand in sacking and approached the box.

Now I have had, at one time and another, a fair amount of experience in trying to get frightened, irritated or just plain stupid animals to feed from a bottle, and I thought that I knew most of the tricks. The Geoffroy's kitten proceeded to show me that, as far as it was concerned, I was a mere tyro at the game. It was so lithe, quick and strong for its size that after half an hour of struggling I felt as though I had been trying to pick up a drop of quicksilver with a couple of crowbars. I was covered in milk and blood and thoroughly exhausted, whereas

1. Gerald as a child.

2. Bungalow in Jamshedpur, India, where Gerald was born in 1925.

3. Gerald gazes at Mouse Island, Corfu, 1936.

4. Durrell family in Corfu, 1938 (*left to right:* Margaret, Nancy, Lawrence, Gerald and Louisa Durrell).

5. Gerald with his beloved dog Roger, Corfu, 1936.

6. Louisa Durrell, Corfu, 1938.

7. Lawrence and Nancy Durrell, 1930s.

8. Gerald's tutor and friend Theodore Stephanides, Corfu, 1930s.

9. Gerald greets Theodore on set of *This is Your Life*, 1983.

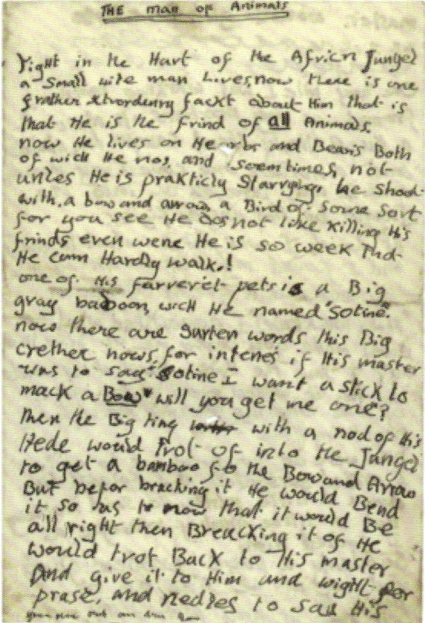

10. First page of *Man of Animals*, Gerald's first known writing, *c.* 1937.

11. Cover of first typescript of *My Family and Other Animals*, by Gerald Durrell, 1956.

12. Leslie, Louisa and Gerald Durrell, Bournemouth, *c.* 1945.

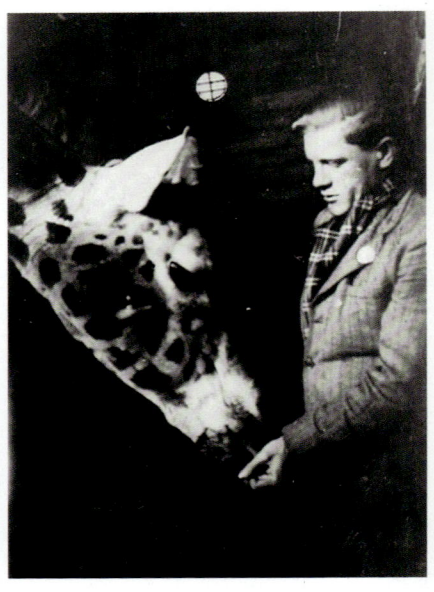

13. Gerald feeding giraffe at Whipsnade Zoo, *c.* 1946.

14. Gerald on riverboat on first expedition to Cameroon, 1947.

15. Gerald with angwantibo from Cameroon, 1948.

16. Gerald with hairy frog from Cameroon, 1949.

17. Gerald with Sarah Huggersack, the young giant anteater, Paraguay, 1954.

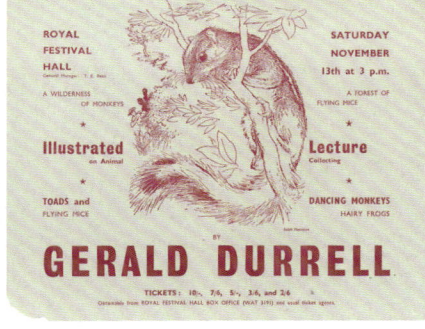

18. Flyer for Gerald's lecture about animal collecting at the Royal Festival Hall, where Sarah made a guest appearance, 1954.

19. Gerald, his wife Jacquie, baby chimp Chumley and other animals from the third Cameroon expedition in Margaret's garden in Bournemouth, 1958.

20. Gerald with Claudius, the tapir, Buenos Aires, 1959.

the kitten regarded me with blazing eyes and seemed quite ready to continue the fight for the next three days if necessary. The thing that really irritated me was that the kitten had – as I knew to my cost – very well-developed teeth, and there seemed no reason why it should not eat and drink of its own accord, but, in this stubborn mood, I knew that it was capable of quite literally starving itself to death. A bottle seemed the only way of getting any nourishment down it. I put it back in its box, washed my wounds, and was just applying plaster to the deeper of them when Luna arrived, singing cheerfully.

'Good morning, Gerry,' he said, and then stopped short and examined my bloodstained condition. His eyes widened, for I was still bleeding profusely from a number of minor scratches.

'What's this?' he asked.

'A cat . . . gato,' I said irritably.

'Puma . . . jaguar?' he asked hopefully.

'No,' I said reluctantly, 'chico gato montes.'

'Chico gato montes,' he repeated incredulously, 'do this?'

'Yes. The bloody little fool won't eat. I tried it on the bottle, but it's just like a damned tiger. What it really needs is an example . . .' my voice died away as an idea struck me.

'Come on, Luna, we'll go and see Edna.'

'Why Edna?' inquired Luna breathlessly as he followed me down the road to Helmuth's flat.

'She can help,' I said.

'But, Gerry, Helmuth won't like it if Edna is bitten by a gato montes,' Luna pointed out in Spanish.

'She won't get bitten,' I explained. 'I just want her to give me a kitten.'

Luna gazed at me with dark, puzzled eyes, but the conundrum was too much for him, and so he merely shrugged and followed me round to Helmuth's front door. I clapped my hands and went into Helmuth's and Edna's comfortable sitting room, where Edna was ensconced over a huge pile of socks, darning placidly and listening to the gramophone.

'Hullo,' she said, giving us her wide, attractive smile, 'the gin is over there, help yourself.'

Edna had a beautiful and placid nature: nothing seemed to worry her unduly. I am sure that if you walked into her sitting room with fourteen Martians in tow she would merely smile and point out the location of the gin.

'Thank you dear,' I said, 'but I didn't come for gin, strange though it may sound.'

'It does sound strange,' agreed Edna, grinning at me mischievously. 'Well, if you don't want gin, what do you want?'

'A kitten.'

'A kitten?'

'Yes . . . you know, a small cat.'

'Today Gerry is loco,' said Luna with conviction, pouring out two liberal measures of gin and handing one to me.

'I have just bought a baby gato montes,' I explained to Edna. 'It's extremely wild. It won't eat by itself, and this is what it did to me when I tried to feed it on the bottle.' I displayed my wounds. Edna's eyes widened.

'But how big is this animal?' she asked.

'About the size of a two-week-old domestic cat.'

Edna looked stern. She folded up the sock she was darning.

'Have you put disinfectant on those cuts?' she inquired, obviously preparing herself for a medical orgy.

'Never mind the cuts . . . I washed them . . . But what I want from you is a kitten, an ordinary kitten. Didn't you say the other day that you were infested with kittens over here?'

'Yes,' said Edna, 'we have plenty of kittens.'

'Good. Well, can I have one?'

Edna considered.

'If I give you a kitten will you let me disinfect your cuts?' she asked cunningly. I sighed.

'All right, blackmailer,' I said.

So Edna disappeared into the kitchen quarters, from whence came a lot of shrill exclamations and much giggling. Then Edna returned with a bowl of hot water and proceeded to minister unto my cuts and bites, while a procession of semi-hysterical girls filed into the room, carrying in their arms groups of kittens of all shapes and colours, from ones still blind to ones that were half-grown and looked almost as wild as my Geoffroy's cat. Eventually I chose a fat, placid female tabby which was approximately the same size and age as my wild cat, and carried it back in triumph to the garage. Here I spent an hour constructing a rough cage, while the tabby kitten purred vigorously and rubbed itself round my legs, occasionally tripping me up. When the cage was ready I put the tabby kitten in first, and left it for an hour or so to settle down.

Most wild animals have a very strong sense of territory. In the wild state, they have their own particular bit of forest or grassland which they consider their own preserve, and will defend it against any other member of their own species (or other animals sometimes) that tries to enter it. When you put wild animals into cages the cages become, as far as they are concerned, their territory. So, if you introduce another animal into the same cage, the first inmate will in all probability defend it vigorously, and you may easily have a fight to the death on your hands. So you generally have to employ low cunning. Suppose, for example, you have a large vigorous creature who is obviously quite capable of looking after itself, and it has been in a cage for a period of a few weeks. Then you get a second animal of the same species, and you want to confine them together, for the sake of convenience. Introduce the new specimen into the old one's cage, and the old one may well kill it. So the best thing to do is to build an entirely new cage, and into this you introduce the weaker of the two animals. When it has settled down, you then put the stronger one in with it. The stronger one will, of course, still remain the dominant animal, and may even bully the weaker one, but as far as he is concerned he has been introduced into someone else's territory, and this takes the edge off his potential viciousness. It's a sort of Lifemanship that any collector has to practise at one time or another.

In this case I was sure that the baby Geoffroy's was quite capable of killing the domestic kitten, if I introduced the kitten to it, instead of the other way round. So, once the tabby had settled down, I seized the Geoffroy's and pushed it, snarling and raving, into the cage, and stood back to see what would happen. The tabby was delighted. It came forward to the angry Geoffroy's and started to rub itself against its neck, purring loudly. The Geoffroy's, taken aback by its greeting as I had hoped, merely spat rather rudely, and retreated into a corner. The tabby, having made the first overtures of friendship, sat down, purring loudly, and proceeded to wash itself with a self-satisfied air. I covered the front of the cage with a piece of sacking and left them to settle down, for I was sure now that the Geoffroy's would do the tabby no real harm.

That evening, when I lifted the sacking, I found them lying side by side, and the Geoffroy's, instead of spitting at me as it had done up until now, contented itself with merely lifting its lip in a warning manner. I carefully inserted a large bowl of milk into the cage, and a plate containing the finely chopped meat and raw egg, which I wanted the Geoffroy's to eat. This was the crucial test, for I was hoping that the tabby would fall

upon this delicious fare and, by example, encourage the Geoffroy's to eat. Sure enough, the tabby, purring like an ancient
outboard engine, flung itself at the bowl of milk, took a long
drink and then settled down to the meat and egg. I had retreated
to a place where I could see without being seen, and I watched
the Geoffroy's carefully. To begin with it took no interest at all,
lying there with half-closed eyes. But eventually the noise the
tabby was making over the egg and meat – it was a rather
messy feeder – attracted its attention. It rose cautiously and
approached the plate, while I held my breath. Delicately it
sniffed round the edge of the plate, while the tabby lifted a face
that was dripping with raw egg and gave a mew of encourage-
ment, slightly muffled by the portion of meat it had in its
mouth. The Geoffroy's stood pondering for a moment, and
then, to my delight, sank down by the plate and started to eat.
In spite of the fact that it must have been extremely hungry it
ate daintily, lapping a little raw egg, and then picking up a
morsel of meat which it chewed thoroughly before swallow-
ing. I watched them until, between them, they had cleaned
both plates, then I replenished them with more milk, egg and
meat, and went to bed well satisfied. The next morning both
plates were spotless, and the Geoffroy's and the tabby were
locked in each other's arms, fast asleep, their stomachs bulging
like two little hairy balloons. They did not wake up until
midday, and then they both looked distinctly debauched. But
when they saw me approaching with the plates of food they
both displayed considerable interest, and I knew that my battle
with the Geoffroy's was won.

Vanished Peoples of Patagonia

In the days when Darwin had visited Patagonia there had still been the remnants of the Patagonian indigenous tribes left, fighting a losing battle against extermination by the settlers and soldiers. These people were described as being uncouth and uncivilized and generally lacking in any quality that would qualify them for a little Christian charity. So they vanished, like so many animal species when they come into contact with the beneficial influences of civilization, and no one, apparently, mourned their going. In various museums up and down Argentina you can see a few remains of their crafts (spears, arrows, and so on) and inevitably a large and rather gloomy picture purporting to depict the more unpleasant side of their character, their lechery. In every one of these pictures there was shown a group of long-haired, wild-looking men on prancing wild steeds, and the leader of the troupe inevitably had clasped across his saddle a white woman in a diaphanous garment, whose mammary development would give any modern film star pause for thought. In every museum the picture was almost the same, varying only in the number of wild-looking men shown, and the chest expansion of their victim.

Fascinating though these pictures were, the thing that puzzled me was that there was never a companion piece to show a group of civilized white men galloping off with a voluptuous indigenous girl, and yet this had happened as frequently (if not more frequently) than the rape of white women. It was a curious and interesting sidelight on history. But nevertheless these

spirited but badly painted portraits of abduction had one interesting feature. They were obviously out to give the worst
possible impression, and yet all they succeeded in doing was in
impressing you with a wild and rather beautiful people, and
filling you with a pang of sorrow that they were no longer in
existence. So, when we got down into Patagonia I searched
eagerly for relics of these people, and questioned everyone for
stories about them. The stories, unfortunately, were much of a
muchness and told me little, but when it came to relics, it
turned out, I could not have gone to a better place than the
penguin metropolis.

One evening, when we had returned to the *estancia* after a
hard day's filming and were drinking *maté* round the fire, I
asked Señor Huichi – *via* Marie – if there had been many indigenous tribes living in those parts. I phrased my questions
delicately, for I had been told that Huichi had indigenous blood
in him, and I was not sure whether this was a thing he was
proud of or not. He smiled his slow and gentle smile, and said
that on and around his *estancia* had been one of the largest
concentrations of indigenous people in Patagonia. In fact, he
went on, the place where the penguins lived still yielded evidence of their existence. What sort of evidence, I asked eagerly.
Huichi smiled again, and, getting to his feet he disappeared
into his darkened bedroom. I heard him pull a box out from
under his bed, and he returned carrying it in his hands and
placed it on the table. He removed the lid and tipped the contents out on to the white tablecloth, and I gasped.

I had seen, as I say, various relics in the museums, but nothing to compare with this; for Huichi tumbled out on to the
table a rainbow-coloured heap of stone objects that were
breath-taking in their colouring and beauty. There were arrowheads ranging from delicate, fragile-looking ones the size of

your little fingernail, to ones the size of an egg. There were spoons made by slicing in half and carefully filing down big sea-shells; there were long, curved stone scoops for removing the edible molluscs from their shells; there were spearheads with razor-sharp edges; there were the balls for the *boleadoras*, round as billiard-balls, with a shallow trough running round their equators, as it were, which took the thong from which they hung; these were so incredibly perfect that one could hardly believe that such precision could be achieved without a machine. Then there were the purely decorative articles: the shells neatly pierced for ear-rings, the necklace made of beautifully matched green, milky stone rather like jade, the seal bone that had been chipped and carved into a knife that was obviously more ornamental than useful. The pattern on it was simple arrangements of lines, but carved with great precision.

I sat poring over these objects delightedly. Some of the arrowheads were so small it seemed impossible that anyone could create them by crude chipping, but hold them up to the light and you could see where the delicate wafers of stone had been chipped away. What was more incredible still was that each of these arrowheads, however small, had a minutely serrated edge to give it a bite and sharpness. As I was examining the articles I was suddenly struck by their colouring. On the beaches near the penguins almost all the stones were brown or black; to find attractively coloured ones you had to search. And yet every arrowhead, however small, every spearhead, in fact every piece of stone that had been used had obviously been picked for its beauty. I arranged all the spear- and arrowheads in rows on the tablecloth, and they lay there gleaming like the delicate leaves from some fabulous tree. There were red ones with a darker vein of red, like dried blood; there were green ones covered with a fine tracery of white; there were blue-white ones, like mother-of-pearl; and yellow and white ones covered with a freckling of blurred patterns in blue or black where the earth's juices had stained the stone. Each piece was a work of art, beautifully shaped, carefully and minutely chipped, edged and polished, constructed out of the most beautiful piece of stone the maker could find. You could see they had been made with love. And these, I reminded myself, were made by the supposedly barbarous, uncouth, and utterly uncivilized people for whose passing no one appeared to be sorry.

Huichi seemed delighted that I should display such obvious interest and admiration for his relics, and he went back into the bedroom and unearthed another box. This one contained an extraordinary weapon carved from stone: it was like a small dumb-bell. The central shaft which connected the two great, misshapen balls of stone fitted easily into the palm of your hand, so that then you had a great ball of stone above and below your fist. As the whole thing weighed about three pounds it was a fearsome weapon, capable of splitting a man's skull like a puff ball. The next item in the box – which Huichi reverently unwrapped from a sheet of tissue-paper – looked as though, in fact, it had been treated with this stone club. It was a human skull, white as ivory, with a great splinter-edged gaping hole across the top of the cranium.

Huichi explained that over the years, whenever his work had taken him to the corner of the *estancia* where the penguins lived, he had searched for relics. He said that people had apparently used that area very extensively, for what particular purpose no one was quite sure. His theory was that they had used the great flat area where the penguins now nested as a sort of arena, where the young men of the tribe practised shooting with bow and arrow, spear-throwing, and the art of entangling their quarry's legs with the *boleadoras*. On the other side of the great sand-dunes, he said, were to be found huge piles of empty seashells. I had noticed these great, white heaps of shells, some covering an area of a quarter of an acre and about three feet thick, but I had been so engrossed in my filming of the penguins that I had only given them a passing thought. Huichi's theory was that this had been a sort of holiday resort, as it were. They had come down there to feed on the succulent and plentiful shellfish, to find stones on the shingle beach from which to make their weapons, and a nice flat area on which to practise with these weapons. What other reason would there be for finding these great piles of empty shells, and, scattered over the sand-dunes and shingle patches, such a host of arrow- and spearheads, broken necklaces, and the occasional crushed skull? I must say Huichi's idea seemed to me to be a sensible one, though I suppose a professional archaeologist would have found some method of disproving it. I was horrified at the thought of the number of delicate and lovely arrowheads that must have been splintered and crushed beneath the Land-Rover wheels as we had gaily driven to and fro over the penguin town. I resolved that the next day, when we had finished filming, we would search for arrowheads.

As it happened, the next day we had only about two hours' decent sunshine suitable for filming, and so the rest of the time we spent crawling over the sand-dunes in curious prenatal postures, searching for arrowheads and other left-overs. I very soon discovered that it was not nearly as easy as it seemed.

Huichi, after years of practice, could spot things with uncanny accuracy from a great distance.

'*Esto, una,*' he would say, smiling, pointing with the toe of his shoe at a huge pile of shingle. I would glare at the area indicated, but could see nothing but unworked bits of rock.

'*Esto*,' he would say again, and bending down pick up a beautiful leaf-shaped arrowhead that had been within five inches of my hand. Once it had been pointed out, of course, it became so obvious that you wondered how you had missed it. Gradually, during the course of the day, we improved, and our pile of finds started mounting, but Huichi still took a mischievous delight in wandering erect behind me as I crawled laboriously across the dunes, and, as soon as I thought I had sifted an area thoroughly, he would stoop down and find three arrowheads which I had somehow missed. This happened with such monotonous regularity that I began to wonder, under the influence of an aching back and eyes full of sand, whether he was not palming the arrowheads, like a conjuror, and pretending to find them just to pull my leg. But then my unkind doubts were dispelled, for he suddenly leant forward and pointed at an area of shingle I was working over.

'*Esto*,' he said, and, leaning down, pointed out to me a minute area of yellow stone protruding from under a pile of shingle. I gazed at it unbelievingly. Then I took it gently between my fingers and eased from under the shingle a superb yellow arrowhead with a meticulously serrated edge. There had been approximately a quarter of an inch of the side of the arrowhead showing, and yet Huichi had spotted it.

However, it was not long before I got my own back on him. I was making my way over a sand-dune towards the next patch of shingle, when my toe scuffed up something that gleamed white. I bent down and picked it up, and to my astonishment found I was holding a beautiful harpoon-head about six inches long, magnificently carved out of fur seal bone. I called to Huichi, and when he saw what I had found his eyes widened. He took it from me gently and wiped the sand off it, and then turned it over and over in his hands, smiling with delight. He explained that a harpoon-head like this was one of the rarest things you could find. He had only ever found one, and that had been so crushed that it had not been worth saving. Ever since he had been looking, without success, for a perfect one to add to his collection.

Presently it was getting towards evening, and we were all scattered about the sand-dunes hunched and absorbed in our task. I rounded a spur of sand and found myself in a tiny valley between the high dunes, a valley decorated with two or three wizened and carunculated trees. I paused to light a cigarette and ease my aching back. The sky was turning pink and green as the sun started to set, and apart from the faint whisper of the sea and the wind it was silent and peaceful. I walked slowly up the little valley, and suddenly I noticed a slight movement ahead of me. A small, very hairy armadillo was scuttling along the top of the dunes like a clockwork toy, intent on his evening search for food. I watched him until he disappeared over the dunes and then walked on. Under one of the bushes I was surprised to see a pair of penguins, for they did not usually choose this fine sand to dig their nest-burrows in. But this pair had chosen this valley for some reason of their own, and had scraped and scrabbled a rough hole in which squatted a single fur-coated chick. The parents castanetted their beaks at me and twisted their heads upside down, very indignant that I should disturb their solitude. I watched them for a moment, and then I noticed something half hidden in the pile of sand which they had dug out to form their nest. It was something smooth and white. I went forward and, despite the near hysterics of the penguins, I scraped away the sand. There lying in front of me was a perfect human skull, which the birds must have unearthed.

I sat down with the skull on my knee and smoked another

cigarette while I contemplated it. I wondered what sort of a man he had been. I could imagine him, squatting on the shore, carefully and cleverly chipping minute flakes off a piece of stone to make one of the lovely arrowheads that now squeaked and chuckled in my pocket. I could imagine him, with his fine brown face and dark eyes, his hair hanging to his shoulders, his rich brown guanaco skin cloak pulled tight about him as he sat very straight on a wild, unshod horse. I gazed into the empty eye-sockets of the skull and wished fervently that I could have met the man who had produced anything as beautiful as those arrowheads. I wondered if I ought to take the skull back to England with me and give it a place of honour in my study, surrounded by his artistic products. But then I looked around, and decided against it. The sky was now a vivid dying blue, with pink and green thumb-smudges of cloud. The wind made the sand trickle down in tiny rivulets that hissed gently. The strange, witch-like bushes creaked pleasantly and musically. I felt that this man would not mind sharing his last resting place with the creatures of what had once been his country, the penguins and the armadillos. So I dug a hole in the sand and placing the skull in it I gently covered it over.

When I stood up in the rapidly gathering gloom the whole area seemed steeped in sadness, and the presence of the vanished people seemed very close. I could almost believe that, if I looked over my shoulder quickly, I would see one on horseback, silhouetted against the coloured sky. I shrugged this feeling off as fanciful, and walked back towards the Land-Rover.

As we rattled and bumped our way back in the dusk towards the *estancia*, Huichi, talking to Marie, said very quietly: 'You know, señorita, that place always seems to be sad. I feel the people there very much. They are all around you, their ghosts, and one feels sorry for them because they do not seem to be happy ghosts.'

This had been my feeling exactly.

Before we left the next day I gave Huichi the harpoon-head I had found. It broke my heart to part with it, but he had done so much for us that it seemed very small return for his kindness. He was delighted, and I know that it is now reverently wrapped in tissue-paper in the box beneath his bed, not too far from where it ought to be, buried on the great shining dunes, feeling only the shifting sand as the penguins thump solidly overhead.

Central America

Jabirus and Jaguars

It is not every day, nor indeed everywhere, that one can swim with and share one's lunch with some thirty handsome pelicans on a deserted tropical island. One can do this, however, off the coast of Belize, a country the size of Wales, nestling in the middle of Central America.

We were staying at a hotel called Rum Point Inn on the southern coast and each day you can be transported out to the small island of your choice, to be marooned there among the pelicans with a plentiful supply of food and drink and then 'rescued' at night. The pelicans were courteous hosts, allowing you to share the reef with them so that you could both fish in your own ways, we with snorkels and they with plummeting dives into the shallow water, followed by much gulping and tail-wagging. Elegant brown and spotless white, floating like toy celluloid ducks on the clear waters, they looked very winsome, their great beaks curved in a shy smile and their dark eyes gazing at you timidly. Yet, when they took to the air, they were enormously impressive and you felt this was the nearest approach to seeing a pterodactyl in flight that you were ever likely to experience.

My wife Lee and I had come to Belize to see for ourselves the wonders that had been described to us, which we felt must be an exaggeration. After all, to us as jaded conservationists, observing the destruction of the world with dismay and frustration, how could we be expected to believe in a small country in Central America (of all places) that had over 70% of its natural and secondary forest left. A country where you could see 425 species of bird, ranging from the giant jabiru stork to hummingbirds smaller than your little fingers, glittering in a dozen colours as though wrought in tiny jewels by the great Fabergé himself; a country that could boast mammals from manatee to jaguar, with armadillos, ocelots and porcupines for good measure; a country that could boast the longest reef in the world, second only to Australia's Great Barrier Reef, and a country, moreover, that was not ruined for the sake of the tourist trade. These reports seemed too good to be true, so we had gone there to see for ourselves and had found that not only was it true, but that it was even better than the descriptions we had been given.

We arrived at the airport, where we were met by our friend Sharon Matola, who runs the excellent local zoo. Knowing the country intimately, Sharon had orchestrated our entire trip. She hustled us out of the noisy, friendly airport, full of smiling faces, and then drove us over bumpy roads, across which flocks of long-tailed Anis flew, black as witches. In next to no time, we had left the town and the airport behind and had come to a halt by a wide placid creek, its banks lined with the multicoloured foliage that only the tropics can produce. We parked and walked down to the edge of the sherry-coloured waters. Here grew an enormous mango tree and on it was a bell. This was pressed to alert our host, Mike Heusner, and he presently arrived, chugging down to us in a stately boat with an outboard engine. As we made our way down the river, we passed boat-billed herons perched in the huge trees, each bird with its large beak looking irresistibly comic, like a sort of chagrined and mournful Donald Duck. Plumbago-blue kingfishers lit up the gloom of the mangroves like lights as they flitted from branch to branch, and brilliant tanagers, gold as chrysanthemums, flirted with each other in the treetops.

Down a side channel, we travelled between lines of red mangroves, their leaves forming a green tunnel, the reddish root structures embedded in the water like the claws of some gigantic dragon. At one time, these lovely and extraordinary trees were thought to be useless except as fuel, but now we have learnt that the great web of criss-crossing roots retains the soil, adding to the land as the mangroves march across the silt and bind it together. These enormous root webs – like fingerprints, no two alike – also serve as nurseries for the baby fish and turtles and other important underwater life. Mike switched off the engine and for a while we drifted over the brown waters between the massed ranks of the mangroves. It was like sliding smoothly down the nave of a huge, gothic cathedral, the only sound being the gentle lapping of the water, as, disturbed by our passage, the ripples ran glinting among the twisted roots.

The next morning, we set off for a place called Chan Chich at a place near the Guatemalan border called Gallon Jug. To accomplish this, Sharon had chartered a four-seater plane that looked as fragile as a butterfly. The pilot was a handsome young man with a toothpaste advert smile and a strong aroma of baby powder. It was not until we were airborne that we began to have any doubts as to our dashing pilot's abilities. We were flying over a vast expanse of virgin forest that looked like a thick green pile carpet, when the pilot turned to Sharon and asked her where we wanted to go. Considerably startled, Sharon said we wanted to be taken to Gallon Jug. The pilot enquired whether she had ever been there. Sharon admitted that she had once flown over it.

'Good,' said the pilot, 'then you'll be able to guide me. I've never been there.'

'Well,' said Sharon, slightly shaken, 'if you could let me have a look at the map . . .'

'Maps?' said the pilot scornfully, 'I haven't got any maps.'

We flew on in an uneasy silence for ten minutes or so and I began to wonder how much fuel we had. At this point, we reached an area where the forest had been felled to make pasture for cattle and through the fields ran a red earth road, neatly fenced, leading to a ranch house.

'Better drop in and ask the way,' said the pilot laconically.

He banked sharply and did a sort of Red Baron dive downwards, leaving all our stomachs behind. For one horrifying moment, I thought he was going to try to land on the road and even I, inexperienced aviator that I am, could see that our wings would be neatly shaved off by the fence posts. However, he swerved at the last minute and landed in a field, whose surface bore as much resemblance to an airstrip as the South Col. We bounced, banged and clattered our way down to the end of the field and stopped in the nick of time some twenty feet away from a large very surprised cow and the large very surprised owner of the beast. The pilot got out and there was much arm waving and pointing which did not seem very conclusive to me. I enquired of Lee, who was occupying the co-pilot's seat, how much fuel we had left and she told me the pilot had just said we had plenty. To say that my faith in him was now shattered was the understatement of the century. I would not have believed him if he told me the sky was blue. I instructed Lee to keep a close eye on the fuel gauge. The pilot got into the plane, mumbling to himself, and we took off, missing the road fences by about three and a half feet. For the next hour we flew round and round aimlessly until even our intrepid pilot was forced to confess that we had practically no fuel left and so we had to fly back to Belize City. Here we changed both planes and aeronaut. I told the handsome young pilot as we left him that if ever I had the misfortune to fly with him again, I would supply him with a white stick and a guide dog.

We eventually got to Gallon Jug and then drove on through magnificent forest to the camp at Chan Chich. To call it a camp, of course, is a misnomer, since it conjures up thoughts of hot tents that fall down in the middle of the night, smelly oil lamps that burst into flames and inedible food that would only be considered haute cuisine in the average English hotel. At Chan Chich, however, nothing could be further from the truth. Here, among some ancient Mayan ruins, beautifully overgrown with lush tropical vegetation, a series of cabins has been built in a most exquisite architectural style, mimicking Mayan houses. They are made out of a local wood which is a warm, reddish rust colour that merges into the jungle backdrop. A feature of these buildings, which I had never seen, is that the walls are slatted like Venetian blinds so you can open up, and see without being seen, each of the walls in your room. Apart from the creature comforts you would expect in a major hotel, every cabin is surrounded by a wide verandah where you can sit at ease and watch birds, mammals and reptiles living their lives out in the intricate mass of green forest thirty or so feet away from your bed. It makes you wonder why places like Butlins and Benidorm were ever invented. In my opinion, Chan Chich is the model that all such places in every part of the world should follow. You can walk – or better still go on horseback – to witness a pageant of birds; not only birds that live in Belize, but all the beautiful, fragile warblers and other species that (because they don't have to worry about money, credit cards, visas or passports) come down from the USA to recuperate and have a holiday after the exhausting task of rearing their young in Massachusetts or Maine, Tennessee or Texas. That is one of the many reasons why these forests are of such importance. If they vanish, the birds that so busily help the farmers in the USA by eating their insect pests will vanish as well. Nature knows no boundaries, neither does conservation. The forests of Belize are as of much importance to the North Americans as they are to the Belizeans.

Down one of the Chan Chich trails, I counted thirty different species of bird, ranging from hummingbirds like flitting chips of opal to toucans with their huge beaks, yellow as bananas, like circus clowns. On one flowering bush the size of a small armchair I counted twelve different species of butterfly feeding, each more glittering and garish than the last, until the whole bush of delicate lacy white flowers looked as unreal as a Woolworths jewellery counter.

It was along one of these trails that we made contact with a jaguar, one of the most beautiful of the cat family. As we were walking along, we must have disturbed it over its kill, for the first thing we knew was the thunder-rumbling threat of a big cat displeased. We could not see it, but the noise was loud and menacing and we moved off quickly, though I am glad to report that we did not actually run. To come between a jaguar and its lunch is something that even the most intrepid of naturalists would hesitate to do, especially as we were armed only with a notebook and a very sharp pencil. After this blood-curdling experience (actually not so blood-curdling, as we knew that any self-respecting jaguar was not going to leave a succulent deer to engulf a smelly human being) we went back to our cabin and, while having sundowners, we watched a parade of ocellated turkeys pass, stately as a group of dowager duchesses, glittering bronze and green in the fading sun, and

then from the darkening depths of the forest we heard the ava-
lanche of sounds which is the nighttime roaring of the howler
monkeys, telling everyone it is *their* territory. Then, when their
raucous sign-posting had finished, the other noises took over in
the warm velvet gloom – the purr of the moths, the crisp vio-
lining of cicadas, the asthmatic croup of frogs, all gentle and
intriguing, all magical. You felt as though you were in a great
cradle of life, intricate and beautiful, that had taken millions of
years to evolve, millions of years to achieve this perfection, but
a perfection as delicate as crystal that could be so easily shattered by the tramping boots of civilisation as it is being trodden
underfoot in so many parts of the world.

We left Chan Chich with great reluctance, for there were so
many wonderful things to see and do and we felt six months
would be too short a stay. However, our adventures were not
over by any means. Through the kindness of Brigadier Lambe,
Commander of the British Forces in Belize, we had arranged
to cadge a lift on one of their helicopters. This fearsome flying
machine was going on a routine duty to deliver supplies to a
group of archaeologists, who were at work excavating an enormous Mayan temple recently discovered deep in the jungle and
said to be even bigger than the fabled Tikal in Guatemala. The
helicopter was piloted by two clean-limbed, sparkling-eyed
young men who appeared to be all of sixteen years old and
who were as ebullient as if they had just won the Battle of Britain
single-handed. These young bloods were obviously delighted
at the chance of taking two beautiful women for a joy ride, but
I fear looked upon my presence as unnecessary, though they
were very polite about my intrusion.

We took off like some malformed but dextrous dragonfly
and were soon zooming over miles and miles of lush green
forest. We were lucky enough to have with us Bill Burley who

was helping the Belize government in its plans for protecting this priceless heritage. As we flew along, Bill gave us a running commentary on which parts of forest were to be used for sustainable, selective timber production and which set aside as strictly protected areas. It was so heartening to hear of a government with such a rich resource making plans to use it wisely for the benefit of Belizeans and for the protection of the ecosystem, and not simply to chop and burn everything in sight, as is happening in so many areas of the Tropics.

Presently, we dropped down almost to tree level and then came to a hole in the canopy that looked just about large enough to put a Mini into. To my astonishment the helicopter then descended into this hole like a well-conducted lift and landed in the clearing below, the blades of our machine missing the surrounding trees by what looked to me like six inches, as supplies for the archaeologists were off-loaded. I began to think I was having more horrifying aerial experiences in Belize than anywhere else in the world that I had been. However, my experiences were not at an end. I suffer from vertigo if I have my shoes resoled, so you can imagine my feelings when our two fresh-faced boys announced they were now going to open the doors on each side of the helicopter so we could get a better view and take photographs. Sitting at two thousand feet, with nothing to prevent you from plummeting to your death but an extremely fragile-looking webbing belt was definitely not my idea of an exhilarating experience.

So we flew, with the doors wide open, over the Cockscomb Jaguar Reserve, the only such reserve in South or Central America, 150 square miles of virgin forest, in which one of the most beautiful of the big cats finds refuge. Near the rim of this important reserve lies the highest mountain range in Belize, crowned by Victoria Peak. Even I had to admit that, although the flight was not for people without nerves of steel, it revealed a spectacle. This huge, saw-edged range, with its feet buried in the forest and the almost sheer sides of its highest peaks bespattered with various coloured lichens and other small plants, was magnificent.

Finally we landed and as I was just congratulating myself on having reached *terra firma* intact, our two heroes who were responsible for my nervous condition took the opportunity to kiss my wife goodbye, an exercise in which she joined with more enthusiasm than was strictly needed or seemly.

So we returned to wintry England, but carrying in our mind's eye many wonderful sights. Jabiru storks mating awkwardly, like stilt walkers, on their huge stick nest. Coral reefs ablaze with fish like a firework display. Orchids and other epiphytes as bizarre and colourful as the birds that flew around them. The miles and miles of forest like a great polychromatic rug, a home to untold millions of life forms. And above all, the charming Belizeans themselves.*

---

* *Our experiences in Belize would not have been possible without the guidance of the extraordinary Sharon Matola, one of the great innovators in the zoo world. The visit also coincided with the early days of an initiative called 'Programme for Belize', dedicated to protecting the country's rainforest ecosystems and sustainable use of forest resources. It gave rise to the World Land Trust, a pioneering UK-based organization which raises funds to purchase land all over the world on behalf of its local conservation partners. We launched 'Programme for Belize' and the World Land Trust in London in 1989. I served on the trust's council for many years and am now an ambassador.*

New Zealand, Australia & Malaysia

Gerry and his first wife, Jacquie, had worked nonstop establishing, managing and funding Jersey Zoo since 1959. In need of a break, they set sail in 1962 for a part of the world furthest from home – New Zealand, Australia and Malaya – to make a television documentary and gather material for a book which Gerry eventually published as Two in the Bush.

Letter to Mother from New Zealand

Australia, May 1962

Dear Mother –

At last I have got five minutes to give you my impressions of New Zealand. The voyage out was o.k. but dull. When we got to Suez I stood on deck straining my eyes for a glimpse of camels, Arabs, pyramids, etc. What did we see at the Gateway to the East? A bloody great hoarding, sixty foot by twenty, informing us in words and pictures that if we drank enough Guinness we should be able to lift an iron girder so large that any intelligent elephant would have left it alone. Our next stop was Aden: very pleasant, but it was dark by the time we could get ashore, and so we couldn't see very much. Then we plunged on and arrived at Auckland. Here, to our astonishment, we found ourselves greeted like royalty. The red carpet was unrolled in no uncertain fashion. We were interviewed, photographed from seventy different angles, recorded, televised, and generally exhausted. We found the Wildlife Department had – to use a New Zealand expression – jacked up our whole tour for us, and had detailed one Brian Bell from the Department to be our guide throughout our stay. Land Rovers had put a brand new job at our disposal, and Brian had brought it up from Wellington with him. We had a couple of days in Auckland, a rather nice, semi-tropical city, which left us feeling dead, for the bloody Press would not leave us alone. At one point we had eight reporters in our hotel room at once, and the room was fairly small. The smell of printer's ink nearly killed us. So we fled the city and sped down North Island towards the place where we were going to meet up with Chris Parsons and Jim Saunders (the cameraman). The countryside is rather English: they have chopped down most of the forest, and so now all you see is grassland with clumps of imported trees, and a sea of bloody sheep. Then, of course, there are all the things they have imported: on every side you see Blackbirds, Skylarks, Goldfinches, etc. We met up with Chris and Jim on the banks of a lake called Fongapay. Here we filmed a huge concentration of Black Swans, which the New Zealanders imported from Australia and have now bred to such an extent they are a pest. The lake was black with them: there were about 100,000 of them. We chased them in a speed boat to get flight shots, and as they took off in clouds the air vibrated with the sound of their wings. Our next stop was a town called Rotorua, a very weird place. It's built on the still quivering remains of a volcano. The whole town smells strongly of sulphur, and apparently it is nothing to get up one morning and find that a geyser of red-hot water has forced its way through your drawing-room floor. Wherever there is a crack in the ground a stream of sulphur smoke pours out, or else a jet of hot water. Everywhere around the town there are mud pools that gluck and gobble like huge cauldrons of porridge, and a special area where the big geysers are found. These can gush up to eighty feet high. We were busy filming one of these when my cine camera (sold to me by an unprincipled Jersey dealer) jammed. Just at that moment the geyser we were next to – called Gertrude or something – went off like a bomb. She only does this once a year or something. As I was unable to film it I was somewhat disgruntled and remarked: 'I suppose the whole f*****g place is going to blow up now . . .' I wondered why everyone kept waving their arms at me frantically, and then I realised that Chris had switched on the recording machine to get the sound of the geyser; I have no doubt when they play the tape through at the BBC the reaction will be interesting, to say the least. Smelling strongly of sulphur we made our way down to Wellington, a deadly dull town, where once again we were driven mad by reporters. However, I amused myself by giving them my views on New Zealand sheep farmers (narrow-minded, bigoted, short-sighted idiots) and New Zealand hotels (where you are treated with the charm and good manners that you would expect from a Mongolian yak herdsman if you had just shot his wife by mistake). To my surprise they printed all this, and Jim, who is a timid soul, was convinced that I would be knocked down in the street by an indignant sheep farmer. However, nothing happened, except that a lot of the local population shook me firmly by the hand and said it was high time somebody said something about the sheep farmers and hotels. While in Wellington another section of the red carpet was unrolled: I was invited to lunch with the Cabinet, forsooth. Can you picture me sitting there surrounded by the Minister for this and the Minister for that?

The fact that ninety per cent of them were sheep farmers only added to the jest. They really were a set of gimlet-eyed sharks. I had only just recovered from this when we were invited to lunch at Government House: as H.E. was really responsible for opening up New Zealand for us we could not refuse. However they turned out to be charming and we enjoyed the lunch. Our next job was to go and film on Kapiti, an island lying about a mile off the coast. We had to get there in a launch, and it was then that we discovered that Jim was not only prone to homesickness, car and plane sickness, but sea sickness as well. Kapiti is a bird sanctuary, and though the birds are wild they are incredibly tame. The first we saw were the Wekas, dumpy brown birds the size of a chicken with very worried expressions. They prowled around our feet, examining us and the equipment with great care, and consulting each other with a most curious noise, like someone beating softly on a tomtom. Then we saw the beautiful green and yellow Bellbird, which has a lovely clear note, and the black Tui with his yellow whiskers, who came and sat in a tree and sang for us. Next to arrive was the Native pigeon, a huge bird and far more beautiful than I had thought it would be, with a snow-white breast and lovely shades of purple and green on the back. Then George Fox, who looks after the island, said he would call the Kakas; these are large parrots, clad in rather sombre shot silk featherings, and with very large, strongly hooked beaks. Fox shouted out for a bit and then, suddenly the birds appeared out of the forest, screeching excitedly. They flew down and perched all over us to eat the dates Fox had provided. One of them decided that my head was the ideal perch, and as their claws are long and sharp I was nearly scalped. But it was a wonderful experience to be able to call wild birds up out of the forest like that, even though my scalp took a week to heal.

WECKA

Our next venture was to a pair of rocks called the Brothers. There is a lighthouse on one of them, with three men in charge. Our reason for going there was to see the Tuatara lizards, which abound there. We got into a launch (much to

Jim's disgust) and wended our way through Queen Charlotte Sound, which was very lovely, not unlike a Scottish loch. On all sides we saw groups of Fluttering Shearwaters, and little clusters of Fairy Penguins, who lay on the surface watching us anxiously, and then, as the boat got nearer, dived below the surface. As the sea was flat and the water clear we could see them perfectly as they swam below the surface, so clearly in fact, that we were able to film them. When we left the Sound the sea became rough, and Brian Bell got a bit anxious, for the only way to get on to the Brothers is to be hauled by crane, in a sort of rope pig net. However, when we got to the rock the weather was not too bad, and they lowered the net for us. I must say it was very unpleasant, for you're hauled up some two hundred feet, revolving slowly, the crane making the most ominous noises, with a delightful view of the jagged rocks that you would fall on to if anything went wrong. Jacquie said it took ten years off her life; I felt the same.

Alan Wright, as soon as we had sorted out the gear, took me down to a hut where, as he said, he had caught up 'a few' Tuataras for us to film. He opened the door of the hut and I was faced with a sea of the things, ranging from ones six inches long to two feet. I was astonished at their colourings, for the ones I had seen in captivity had been drab brown. But these were mottled and speckled with vivid sage green, mustard yellow and rich fawn. They made quite loud purring grunts when you held them, and were very active.

It really was thrilling that evening, for as dusk fell all the birds whose burrows the Tuataras share came back to the island; Petrels, Shearwaters, Prions and Penguins. They crept into their burrows and had prolonged conversations with each other, grunting, squeaking, gargling, braying, until the whole island vibrated. In and out of the short scrub the Tuataras prowled, their eyes gleaming like jewels in the torch beam. There were also Giant Geckos all over the rocks, and I collected a number of these, which I sent off by air and which I hope are now settled in happily at Jersey. All five of us had to sleep in a tiny hut that night, and our slumbers were not of the sweetest as two pairs of Fairy Penguins had their nest burrows under the floor, and spent the whole night braying at each other like four donkeys; even banging on the floor with a boot did not have the slightest effect on their singing.

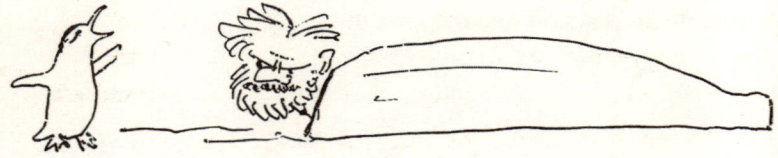

When we left the Brothers we were praying for fine weather, not only so that we could get off the damn place, but also so that we could get on to the White Rock: this is a lump of rock about the size of a small block of flats, and is one of the only three breeding colonies of the King Shag, of which there are only three hundred and fifty members left in the world. Fortunately the sea was very calm and we were able to get up on to the rock. It is so soft that you can crumble it up in your hands like a biscuit: given a couple of days you could demolish the whole thing without tools. The Shags were very large birds, almost the size of a goose, with white shirt fronts and huge, flat feet. They were very ungainly on land, shuffling about like penguins. We saw a number of them collecting nesting material, and doing a bit of courtship. Eventually the whole of the White Rock will be eaten away by wind and waves, and then God knows where the poor devils will breed.

After this we paid two quick visits to various parts of the coast, one to see the Royal Albatross colony, and one to see the Yellow-eyed Penguins. The Albatross chicks were delightful, like huge, indignant powder puffs, squatting regally on the cliffs. The Yellow-eyed Penguins were wonderful birds: slate blue on the back, with bright yellow feathers forming a sort of army cap on their heads, and amber yellow eyes. They are probably the rarest of the Penguins, only about a thousand left.

Baby Albatross

After this came the highlight of our trip: we had been granted permits to go into the Notornis Valley. The Notornis (Takahe) is that bird that they thought was extinct until they rediscovered it in this remote valley in the mountains. They think there might be about four hundred pairs. The valley is, of course, strictly protected, and no one is allowed to go in without permission.

Operation Takahe

In 1948 a discovery was made in New Zealand that shook the ornithological world out of its usual comatose condition in an incredible manner – no less than the discovery (or re-discovery) of a bird that had vanished, a bird that had, for the last fifty years, been believed to be extinct. It was, to give it its full title, the notornis or takahe (*Notornis mantelli*), and the whole history of this bird is one of the most fascinating in the annals of ornithology.

The first takahe fossils were discovered in 1847, and excited even the staid naturalists of those days. The bird had been known to the Maoris from both North and South Islands, but in North Island it was only known from fossil remains. In South Island, the Maoris said, the takahe had been common, particularly around the shores of Te Anau and Manapouri, two large glacial lakes. It was so common, in fact, that the Maoris used to organise annual hunts during the winter, when the snows up in the mountains drove the birds down to lower levels in search of food, but by the time the Europeans came to the area, only fossil remains could be found. Then, in 1849, the first live one was caught on Resolution Island in Dusky Sound by a party of sealers, who did what human beings usually do in these circumstances: they ate it. Two years later another takahe was discovered and presumably suffered the same fate, but fortunately the skins of both these birds were obtained by a gentleman called Mantell, who sent them to the Natural History Museum in London. For twenty-eight years after this the takahe vanished again, as mysteriously as it had reappeared, then, in 1879, another specimen was caught near Lake Te Anau, and in 1898 yet another was caught by a dog in the same vicinity. Now it seemed as though the takahe was really extinct, that it had followed in the footsteps of that other famous flightless bird, the dodo, for fifty years passed and there was no sign of it at all.

But there was a Dr G.B. Orbell who did not believe that the takahe had suffered the fate of the dodo, and in 1948 he set out on an expedition to see if he could find it. The place he chose was an old glacial valley which lay high up in the mountains on the western shores of Lake Te Anau. His expedition was not a success for, apart from seeing some ill-defined footprints and hearing some unusual bird calls, he found no proof that the takahe was still in existence. Nothing daunted, he went back to the valley seven months later, and there he found a small breeding colony of the elusive bird. This is the sort of discovery that every naturalist dreams of making, but only one in a million achieves, and so I can understand and envy the delight which Dr Orbell must have felt when he caught his first glimpse of a real, live takahe. The day after his discovery, of course, the reappearance of the takahe was headline news all over the world, and the New Zealand government, fearing a sudden influx of sightseers, ornithologists and other fellow travellers into this tiny valley – thus disturbing the colony – stepped in with commendable promptitude and immediately declared the whole area a vast sanctuary, making it out of bounds to anyone who was not an accredited scientist or naturalist, and even their visits were under government and Wildlife Department supervision. So the takahe (numbering, as far as he could judge between thirty and fifty birds) was secure in its own sanctuary at last, a sanctuary measuring some seven hundred square miles.

Shortly after we had arrived in Wellington I had met Gordon

Williams who, at the time the takahe was rediscovered, was a biologist attached to the New Zealand Wildlife Service. He told me about the second part of the takahe story which was, if anything, even more remarkable than the first.

The birds in their remote valley were certainly anything but safe, in spite of the fact that the whole area had been designated a sanctuary and no unauthorised person was let in. To begin with, their numbers were minute and it was quite possible for a sudden influx of the introduced stoat and weasel to wipe them out, or for a similar influx of introduced deer or opossums to do much the same thing by their damage to the trees, thus altering the whole habitat of the bird. So, once again, one of New Zealand's native birds was being threatened by introduced animals. It was obviously impossible to patrol the valley to make sure that predators, deer and opossums did not get into it, so there was only one thing to do to ensure the safety of the takahe, and that was to try to establish a breeding colony of them in captivity; but this was not quite so easy as it appeared on the surface. First, a site for the experiment had to be chosen which closely resembled the Takahe Valley; then public opinion had to be weaned on to the side of the experimenters, for a lot of well-meaning people – not fully understanding the ramifications of the problems and the dangers that faced the newly rediscovered birds – were against 'putting them in cages'. The first problem was solved by finding a very suitable area up at Mount Bruce, some eighty miles from Wellington, and public opinion was at last persuaded that the whole scheme was for the good of the birds. So Operation Takahe came into being.

Now, as Gordon Williams explained, came the hardest part of all. In those days the only way to get into and out of the valley was to climb from the shores of Lake Te Anau up the steep, thickly forested slopes over extremely difficult terrain until you reached the narrow gorge entering the valley, two thousand five hundred feet above. This was difficult enough (as previous expeditions had found out) even if you were just going up there to film or collect scientific data; but to climb up there, collect live takahe and bring them down again, was a feat that would make even the most hardened collector blanch. It was obvious that these difficulties ruled out the capture and transportation of fully adult birds, for everything taken up into or brought down out of the valley had to be transported by pack, and it was felt that the adult birds would not survive the journey; therefore, the only thing to do was to get chicks. Now this decision in itself brought up a whole host of new problems; firstly the chicks would have to have a foster-mother and it seemed that bantams, the time-honoured domestic breed of fowl for this job, were the ideal choice. But even the most phlegmatic of bantams was not going to take kindly to suddenly having a lot of takahe chicks shoved under her, and being told to keep them warm. So the answer was to get takahe eggs and put them under bantams, but then, as somebody pointed out, even the most well-behaved bantam, brimming over with mother love, could hardly be expected to sit tight on the eggs while being bumped and jolted all the way up to and down from Takahe Valley. Gloom and despair settled over the instigators of Operation Takahe and it seemed as if it really was going to be impossible to get any of the birds out of the valley to safety. Then somebody (I suspect Williams himself, for he was so desperately keen on the project) suggested that the bantams be 'brain-washed' – that is to say, that a series of bantams be taught to sit tight on a nest of eggs no matter what the circumstances were. It was a long shot but well worth trying, and now began a careful selection of bantams. Out of a hundred or so, a handful were chosen either for their dim-wittedness or their basically phlegmatic characters, and these birds had to undergo what was, to all intents and purposes, a sort of avian assault course. They each had a clutch of chicken eggs to sit on in a cardboard box, and once they were sitting firmly they were then subjected to every form of shock that they might have to cope with on their trip to and from the valley. The boxes were jolted about, they were dropped, they were driven in cars over bumpy roads, taken in trains, speedboats and aeroplanes. Gradually the bantams of weaker moral fibre started to crack, and desert their eggs, so that at the end of the experiment only three were left. Of these, one was chosen for the simple reason that sitting on her eggs in a cardboard box, she had been placed on top of a car and a low branch had swept box, bantam and eggs straight off the roof – a piece of basic training that had not been included in the curriculum. The box, after rolling over and over for several yards, came to a halt the wrong way up, but when it was opened they found the bantam still sitting on her eggs with grim determination – and not one of the eggs was broken, for presumably they had been cushioned against the shock by her body. So this dutiful bantam was chosen for the task of being the most important member of the Operation Takahe expedition.

It must have been a nerve-racking trip for the members of the team. Firstly, they had no means of knowing that a bantam who had behaved so beautifully down below was going to behave in the same way up in the valley, and they all knew that if they failed in their mission there would be such a sentimental public outcry that their chances of having a second attempt would be nil. To their infinite relief and credit, however, the whole thing went off without a hitch. The takahe eggs were obtained, the bantam sat like a rock, and after giving a day or so to make sure, they started down the hazardous, slippery mountainside towards Lake Te Anau. Once they reached the shores of the lake there was a speedboat waiting to rush their precious cargo to the nearest road; here the bantam and eggs were put in a car and dashed down to Picton, there to be loaded on to a plane that flew them to Wellington; then another car ride, and at last the faithful bantam and her eggs were safely installed in the sanctuary at Mount Bruce. After this epic and nerve-racking trip, all the team could do was sit back and wait for the eggs to hatch, while offering up prayers that they would be fertile. In due course, however, two chicks hatched, and the team and the bantam began to look rather smug about the whole business. At last, they felt, they had achieved success. But now a new obstacle reared its ugly head. The bantam foster-mother, of course, treated the takahe chicks exactly as if they were her own. She led them about, scratching up the leaf-mould vigorously and pecking at whatever tit-bits appeared, fondly imagining that the baby takahes – like bantam chicks – would learn by her example, but the takahes were not bantam chicks and followed their foster-mother about in a bewildered fashion, piping for food but unable to learn the bantam method of feeding. It was obvious that the female takahe feeds her babies, and does not show them how to feed for themselves as the chicken does. Now the problem of feeding them was in itself a task, for it was found that baby takahe do not gape at the mother as normal birds would do; the food is offered in the mother's beak and the babies take it from there in a sideways manner. At length a satisfactory method was worked out: the takahe chicks were fed on blow flies and similar delicacies impaled on the end of a pencil. With this method of food intake and with the bantam to supply them with mother love and warmth at night, they grew and throve.

Australian Friends

Before going to Australia, I had always been under the impression that by far the most engaging of the marsupials was the Koala Bear. At the risk of alienating all my Australian friends I must confess that in my opinion the Koala Bear is one of the most dim-witted creatures that it has ever been my misfortune to meet. They are rather like a film starlet – charming to look at but apparently completely devoid of personality or brains. I must admit, however, that we did not see Koala Bears under the best circumstances.

It was down in Victoria on a freezing-cold day, with grey skies, and bursts of icy rain, when we were taken by the wildlife department to witness the capturing of some Koala Bears. At one time, a combination of bushfires and fur hunters had so decimated the Koala Bears that they were in grave danger of extinction. Now, however, under rigid protection, their numbers in certain areas have recovered. Once the population in a certain area rises above a certain level the Koalas are in danger of eating all the available food-stuff and thus perishing; so the wildlife department goes to the area, catches up all the surplus Koalas and transports them to another suitable habitat in a different part of the region.

The techniques of Koala-catching are interesting. Teams of five or six people make their way out to the area with cages, a fireman's sheet and a long sectional aluminium pole with a noose on the end. The noose is fixed with a knot so that there is no danger of its getting too tight and strangling the animals.

Once the Koalas have been located, one member of the team shins up the tree, carrying the pole, and slips the noose over the Koala's head. The Koala's reaction is to stare at its captor with a vacant expression, to clutch the tree more firmly and to utter a series of strange wheezing growls vaguely reminiscent of a highly indignant and asthmatic Brigadier-General. As the noose pulls it gradually down the tree, the growls get louder and louder and then finally the Koala gives up in despair, releases its hold on the tree, and falls with a soft thud into the fireman's sheet which the other members of the team have been holding out in readiness. It is then picked up and put into a waiting cage. Picking up a Koala can be quite an unpleasant business, for although they look so soft and cuddly and harmless, they can, in fact, give you a wicked bite and severely slash you with their razor-sharp claws. It was not long before in my kind attempt to help a Koala up a tree I had my thumb slashed open with a speed and ferocity that would have done credit to a leopard. When the correct number of Koalas has been captured, they are transported to the new area and there the cage doors are opened and they are tipped out onto the ground. They sit for a moment or so looking slightly dazed, and then set off for the nearest trees at a shambling run. From the back they look exactly as though they were wearing long dirty grey combinations. They shin up the first tree they come to with tremendous speed and skilfulness and then they perch among the branches complaining to each other about the indignity of being captured, with high wailing cries, like a group of heartbroken children.

When you consider that these charming-looking little marsupials were once slaughtered for their furs to the extent that two million were killed in one year, it is heartening to think that they are now on the increase and that their only enemies nowadays are bushfires and the odd speeding motorist who runs them over at night when they are crossing the road.

One of the most engaging Australian animals that we met was the Duck-billed Platypus. I knew how fascinating, biologically speaking, this creature was before I met it, but what I was not prepared to find was that they have tremendous personality. It is rather as though Donald Duck had come to life. They have, peering out from behind their rubbery beak, tiny twinkling humorous eyes. They have the most engaging walk, and their fur is so soft and their skin so loose that when you pick them up they appear to be clad in a moleskin fur coat seventeen sizes too big for them. One of the curious things about the male Platypus is the pair of spurs on its hind feet. These long, curved spurs are connected with a venom gland, and work on much the same principle as the venomous teeth of the snake. This venom is very powerful, and I heard of one case of a man who was struck by a Platypus spur in his hand and has lost the use of the whole left-hand side of his body. So when handling a male Platypus it pays to be circumspect. We saw the Platypus at David Fleay's remarkable fauna sanctuary in Queensland. Fleay is probably one of the foremost authorities on marsupials, and it was he who first successfully bred the Platypus in captivity. This is a remarkable feat, for not only is the Platypus a difficult animal to keep but it is so highly nervous that any loud noises will worry it to the extent where it will go off its food and die. They have a voracious appetite and will consume their own body-weight in food each day, a succulent diet consisting of worms and yabbies, a small species of fresh-water crayfish. To provide a pair of Platypus with sufficient food to keep them healthy is a Herculean task.

While we were in Victoria, it was, fortunately for us, the

time of year when Lyre Birds display, and we were taken by the wildlife department to Sherbrooke Forest, a small natural reserve where the Lyre Birds have become so used to human spectators that they will perform their extraordinary song and dance routine within a few inches of you. The cock-bird clears a dancing ground for himself among the bushes, scraping up the earth into a mound on which to do his displays. He generally has several of these little dance-halls and will visit them each in turn. A rather drab, brown bird, somewhat pheasant-like to look at, the beauty of the Lyre Bird lies in his tail. Two long delicately scalloped white feathers curve out gracefully in the shape of a lyre, and fine hair-like feathers criss-cross between these two to form the 'strings'. This beautiful, shimmering tail stands straight up and droops slightly over the bird's back as he throws back his head and gives his fantastic song. Not only does he have his own song, but he is an accomplished mimic and will include the most unlikely noises in his repertoire. So a burst of beautiful liquid trills may be followed by the harsh laugh of a Kookaburra or the sound of a tin can being kicked over stony ground.

Although it was bitterly cold watching the Lyre Birds' display, it was one of the high spots of our Australia trip. To have managed to get such secretive and timid birds so tame is a remarkable achievement. At one point I was crouching down by a displaying bird and holding a microphone within a foot of his beak to record his fantastic songs, and he actually turned a little towards me, almost as if he felt appreciative of having such a close audience. It was wonderful to see groups of people wandering through the forest, clergymen, elderly ladies, boy-scouts and schoolchildren, all moving from dancing ground to dancing ground and standing enraptured as these fabulous birds sang to them. Sherbrooke Forest must do more to instil in people the importance of animal conservation than practically any other place in Australia. For a city-dweller to be able to take an hour's car drive and observe and listen to one of the most extraordinary ceremonies in the bird world is a rare and important privilege.

On our journey through New South Wales, it was brought home to us quite vividly that not all Australians feel that their wildlife should be preserved. On a fence marking the boundary of a farm we discovered twenty-eight dead Wedge-tailed Eagles that had been crucified along the wire with their wings outstretched. They were all young birds. While it is obvious that the Wedge-tailed Eagle must be to a certain extent a pest, one cannot help wondering how long even the most prolific species can put up with this kind of slaughter.

In direct contrast to this we went up to an area of Mallee country which is a curious form of scrub, eucalyptus growing on a rather poor soil. Great tracts of Australia are covered by this Mallee scrub and up to now it has been considered quite useless. Even if the scrub was felled, the soil was not sufficiently rich for growing crops. However, it has recently been discovered that with the addition of certain chemicals the Mallee soil can be turned into good wheat-growing country. In consequence, vast areas of Mallee hitherto considered unproductive are now being felled and cleared to make way for vast areas of wheat. The Mallee scrub, being totally unlike the other gum forests of Australia, has produced its own curious adaptations of animal life, rather as many islands have done in the oceans of the world. One of the most peculiar of the Mallee's inhabitants is the Mallee hen – this is an attractive, turkey-like bird, with mottled or autumnal plumage. The astonishing thing about these birds is their nesting habits. The cock-bird digs a gigantic hole in the soft earth under the

Mallee trees which in the early stages looks like a small bomb crater; this hole he then fills with dead leaves and carefully covers with earth. The leaves gently rotting in this compost heap provide the heat to incubate the eggs. When the females have been mated with, they come to the nest built by the cock-bird, lay their eggs and leave the rest to him. He carefully buries the eggs in the rotten leaf mould and watches over them until they hatch. The cock-bird is most assiduous in his guarding of the nest. He watches the temperature most carefully, controlling it by removing or adding more leaf mould.

In the area we visited which was near a town called Griffith we came across a wonderful example of conservation. The local townspeople knew about the Mallee fowl and its extraordinary nest-building habits. They even occasionally used to go out and watch the cock-bird digging his great egg-oven. It occurred to them that with the disappearance of the Mallee scrub, the Mallee hen would disappear as well. Rather than allow the disappearance of the fowl which they knew to be of great scientific interest and importance, they clubbed together and purchased a section of Mallee scrub to set aside as a permanent sanctuary. So many areas in the world wake up one morning to find that some animal species and its habitat have been lost to them for ever because they did not realize in time the importance of taking measures to conserve it. So the town of Griffith deserves a special accolade for its good sense in ensuring that future generations in that area will also have the pleasure of watching this strange bird.

One of the biggest bones of contention in the conservation field in Australia is the Kangaroo. This is considered by the average farmer to be the most tremendous menace. In certain areas this is indeed true, for the farmer has sunk wells and cultivated land which would have been arid wastes. In consequence the Kangaroos moved in and, finding an unlimited supply of water and food, their numbers increased to such an extent that they have become a serious pest. Farmers claim that one Kangaroo will eat the equivalent amount of food for five sheep. This has never been scientifically proven, but it has been repeated so often, by so many farmers, that you stand as much chance of refuting it as you would in convincing people that grass is pink. Nobody, not even the most ardent conservationist, would suggest that Kangaroos ought to be preserved to the detriment of the farmer. However, it might well be possible for both the Kangaroo and the sheep to exist side by side. At the moment the slaughter of Kangaroos is on a vast and rather cruel scale, and it is possible in many places to come across hideously maimed Kangaroos that have been shot but not finished off. The danger of allowing indiscriminate shooting of the Red and Grey Kangaroos is that the average farmer has not time to be a naturalist and therefore as far as he is concerned everything that hops is a 'roo and should be slaughtered. In consequence a great number of the smaller Wallabies and Padymelon, some of which are excessively rare, pay the price of the damage that the larger and more numerous marsupials effect. The average female Kangaroo is apparently a sort of Ford production belt for baby 'roos. They, like a number of mammal species, are capable of delayed implantation, which means that a female Kangaroo can retain the spermatozoa while in the uterus there is a baby Kangaroo developing, and while there is another half-grown one suckling in her pouch. So at any time the mature female Kangaroo can be the mother of three different babies of different ages and of different parentage.

The adult female Kangaroo can stand about five feet high yet the baby, when it is born, is only the size of the last segment of your little finger. I have always wanted to witness the birth of a Kangaroo, but I always imagined that this would be an impossibility. However, when we got to the Canberra research station, I discovered to my delight that they had several pregnant females which were due to give birth, and that it would be possible for me to watch and film it. The one we chose was a rather sedate matronly creature who rejoiced in the name of Caroline.

The hour of birth can be fairly accurately estimated by the behaviour of the female. The first sign is that she spring-cleans her pouch, which becomes clogged and dirtied with a black substance similar to the wax from a human ear. We watched, fascinated, while Caroline solemnly turned her pouch inside-out and cleaned it thoroughly, looking not unlike a rather frantic elderly lady searching through her shopping basket for a mislaid train ticket. Having cleaned out her pouch to her satisfaction, she then appeared to be suffering some discomfort, which considering the size of the baby she was to produce struck me as being rather strange. Eventually after two or three hours of waiting the baby was rapidly and very easily born. Now came the really extraordinary part of the whole experience. The embryo is so minute that you could hardly see it, it is deaf and blind, its hind feet have no power of movement, yet by some extraordinary means, presumably a sense of smell, it crawls up through the thick fur of the mother's stomach until it reaches the rim of the pouch. It disappears inside and then has to search for the teat to which it will fasten itself. It is rather as if you were blind and deaf and with paralysed legs, and you were set the task of climbing Mount Everest, and then, having reached the summit, you were requested to grope and fumble your way round an area the size of a cathedral in order to find a small packet of sandwiches that you need to keep you alive. I have witnessed quite a number of animal births at one time and another but nothing has affected me as strongly as the tenacity of this minute cochineal-pink blob of life, fighting its way grimly through that tremendous forest of fur. As I watched it making this exhausting trek, I felt that even the most hardened anti-roo Australian farmer would have had his attitude towards these the largest marsupials slightly softened. It was for me one of the most moving and intriguing things that I have ever seen.

Great Barrier Reef

Manny and Doreen lived at Port Douglas, a tiny place that has a lovely, relaxed, beach-combing air about it; it reminded me very much of John Steinbeck's *Cannery Row*. From here we went in Manny's boat out to the Low Islands. There are in fact two of them, one of which is completely uninhabited, and the other of which has a lighthouse and a series of houses for the lighthouse keepers and warden. We anchored the boat in about ten or fifteen feet of water between the two islands and then Manny rowed us in a small boat to the uninhabited island. At first the only noise we could hear, apart from the plash of the oars, was the cries of the gulls. But then as we drew closer to the island we became aware of an extraordinary throaty purring noise. This was the cry of the Torres Straits pigeons, the most beautiful milk-white birds with black edges to the wing and a black band on the end of the tail, and great lustrous black eyes. The island beaches were white, dazzling white, and the mangrove undergrowth that covered the bulk of the island stood on great basket-like roots that were a bright fox-red. As we landed, we found a turtle lying dead upside-down in the shallows. I don't think he'd been killed by human beings because he'd have been eaten, but he'd got a great slash on his underside and his bowels had been dragged out and were providing food for fish. Every mangrove bush, it seemed, had two or three nests of the Torres Straits pigeons – if you can dignify them with the term nest, because they were just the usual pigeon-type nest which means three twigs flung in a rather haphazard and absent-minded manner across a branch, and you wondered how the egg ever stayed in it, let alone the young birds. The pigeons themselves were reasonably tame but would only allow you to approach up till a certain distance, and they would watch you, turning their heads and arching their necks, their dark eyes glistening, and then they would fly off in a great flap and flutter of wings – a heavy flight, typically pigeon. The young in the nests looked like unshaven semi-bald octogenarians with scrawny necks. Here it would be a good idea to quote from the book about the killing of Torres Straits pigeons because this is one of the last areas where you can see them in any quantity. Manny reckoned that there were between four and five thousand on this island. But at one time all the islands that stretch down the coast had these pigeons in hundreds of thousands, so many that the trees were white with them as though covered with snow.

We walked along the beach in the blazing sun for a bit and your feet crunched on the pieces of washed-up Stag's Horn coral, so that you walked on what appeared to be a graveyard of mammoths or, when you looked down, it was as though you were tromping underfoot a million snow-covered Christmas trees. Along the beach great shells, sea-shattered, lay bleached by the sun like the remnants of some strange underwater dinner service. We left the beach and waded through the shallow water. It was as hot as a bath. And here we saw any number of the clams about the size, or perhaps a little smaller, of a football. They are called the Horse Hoof clam because if you look at the part where the hinge is – the base end, as it were, of the clam – it bears a very close resemblance to the hoof of a horse. But these ends were buried in the mud and sand and only the filigreed edge of the clam, half open, was displayed. Overlapping this were the mantles of the animals themselves, which were of the most exquisite iridescent colours; some were peacock-blue with a gold filigree, others were the most vivid dragon-green, again with a gold motif worked onto them; they were quite beautiful.

There were a number of Stingrays, which zoomed away from us as we walked through the water. They were, for the most part, a sort of bluey-grey, some with reddish-gold spots on them. They seemed far more afraid of us than we were of them. Indeed, as I ventured into the mangroves I almost trod on one and he was off in a second in a great flap and flurry. Also in the shallows there were some baby sharks – at least, Manny called them babies; they were four to six feet in length. And they, as well, seemed far more afraid of us than we were of them.

After we had toured the island for a time we went back and rowed out to the boat in the dinghy. On the way we spotted a baby turtle. He was about the size of a silver salver and he was quite peacefully sleeping on the surface until we arrived. He then dived and swam as rapidly as he could, but Manny put the engine on full speed and we followed him. He lodged himself on the sea bed hoping to escape detection, but he was in a rather prominent position and Manny manoeuvred the boat over to him. I was just about to dive to see if I could catch him when he realized that we'd seen him and he zoomed off again. We chased him for some time and then he went under a rock with a pile of weed growing on top of it. Here he was beauti-fully camouflaged, and if you hadn't known he was there you would have passed over him. Manny stopped the boat and I dived overboard and managed to catch him. He flapped his flippers indignantly and waved his head from side to side as I picked him out of the water. He was a lovely yellow with darker markings, large, benign, intelligent eyes and the strange hooked upper lip of his breed. When I let him go he zoomed off at a rate of knots.

After we'd had lunch we went swimming with snorkels to look at the reef area that spread around the islands. Here was an interesting thing which I didn't fully realize the implications of until later. There were once a lot of hard corals but all these had been eaten by the Crown of Thorns starfish. In fact, the dinghy went over a piece of Brain coral which was almost the size of a double bed, and an enormous smooth white cranium it appeared until you dived down and saw the little pock marks where the polyps lived before they had been sucked out by the starfish. So we saw no living hard coral, but in its place had come the soft coral which looked as though it should be hard until you touched it and found that it is soft, spongy, rather like damp cardboard.

The soft corals were everywhere; they were fringed, fili-greed, tessellated, growing in great towers. They were like the multicoloured fingers of some strange medieval city – castle, monastery and dwelling houses for fish of every hue. There were the brilliant Parrotfish with their ridiculous little fins that flapped up and down, and quite apart from their colouring, their flight, as it were, was extraordinary. There were plenty of sea slugs lying, dimly meditating on the bottom amongst the corals, and presently Manny found a gigantic one. It must have been a good eighteen inches in length, and so I dived for it. As soon as I lifted it above the surface of the water it suddenly appeared to disembowel itself; it exuded from one end of its sausage-like shape a great thick column of white, rubbery material. Manny told me to be careful not to get it on me as he said that it stuck, so I released the sea slug, but unfortunately a few strands of this strange secretion had floated threadlike in the water and wound themselves around various parts of my anatomy, and later on – when I was on the boat and these had dried out – I discovered them sticking to the hairs on my legs and on my arms, and they were exactly like Latex and extraordinarily difficult to remove. So inextricably entwined had they become on the hairs of my thighs that I was forced to borrow a pair of nail scissors from her ladyship and cut myself free from this rubbery self-defence.

We contacted a man called Johnny D'Urso and he promised to take us out to see Feather Reef and another area and then part of Nathan Reef. In these three areas he said that he could show us parts that had been completely destroyed by the Crown of Thorns, parts that were in the process of being destroyed, and parts which the Crown of Thorns had not yet penetrated. So we made our way up early in the morning and eventually arrived at Johnny's house. He was a slight but very muscular man, with a pointed face and brilliant eager eyes, and possessed an extraordinary volubility on the subject of the reef, and on the Crown of Thorns in particular. We got on his rather nice little boat and started chugging down the river where there were some beautiful curves covered with mangroves and other vegetation, and then eventually we were out in the open sea and heading towards Feather Reef. As Johnny explained, it was going to be high tide so the reef wouldn't be exposed, but it would be under only six to ten feet of water in places.

I asked Johnny about the Crown of Thorns, and he said that the situation in his opinion was so serious that he doubted whether anything could be done about it. But he said certainly nothing could be done if people were not getting sufficient funds to do the research work necessary. I asked him what he thought the cause was, and he said he didn't like to commit himself but he thought some sort of human interference had probably created this population explosion. He said that practically everything that was done on the reef interfered with it in some way – even the shell collectors, though they were confined to certain areas.

'What I would like to see,' he said, 'is the Barrier Reef closed for ten years – even though it would put me out of business; I could always get another job. But you see, over the last five or six years the fishing has dwindled and I attribute that to the Crown of Thorns as well . . . Shells are not as easy to find now, and I'll show you later when we get there that areas that should be absolutely clear, and if populated by live coral are in fact clear, are now sort of murky and milky and you can't really see through the water.'

Eventually we sighted Feather – at least, we could tell it was there by the flash like a sword blade, as the great surf raised itself and then broke on the outer edge of the reef. Now the water grew shallower and Johnny could look down and pick his way in between the great beds of coral; then eventually he threw the anchor over and we all got into the water and started to swim around while Johnny showed us what he meant. Here again, as we had seen with Manny, there were a lot of soft corals. These are, indeed, very beautiful and in most places in fact it is the soft coral that is shown to the tourists and they don't realize it. But interspersed with the soft coral were masses of other coral – Brain coral and particularly the Stag's Horn coral. These were just whitened husks. Johnny dived down and plucked a branch and brought it up so that we could see. The tips of the branches were a very beautiful royal purply-mauve colour. This part was still alive and this is how the whole of the coral should look, but the rest of it was pure stone-white. Johnny explained that a lot of people, seeing the tips of the coral, were under the impression that the whole of the Stag's Horn was regenerating. But this, in fact, was quite untrue. It was simply due to the fact that the Crown of Thorns, when it crawled over the coral sucking the polyps out of their little holes, couldn't, for some reason, get up and over the very tip of the Stag's Horn, and so they left that piece. But that would eventually die off because while the great delicate tracery was no longer held in place by the mucous-like substance of the polyps, and therefore had no resistance to the surf and to the currents, it could be snapped off at the base by the first big wave that came along.

From Feather we went to the tip of Nathan where there was a little outcrop of reef. Here, Johnny said, some eight weeks previously, the starfish had just started to eat it out and he wanted to see how it was getting on. Well, we dived there and again it was the same sorry tale. All the beautiful hard coral was whitened, broken and being pummelled by the waves and currents. They'd done a good job of it in eight weeks, according to Johnny, for they'd only just started when he'd last seen it. Then we went on along the reef and I could see immediately what he meant about the clarity of the water, for here the coral had not been attacked and was still living, and the water was clear and beautiful, whereas on Feather and the little outcrop on Nathan the water was murky. His theory is that the coral is constantly pumping the water in, filtering it and then pumping it out again so it keeps it clear. There could be something in this in an area where the whole mass of coral in the water acts like a giant filter bed. We swam and swam and really you get dizzy after a time; there are so many shapes and colours, not only of the coral itself, but the fish and everything else in the sea. You suffer from a sort of surfeit of it. There were brilliant blue-green fish; and then the Parrotfish again, and the beautifully striped, rather pouty faces of Anemonefish living in the giant anemones with their stinging tentacles moving gently to and fro. Then there were pure white cowries which Johnny dived for and brought up, with a beautiful black mantle on the ivory-white of their shell. And then there was the giant clam some three foot across with a rather disappointing mantle; it wasn't as highly coloured as the ordinary clams which glowed and glistened gold and green and red. Then there were beautiful, bright-blue starfish, some six or eight inches across. Johnny brought up one piece of Stag's Horn that had no fewer than five Crown of Thorns on it, varying in size from those as big as a coffee saucer to those the size of a hefty soup plate.

On the way out to Feather and Nathan we had seen two species of sea snake, both passing quite close to the boat. One was, I suppose, about four foot long, banded black and white and very handsome. And the other, which was about six foot long, appeared to be yellow and black but he dived and we only caught a glimpse of him. Then we passed a very large turtle who lay, blinking, on the surface of the waves, obviously having just roused himself from a deep sleep and not quite sure what was happening, for we passed him so close that the wake of the boat jogged him up and down as he peered at us with his rather soulful eyes. When we had finished looking at the inner part of Nathan Reef, Johnny took the boat out to the very edge of the reef where it fell down into an abyss of some four hundred fathoms. Here, holding the small boat in the lift and surge of the waves, we got out and swam on the very edge of the reef. There was a lovely great blue push from the waves and as you swam over the edge, the dark depths seemed to go on and on, downwards and downwards, until you could no longer see coral or anything else. In one crevice Johnny showed me an enormous Stag's Horn. It was as big as a large bush and it was partly white and partly the mauvey-blue that it should be. And then you could see, in the whiteness of its branches, lurked the Crown of Thorns.

The last leg of the arduous 45,000-mile filming expedition in 1962 was to Malaya, to be renamed Malaysia the next year. The first part of the visit was to the vast rainforest of Taman Negara, followed by a journey to the east coast to film the spectacle of leatherback turtles laying their eggs.

Dragons and Giants from the Sea

Most people think of a tropical forest as an evil, ugly and dangerous place, and to them the idea of wanting to conserve large sections of this forest and its wildlife is incomprehensible. Much better, they say, to chop it all down and have nice sedate rubber plantations or coconut groves. A tropical forest (whether you like it or not) is a magnificent thing that should be preserved, for it is nature at her most flamboyant, prolific and beautiful.

The first thing that strikes you on entering the forest is the wealth of vegetation. Trees groan under the weight of epiphytes and orchids that cling tenaciously to their bark. Giant lianas coil through the gloomy undergrowth like great dark snakes, chaining each tree to its neighbour with their strangling lengths. The floor of the forest is thick with leaves, leaves of all shapes and sizes, from the size of a soup tureen to ones the size of your little fingernail. Everywhere there are plants with spikes, hooks and barbs, cunningly concealed to trap the unwary. It is a bewildering display of vegetable inventiveness.

Then you notice the apparent *lack* of life. There are insects, of course, everywhere. Cicadas with shimmering wings cling to every tree, uttering their incessant sawmill-like cries. Spiders festoon the bushes with webs, spiders of every conceivable colour and shape, some so ornamented with spikes and knobs that at first glance you cannot tell which end is which. Great beetles prowl among the trees, each one three or four inches long, waving their thin, delicately jointed antennae, as long as a pencil. Butterflies the size of birds suddenly appear out of the dark undergrowth, play around you briefly in a fire-work display of colour, and then disappear as silently as they came. On the damp leaf mould of the forest floor you will soon see the commonest and most unpleasant of the forest creatures: the leeches. Choose a nice bare area of forest floor, make sure it contains no life and then sit down. Within minutes, by some magic of their own, the leeches are aware of your arrival. They appear out of the undergrowth, humping their slender, hungry bodies eagerly towards you. Every now and then they will climb to the top of a twig or grass blade and stand on end, waving their heads to and fro in the air as if looking for you. Having got their bearings, they will set off once more in your direction. The main trouble with leeches is that they move with such gossamer lightness that a hundred could crawl onto you and you would be completely unaware of their presence. No clothing seems to stop them, for they can elongate their rubbery bodies into fine threads and crawl through a minute crack or hole with the ease of ink soaking into blotting paper. Once they have sunk their jaws into your skin and are feeding thirstily on your blood there are only two ways of dealing with them: a lighted cigarette end, or a pinch of salt. If you pull them off they leave their mouth parts imbedded in your skin, and this can fester and go septic. Regular 'leech inspection' when you are in the forest becomes an automatic action.

So your first confused impression of the forest is one of a tangled mass of plants and trees inhabited solely by insects and leeches. But as you explore the forest by day you start to see the other inhabitants. Some of these are not at all what they seem at first sight. I noticed a small, slender brown lizard once on the bark of a tree. He matched the bark so closely that I would not have noticed him if he had not kept nodding his head with a knowing air, and inflating a whiteish sack, like an elongated strawberry, beneath his throat. To me he was just a small brownish lizard with an unusual throat sack, but then, quite suddenly, I discovered that he was a creature I had always longed to see. He nodded his head two or three times with great vigour, and then hurled himself off the tree and into the air. I expected to see him drop to the ground like a stone, but, as he was falling, two 'wings' of thin skin, supported by umbrella-like ribs, bloomed along the sides of his body and he glided off through the forest like a paper dart, to land on a branch some thirty feet away. He was a Flying Dragon, one of the most unusual lizards in the world. The 'wings' along the sides of the body are so neatly furled when the reptile is at rest that, even if you handle it, they are very hard to see. When they are open the wingspan is about five inches.

As we explored the forest we discovered that both by day and by night there were a host of creatures on the move, but by and large they were so quiet and so cautious that you had to use all your patience and skill to see them. A faint whisper of leaves a hundred feet above you would mean that you were standing under a troupe of fifty or so monkeys the size of large dogs – Leaf Monkeys – but they would be squatting there, watching you, so silently that you could walk under them without noticing them. Once they knew you had spotted them the whole troupe would make off rapidly, crashing through the treetops with a noise like surf breaking on a rocky shore. Some of the animals, of course, were far from silent, and would advertise their presence in what seemed to me the most blatant manner. The Gibbons, for example, were always hooting and tittering in the trees, so that you could hear them miles away.

But the first prize for vocal effort undoubtedly goes to the Siamang, the largest of the Gibbons, a slender ape with coal black

fur and a sad black face. The first time we were treated to a Siamang chorus was one day when we had spent some hours,
sweaty and leech covered, lugging the cameras through the
forest in search of some shots we needed. Suddenly, right over
our heads, an extraordinary noise broke out, a series of ringing
cries that sounded like 'Wharrr . . . onk'. The 'Wharrr' part was
rich, musical and strangely bird-like, while the 'onk' part sounded
like a huge suppressed belch that seemed more like a vibration
than a cry. The forest rang and echoed with this cacophony of
cries. We moved round cautiously until we could see up above
us a small group of five Siamang. Three of them – two adults
and a youngster – squatted in the branches watching the remaining two who were doing the singing. The songsters were hanging
from the branches by their long, slender arms, swinging to and
fro like black pendulums, while their throats were swollen with
song, the skin bulging out of the fur like an orange. As suddenly
as they had begun they stopped singing. There was a few minutes' silence while their audience watched them closely. Then
the audience, including the baby, started a series of squeaks and
screams which got faster and faster and more and more excited.
The effect on the two singers was remarkable. They started to
swing faster and faster, uttering loud, reverberating 'onks' that
got louder and louder, until they burst into full song again. The
audience, having encouraged them, fell silent and listened atten-
tively. It was a remarkable sight.

As evening approached, the day animals started to make
their way to their beds, and the night animals started to stir
into wakefulness. As a signal that the night shift, as it were, was
about to take over, the green evening sky became suddenly
freckled with bats, flying in a steady stream from their daytime
roosting places into the deep forest to feed on the wild fruits.
When the last of them passed overhead the sky was so dark

that you could hardly see them. As night fell, the large animals of the forest came into their own. The leopards, beautifully marked, yawned, stretched and prepared for a night's hunting. The Seladang herds, the great black heavy cattle with thick sweeping horns and white marks on their legs that made them look as though they were wearing white socks, moved ponderously out of the deep undergrowth where they had spent the heat of the day and into the grassy clearings scattered here and there among the tall trees. After them, sliding through the undergrowth as silently as ghosts, for all their bulk, came the elephants, moving slowly, uprooting plants with casual strength and stuffing them delicately into their mouths.

So we discovered that the forest both by day and by night was never as lifeless as it appeared; all around you the animals went about their business, quietly and efficiently and unobtrusively. It was such a fascinating and complicated world that we were sorry that we had not got longer to investigate it. But the time had come for us to make our way over to the east coast of Malaya, to film the most extraordinary exodus from the sea that I have ever witnessed.

Once a year on a special strip of sandy beach the giants of the reptile world drag themselves out of the sea into an alien environment in order to perpetuate their race. These are the Leatherback Turtles, measuring between six and eight feet long, who come ashore to lay their eggs. There are only two other known breeding places of these creatures in the world, one in Ceylon and one in the West Indies. Both these breeding beaches have been so exploited that the turtles no longer visit them, so this remote Malayan beach is the last stronghold of one of the biggest reptiles known to exist.

We knew that the female turtles were due to start laying at any moment, so we had to get our cameras and equipment ready for when they appeared. We drove down the beautiful, palm-fringed coastline until we came to a small village that sprawled along either side of the road. This marked, we had been told, the turtle beach. Why they preferred this beach to the others scattered along the coast was a mystery. My own theory is that the bottom shelves very rapidly from the edge of the water, thus making it easier for the ponderous creatures to get out of the water onto the beach. We got our cameras and lighting ready and then had to wait until dark, for we were assured, the turtles never appeared before nine p.m.

We went and got something to eat, and then drove back to the village when it was dark and the sky was freckled with stars. We were greeted by excited and grinning villagers who informed us that the first of the sea-turtles was at that very moment coming ashore. We hurried down to the beach and there, struggling at the edge of the surf, was an enormous black object that looked, at first sight, like an overturned dinghy. The great carapace, shining as the waves broke over it, gleamed like well dubbined black leather, and from one end of it peered a head that was quite astonishing. The head of a tortoise magnified to the size of a Shetland pony takes some assimilating. The parrot-like look of the mouth, the eyes as big as hen's eggs, soulful and worried, the thick neck with its folds and dewlaps of skin, all these I noticed as, with much effort and deep sighs, the Leatherback Turtle hauled herself clear of the waves and onto the beach. She paused for a moment to get her breath, and then slowly made her way up the sloping beach with many pauses to rest, during which she gasped and sighed with open mouth. The glutinous substance that protected her eyes underwater now started to flow from her eyes and hang in thick strands like gelatine, giving the ludicrous and pathetic impression that she was crying bitterly at the task of climbing the beach.

Presently she reached an area of beach which she thought was suitable, and there she started to dig. She used her front flippers, each as wide as a garden spade, throwing up a great heap of sand, some of which fell on her shell. Soon she had excavated a hole some three feet deep, but it was only a rough hole. Now she turned round and with her smaller hind flippers completed the work. The hind flipper (unlike the front ones which are like paddles) can be cupped like a human hand, and so steadily and carefully she smoothed and rounded the hole for the reception of her eggs. Throughout this hard work she paused frequently and gave deep, heartrending sighs.

When the hole had been smoothed and patted to her satisfaction she had a short rest and then commenced to lay. With apparently little or no effort the eggs poured forth, dropping like white billiard balls into the sandy hole, five, ten, twenty, thirty, until some eighty eggs formed a neat pyramid at the bottom of the nest. Again she rested before starting to fill in the hole. She shovelled the sand back with her great oar-like flippers, and padded it down with the bulk of her body, turning round and round so that the sand was evenly spread. Then, satisfied that her task had been well done, she made her way down to the sea again. She paused at the edge of the surf, letting the waves break over her head, washing off the glutinous, sand-encrusted tears that trailed forlornly down her cheeks. Then, summoning up her strength, she lumbered into the sea. A wave curved up over her, and she turned on her side to meet it. As she did one huge flipper came out of the water and waggled. It looked as though she was – rather skittishly – waving goodbye to us. The wave broke over her and then she was in deep water, back in her element. Swiftly and gracefully she plunged beneath the surface and was gone, into the vastness of the ocean.

Mauritius & Madagascar

The islands of the western Indian Ocean held a special fascination for Gerry. Above all others was Mauritius, the land of the dodo, because Gerry had chosen the dodo as the emblem of his conservation trust. The dodo was a huge flightless pigeon that had evolved on Mauritius several million years ago, but became extinct in the twinkling of an eye due to the actions of a handful of humans only a few hundred years ago. For Gerry the dodo was a symbol of the fragility of nature. On his watch, he would not let other creatures follow it into oblivion. The passage that follows, however, is not about the fate of the dodo but is rather a celebration of the diversity of life to be found in the seas around Mauritius.

The other island he was enamoured with was Madagascar, a crucible of evolution in its 90 million years of separation from other land masses, yielding a fauna and flora literally a world apart. It was astonishing that Gerry had never been to Madagascar on his many travels, but after I came on the scene we visited the Great Red Island four times together. Gerry fell in love with it from the very first trip.

The Enchanted World

Outside the French windows that led from the sitting-room of the hotel suite lay a spacious and cool verandah. Step off this, and one walked twenty yards or so across coarse grass planted with tall casuarina trees that sighed like lovers in the wind, until one came to the wide, frost-white beach with its broken necklace of corals and coloured shells, lying wavering across the shoreline. In the distance lay the reef, white and thunderous with surf, and beyond it the royal blue of the Indian Ocean. Between the white beach, decorated with its biscuit-brittle graveyard of coral fragments, and the wide reef with its everchanging flower bed of foam, lay the lagoon. Half a mile of butterfly-blue water, smooth as a saucer of milk, clear as a diamond, which hid an enchanted world like none other on earth.

Any naturalist who is lucky enough to travel, at certain moments has experienced a feeling of overwhelming exultation at the beauty and complexity of life, and a feeling of depression that there is so much to see, to observe, to learn, that one lifetime is an unfairly short span to be allotted for such a paradise of enigmas as the world is. You get it when, for the first time, you see the beauty, variety and exuberance of a tropical rain forest, with its cathedral maze of a thousand different trees, each bedecked with gardens of orchids, epiphytes, enmeshed in a web of creepers; an interlocking of so many species that you cannot believe that number of different forms have evolved. You get it when you see for the first time a great concourse of mammals living together, or a vast, restless conglomeration of birds. You get it when you see a butterfly emerge from a chrys-alis; a dragonfly from its pupa; when you observe the delicate, multifarious courtship displays, the rituals and taboos, that go into making up the continuation of a species. You get it when you first see a stick or a leaf turn into an insect, or a piece of dappled shade into a herd of zebras. You get it when you see a gigantic school of dolphins stretching as far as the eye can see, rocking and leaping exuberantly through their blue world; or a microscopic spider manufacturing from its frail body a trans-parent, apparently never-ending line that will act as a transport as it sets out on its aerial explorations of the vast world that surrounds it.

But there is one experience, perhaps above all others, that a naturalist should try to have before he dies, and that is the astonishing and humbling experience of exploring a tropical reef. It seems that in this one action you use nearly every one of your senses, and one feels that one could uncover hidden senses as well. You become a fish, hear, and see and feed as much like one as a human being can; yet at the same time you are like a bird, hovering, swooping and gliding across the marine pas-tures and forests.

I had obtained my first taste of this fabulous experience when I was on the Great Barrier Reef in Australia but there, unfortunately, we had only masks and no snorkels, and my mask let in water. To say that it was fascinating, was putting it mildly, for there below me was this fascinating, multi-coloured world and I could only obtain glimpses of it, the duration of which was dependent upon how long I could hold my breath and how long it took my mask to fill and drown me. The tan-talising glimpses I did get of this underwater world were unforgettable and I determined to do it properly at the first available opportunity. This came in Mauritius, for there at the

Le Morne Brabant Hotel, the lagoon and its attendant reef were literally on my doorstep. I could not have been closer without moving my bed into it.

The first morning, I made myself a pot of tea and carried it out on to the verandah, together with one of the small, sweet Mauritian pineapples. I sat eating and watching the boats arrive farther down the beach, each piloted by handsome, bright-eyed, long-haired fishermen, wearing a variety of clothing in eye-catching colours that shamed the hibiscus and bougainvillaea flowers that flamed in the gardens. Each boat was loaded down with a cargo of snow-white pieces of coral and multi-coloured, pard-spotted cowries and cone shells. From sticks stuck in the gunwales, hung necklaces of tiny shells like glittering rainbows. The sun had just emerged from the mountains behind the hotel. It turned the sky and the horizon powder-blue; gilded a few fat, white clouds that sailed in a slow flotilla across the sky; gave a crisp, white sparkle to the foam on the reef and turned the flat, still lagoon transparent sapphire.

I finished my tea and then, taking my mask and snorkel, made my way slowly down to the shore. I reached the sand and the ghost crabs (so transparent that when they stopped moving and froze, they disappeared) skittered across the tide ripples and dived for safety into their holes. At the rim of the lagoon, the sea lapped very gently at the white sand, like a kitten delicately lapping at a saucer of milk. I walked into the water up to my ankles and it was as warm as a tepid bath.

All round my feet on the surface of the sand were strange decorations that looked as though someone had walked through the shallow water and traced on the sandy bottom the blurred outlines of a hundred starfish. They lay arm to arm, as it were, like some strange, sandy constellation. The biggest measured a

foot from arm tip to arm tip, and the smallest was about the size
of a saucer.

Curious about these ghostly sand starfish, I dug an experi-
mental toe under one and hooked upwards. It came out from
under its covering and floated briefly upwards, shedding the
film of sand that had been lightly covering it and revealing itself
to be a fine, robust starfish of a pale brick-pink, heavily marked
with a dull white and red speckling. Though they looked attractively soft and velvety – like a star you put on top of a Christmas
tree – they were, in fact, hard and sandpaperish to the touch.
The one I had so rudely jerked out of its sandy bed with my
toe performed a languid cartwheel in the clear water and drifted
down on to the bottom, landing on its back. Its underside was
a pale, yellowish ivory, with a deep groove down each arm that
looked like an open zip-fastener. Within this groove, lay its
myriad feet – tiny tentacles some four millimetres long, ending
in a plate-shaped sucker. Each foot could be used independently so that there was a constant movement in the grooves
and the tentacles contracted and expanded, searching for some
surface on which the suckers could fasten.

Discovering none, and presumably concluding that it was
upside down, the starfish curled the extreme tip of one arm
under itself. Finding a foothold, it then curled its arm further in
an effortless, boneless sort of way. At the same time, it curled
under the two arms on either side of the first one, and slowly
and gently, the animal started to lift itself with this triangle of
arms. The arms on the opposite side of its body curled and
spread upwards like the fingers of a hand to support it, and
soon the body was vertical like a wheel, supported by the ever-
stiffening arms. The arms on the farthest side now spread wide
and the body sank towards them slowly and gracefully like a
yogi completing a complicated and beautiful asana. The body

was now turned upright; it remained only for the starfish to pull out its remaining arms from underneath it and the animal was the right side up. The whole action had been performed with a slow-motion delicacy of movement that would have brought tears to the eyes of any ballet dancer.

Now, however, the starfish did something that no ballerina, be she ever too talented, could have emulated. It lay on the sand and simply disappeared. Before my eyes, it vanished and left behind it, like the Cheshire Cat left its smile, merely a vague outline, the suggestion of a starfish, as it were, embossed upon the sand. What had happened, of course, was that while the starfish remained apparently unmoving, its hundreds of little feet, out of sight beneath it, were burrowing into the sand, so the animal simply sank from view and the white grains drifted to cover it. The whole thing, from the moment I had unearthed the creature until it disappeared, had taken no longer than two minutes.

Determined not to be sidetracked again, I waded out waist-deep into the water, put on my mask and plunged my head under the water to get my head and back wet and protect it a little from the sun, which was hot even at that early hour. As my mask dipped below the surface, the sea seemed to disappear and I was gazing down at my feet in the submarine territory that immediately surrounded them.

Instantly I forgot my firm resolve to swim out into deeper water, for I was surrounded by a world as bizarre as any science fiction writer had thought up for a Martian biology. Around my feet, a trifle close for comfort, lay six or seven large, flattish sea urchins, like a litter of hibernating hedgehogs with bits of seaweed and coral fragments enmeshed in their spines so that, until one looked closely, they appeared to be weed-covered lumps of dark lava. Entwined between them were several curious structures, lying on the sand in a languid manner, like sunbathing snakes. They were tubes some four feet long and about four inches in circumference. They looked like the submarine parts of a strange vacuum cleaner, apparently jointed every three inches and manufactured out of semi-opaque, damp brown paper that had started to grow a sort of furry fungus at intervals along its length.

At first, I could not believe that these weird objects were alive. I thought they must be strange, dead strands of some deep-sea seaweed now washed into the shallows by the tide, to roll and undulate helplessly on the sand to the small movements of the sea. Closer inspection showed me that they were indeed alive, unlikely though it seemed. *Sinucta muculata*, as this strange creature is called, is really a sort of elongated tube, which sucks in water at one end and with it microscopic organisms, and expels the water at the other.

As well as *Sinucta*, I saw some old friends lying about, placid on the sea bed – the sea slug that I had known from my childhood in Greece, thick, fat, warty creatures, a foot long, looking like a particularly revolting form of liver sausage. I picked one up; it was faintly slimy, but firm to the touch, like decaying leather. I lifted it out of the water and it behaved exactly as its Mediterranean cousins did. It ejected a stream of water with considerable force, at the same time becoming limp and flaccid in my hand. Then, having exhausted this form of defence, it tried another one. It suddenly voided a stream of a white substance that looked like liquid latex and was sticky beyond belief, the slightest portion adhering to your skin more tenaciously than Sellotape.

I could not help feeling that this was a rather futile form of defence for should an enemy be attacking, this curtain of adhesive, rubber-like solution would only serve to bind it more closely to the sea slug. However, it seemed unlikely that any weapon as complex as this would have been evolved in a creature so primitive unless it had fulfilled a necessary purpose. I released the slug and he floated to the bottom, to roll gently on to the sand, fulfilling the gay, vibrant, experience-full life that sea slugs lead, which consists of sucking the water in at one end of their being and expelling it at the other, while being rolled endlessly by the tide.

Reluctantly, I dragged my attention away from the creatures that lived in the immediate vicinity of my feet, and launched myself on my voyage of exploration. That first moment, when you relax and float face downwards, and, under the glass of your mask, the water seems to disappear, is always startling and uncanny. You suddenly become a hawk, floating and soaring over the forests, mountains and sandy deserts of this marine universe. You feel like Icarus, as the sun warms your back, and below you, the multi-coloured world unfolds like a map. Though you may float only a few feet above the tapestry, the sounds come up to you muted as if floating up from a thousand feet in still air, as you might be suspended and hear sounds of life in the toy farms and villages below a mountain. The crunch of the gaudy parrot fish, rasping at the coral with its beak; the grunt or squeak or creakings of any one of a hundred fish, indignantly defending their territory against invaders; the gentle rustle of the sand moved by tides or currents; a whisper like the feminine rustle of a thousand crinolines. These and many more noises drift up to you from the sea bed.

At first, the sandy bottom was flat, littered with the debris of past storms and hurricanes; lumps of coral now covered with weed, and the abode of a million creatures; pieces of pumice stone. On the sand lay battalions of huge, black sea urchins, with long, slender spines that move constantly like compass needles. Touch one of them, and the spines moving gently to and fro suddenly become violently agitated, waving about with ever-increasing speed like mad knitting needles. They were very fragile as well as being sharp, so that if they penetrated your skin, they broke off. They also stained the immediate area of the puncture, as though you had been given a minute injection of Indian ink. Although they looked black, when the sunlight caught them, you found that they were a most beautiful royal blue with a green base to each spine. This species was fortunately flamboyant enough to be very obvious and, although some lay in crevices and under coral ledges, the majority lay on the sand, singly or in prickly groups, and were very apparent.

I swam on and, quite suddenly, like a conjuring trick, I found I was swimming through and over a large school of extraordinary looking fish. There were about fifty of them; each measured some three to four feet long and was coloured a neutrally transparent grey, so that it was almost invisible. Their mouths protruded almost into an elongated spike, as did their tails, so that it was difficult to tell at first glance which way they were pointing until you saw their round, rather oafish eyes staring at you with caution. They had obviously been doing something very strenuous and were now exhausted. They hung, immobile in the water, facing the current, meditating. They were most orderly, for they hung in the water in ranks, like well-drilled, if somewhat emaciated soldiers. It was interesting to note that they hung in exactly the right juxtaposition to each other, like troops on parade, so many feet between the fish in front and behind, and the same distance between the one above and the one below and the ones on each side. My sudden presence caused a certain amount of panic in their ranks, like someone marching out of step on an Armistice Day parade, and they swam off in confusion. As soon as they put enough distance between themselves and me, they re-formed ranks, turned to face the tide, and went into a trance again.

Leaving these fish, I swam on, gazing enthralled at the sandy bottom, barred with broad stripes of gold by the sun and these, by some optical alchemy, spangled all over with golden, trembling rings. Then, looming up ahead of me, I saw a shape, a dim blur which materialised into a massive rock some nine feet by three, shaped like the dome of St Paul's Cathedral. As I got closer, I saw that the whole rock was encrusted with pink, white and greenish corals and on top of it there were four huge, pale bronze sea anemones, attached like flowers to a monstrous, multi-coloured bonnet.

I swam over this fascinating rock and anchored myself against the slow pull of the tide by catching hold of a projecting piece of coral, having first examined it carefully to make sure that there was nothing harmful lurking on, or under, or in it. That this was a wise precaution, I soon realised for as soon as my eyes got focused, I saw lurking, almost invisible, in the coral- and reed-encrusted grotto, a foot or so away from my hand, a large and beautifully coloured Scorpion fish whose dorsal spines can cause you agony and even, in rare cases, death, should you unwittingly touch it and it jabs them into you. He was some seven inches long, with a jowly, pouting face and huge, scarlet eyes. His predominant colours were pink and orange, with black bars and stripes and specklings. His pectoral fins were greatly elongated so he looked as though he had two pink hands growing out from under his gills, with attenuated fingers. Along his back was the row of scarlet spines that could prove so lethal. Altogether, he was a most flamboyant fish and, once you had spotted him, he glowed like a great jewel; yet until I had noticed a slight movement from him, he had, with his striped and spotted livery, melted into the background. Now, realising he had been spotted, he moved his great trailing fins gently and gradually edged his way round and down the rock away from me. Beautiful though he was, I was relieved not to have him at quite such close quarters.

Living in and around the anemones, were some handsome Clown fish, about three inches long, a bright orange colour, banded with broad stripes of snow-white. These pretty little fish have a symbiotic relationship with the anemones. They live among the stinging tentacles which would kill other fish, and so the anemone becomes their home; a formidable fortress in which the Clown fish takes refuge in moments of danger. In return for this protection, the fish, of course, drops some of its food which then becomes the anemone's lunch. Why, or how, this curious relationship came about, is a mystery. Anemones can hardly be described as having scintillating intellects, and how they managed to work out the usefulness of the Clown fish and refrain from stinging them, is a puzzle.

Wedged deep into the coral here and there were a number of large clams. All that could be seen of them were the rims of their scalloped shells, over which the edge of their mantle protruded, so they appeared to be grinning at you with thick, blue and iridescent green lips. These, each about the size of a coconut, were, of course, relatives of the famous giant clam found farther out on the reef – a monstrous shell that could weigh up to two hundred pounds and measure three feet. Many blood-curdling stories have been written about unfortunate divers who by chance have put their foot into one of these shells, which immediately slammed shut like a man-trap (as all clams do in moments of stress) thus consigning the diver to death by drowning. There does not appear to be an authenticated record of this ever having happened, although of course it is perfectly possible, for the shell could snap shut and unless the diver had a knife with which to cut the massive muscle that acts as both hinge and lock on the two halves of the shell, it would be as immovable and unopenable as a castle door. Again, in the case of these highly coloured clams, there is a curious symbiotic relationship, for in the brilliant mantle there are a number of small, unicellular algae, called by the rather attractive name of *Zooxanthellae*. These minute creatures obtain their sustenance from the food the clam sucks in, and in payment they give the clam an additional supply of oxygen. It is rather like paying for your daily bread with air, a thing most of us would like to do.

I shifted my vantage point to the other side of the rock, making sure of the whereabouts of the Scorpion fish, and came upon yet another symbiotic relationship. There was a small shoal of various multi-coloured fish, which included a Box fish and three canary yellow Surgeon fish. The Box fish was quite incredible. He was only three inches long, vivid orange with black polka-dots all over him; but it was not the colouration so much as the bizarre shape of the creature which amazed me, for the whole body is like a square box of bone and through holes in this protrude the creature's fins, vent, eyes and mouth. This means that the tail has to wave around like the propeller of an outboard engine. This mode of locomotion, coupled with the fish's big, round, perpetually surprising-looking pop-eyes, its square shape and polka-dot suiting, combine to make it one of the most curious inhabitants of the reef.

The Surgeon fish were quite different. Their yellow bodies were roughly moon-shaped, they had high domed foreheads and their mouths protruded, almost like the snout of a pig. They get their name from the two sharp, scalpel-like knives set just behind the tail. These dangerous weapons can fold back like the blade of a pocket knife into a hidden groove.

But, fascinating though these two species of fish were, it was what was happening to them that was so curious. The two Surgeon fish were close to the rock, hanging in a trance-like state while the Box fish puttered to and fro like some weird, orange boat, occasionally coming to a standstill. Among them darted three lithe little fish, small gobies with bright Prussian-blue and sky-blue markings. They were cleaner fish and they worked assiduously on their three customers, zooming in to suck the parasites off their skin and then, as it were, standing back to admire their handiwork before dashing in again, rather like effeminate hairdressers admiring the creation of a new hairstyle. Later on, on the big main reef, I sometimes saw queues of fish waiting their turn at the barber's shop, where the little blue barbers worked in a frenzy to keep up with their customers.

So captivated had I become by all I had seen, for every inch of what we came affectionately to call 'St Paul's' was covered with tiny anemones, sea fans, feather worms, shrimps, crabs and a host of other things, that I discovered I had spent over an hour suspended in one spot and even then, had been unable to take it all in. Here, on this one rock, was a myriad of life which would require a naturalist to spend a dozen lifetimes even to start to unravel it. What, I wondered, as I swam slowly back to breakfast, was the reef going to be like? I was soon to know. It was overwhelming.

Miraculous Madagascar

Madagascar is one of those parts of our planet that any self-respecting scientist would be overjoyed to find one Christmas morning that Santa Claus had put into his stocking, because it would not matter if his interests were primarily zoological, botanical, anthropological or geological, for this great island – the fourth largest in the world – could be called, scientifically speaking, a multi-purpose present. It is so rich in all these things and more, so bristling with strange forms of life and the enigmas that go with them that, biologically speaking, it is one of the most important parts of our world.

It lies athwart the southern and eastern coasts of Africa looking (if one must be truthful) like a badly made and served omelette, a thousand miles long and some three hundred miles across at its widest point. It was supposedly formed at the time in the world's history when the great land masses were shaping, merging and parting again like huge granite rafts on a skating rink, eventually merging to form the great Gondwanaland continent. This then split up once more, forming the continents more or less as we know them today. When Gondwanaland was in existence, of course, animal species could wander and merge over a wide area, but after the break-up each continent was rafted away with its own crew of creatures that evolved along different lines. About 100 million years ago, Madagascar broke away from Africa, so the bulk of its wonderful selection of plants and animals dates back to this ancient era, but as recently as 60 million years ago the island was still within colonising distance of Africa and it received rafts in the shape of giant trees that carried not only seeds and spores but the earliest types of monkey, the prosimians, as well as other mammals and reptiles. So Madagascar became a sort of living animal museum with types of creatures that go back to the time of Gondwanaland.

For millions of years, unmolested by man, the fauna of this huge island evolved into a fantastic array of creatures from huge lemurs the size of a calf to ones the size of a mouse. Pigmy hippos lolled in the swamps and ten-foot-high Elephant birds thumped their way ostrich-like through the forest glades and made nests in which they laid their eggs the size of footballs (suitable for an omelette for 75 people) and giant tortoises lumbered everywhere. Then into this zoological and botanical paradise came man, rafting in his own way (though not on tree roots) across the Indian Ocean from homelands in some part of Indonesia. Inevitably the rate of extinction rose, as it does everywhere with the advent of *Homo sapiens*, the super predator and destroyer of wild habitat. Ten species of giant lemur vanished, together with the giant tortoises, Elephant birds and Pigmy hippo. Having exterminated these, man then set about finishing off the forests. At one time, Madagascar was covered almost entirely in forest, from the moist rainforest in the east to the dry deciduous forest in the west. With the advent of wasteful slash and burn agricultural methods and the introduction of a zebu, whose over-grazing prevented any forest regeneration, in a very short time the island was in very bad shape and this has deteriorated to the present day. Now less than one-fifth of Madagascar's forests remain. As the forests vanish so erosion takes over. If the present rate of forest destruction goes on unchecked, in twenty years' time the island will be nothing more than a giant red cinder, unable to support its ever-mounting population.

My wife, Lee, and I went to Madagascar in 1981 to make some television films and to see which species of mammals, birds and reptiles could benefit from having breeding colonies set up in our sanctuary on the island of Jersey. As you fly across Madagascar to the Antananarivo airport, you can see the effect of man on this environment. Eroded hillsides that look as though they have been scratched by the claws of a gigantic cat dribble the laterite soil into the rivers so that they run, red as blood, to the sea where they stain the ocean like severed arteries. Shrouds of smoke hang here and there where precious forests and grasslands are still being burned and the whole island seems to glower at you under a brilliant flax blue sky.

I must say the drive to Antananarivo from the airport is simply enchanting. In what other country, for example, would you be held up by a traffic jam of zebus, great, glossy, multicoloured beasts, swaggering along the road in a formidable glittering forest of huge horns? On every side there were bright green paddy fields, contrasting with the curious Malagasy architecture – small verandahed houses with steep pitched roofs, built out of pale rose brick.

Antananarivo was as vibrant and noisy as an overturned beehive, for it was Zoma Day, the great Friday market when everyone converges on the capital bringing their multitudinous wares with them. The streets and boulevards burst into a mushroom bed of white umbrellas that sheltered both the shopkeepers and their produce from the sun. Everywhere there were huge yellow and green piles of plantains and bananas, red and green peppers shining as though just varnished, mounds of rice, lentils and chickpeas, mounds of various spices like miniature volcanoes, cabbages, sugar cane and sweet potatoes as orange as winter suns; shuffling, cackling carpets of ducks, geese and chickens, their legs tied together but each bird within reach of a bowl of fresh water. There were piles of multicoloured straw mats and what seemed like acres of straw hats of every size and shape. There were stalls selling precious stones, glittering like chips of rain-bows, iron pots and pans, baskets, wood carvings and a host of other items. Moving through this enormous display of prod-uce were the Malagasy from all over the island, some in national costume, some in quasi European outfits, most of them wear-ing small straw hats with coloured patterns woven into them, each denoting their tribe – the Malagasy equivalent of the old school tie. You might see some Tsimihety (Those Who Do Not Cut Their Hair), Antandroy (People of the Thorn Bush), Antaifasy (People of the Sun), Bezanozano (Those with Many-Braided Hair), or Mahafaly (the Joyful People) and many others – a sea of handsome faces and glittering smiles. An inveterate market-goer all over the world, I think the Zoma is one of the most colourful and enchanting markets I have ever encountered and after an hour wandering through it you became drugged with all the different scents, sounds and col-ours and emerged like a satiated bee from an exceptionally lush herbaceous border.

Our first trip was to the south of the island, to Berenty and Hazafotsy. Berenty is of particular interest for it is a section of lush riverine forest that has been set aside by its owner, Mon-sieur DeHeaulme, as a lemur reserve and in it dwell colonies of what must be the best-studied lemurs in the world as well as many other creatures that benefit from the Reserve. Berenty is an incredible place, for the animals who live there are so used to hosts of earnest scientists plodding through the forest, that they have become exceedingly tame and pay little attention to you, treating you as if you were just another tree. So it was wonderful to be able to squat on the ground and have a troupe of some twenty Ring-tails forage around you, almost oblivious to your presence, back and white tails held aloft like furry caterpillars, bickering or yodelling, stuffing their mouths full of leaves, occasionally pausing to mark their territory by slashing the bark on branches with the aid of a hard, horny spur on their forearms. Their lovely grey and white decor with a pinkish tinge on the grey fur, their prick ears, boldly ringed tails and great golden eyes made them look like an animal that had been designed by a very up-market interior decorator.

Berenty was a fascinating piece of forest. Hundreds of Kites flew down to the river to fish and bathe and then sat and, as it were, hung themselves out to dry on the branches of the great dead trees along the riverbank. In the gloom of the forest Giant couas in Oxford and Cambridge blue feathering and with long tails like magpies scuttled along the ground searching for fruit and insects. In the leafmould lives the big Malagasy 'singing' cockroach, a beast the size of a small tangerine, with a formidable array of spikes and spines on his chocolate brown body and legs. When captured, this strange insect emits a loud purring noise, the sort of sound a clockwork train makes when lifted from the rails. So loud and startling is this 'song' that it has an immediate and frightening effect on any would-be predator. In the bushes prowled and swayed foot-long stick insects looking more like branches than the branches they clung to, and multicoloured butterflies glittered in the gloom as they flew from flower to flower. Altogether, it was an enchanted forest with the soft calls of the couas echoing around you, the gold bars of sunlight slanting through the trees like spotlights illuminating the pirouetting flocks of parti-coloured lemurs, mewing to each other like cats as they made their way through the forest.

In complete contrast to this was our next stop in the Didiera forests at Hazafotsy, a little north of the river. Didiera is a strange plant that resembles a 40-foot-high candelabra cactus. Its trunk and arms are closely covered with darning-needle-long spines and little fleshy plate-shaped leaves the size of a thumbnail on a minute stalk. It was a strange otherworldly sort of forest, the kind of thing you would expect to find on a distant planet. The inhabitants were equally strange, for it was the home of the Sifaka, a lemur the size of a small dog with long limbs and eyes that are blazing orange. An amazing thing about the Sifaka was their ability to bound through the Didiera forest, leaping 20 or 30 feet from one spiny plant to another without apparently suffering any ill effects, even though they had to clasp the upright stem close to their bodies with hands and feet. It was an incredible sight to see these white ghostly forms bounding through the Didiera like circus acrobats, never missing a hand or foot hold, jumping upwards and downwards with equal ease.

Soon we left this strange forest and headed up to the north of Madagascar to visit the offshore island called Nosy Komba. On this island lives a colony of Royal Black lemurs and the story of their establishment is a curious one with an almost fairytale-like quality. In the distant past, Nosy Komba was conquered by one of the mainland kings and in order to make sure it remained in his possession he sent one of his daughters and her retinue to live there. So that she would not be lonely, this princess took with her a group of her pet Black lemurs and it is from these animals that the present-day colony is descended. They are treated with great reverence by the inhabitants of Nosy Komba and – rather like sacred cows in India – are allowed the run of the village, where they enter the huts, steal food and generally behave like naughty children but are never molested because of their lineage.

It took a couple of hours to reach the island which proved to be so idyllic that you would have thought it had been designed by Hollywood. A thick grove of palms and other trees lined the snow-white beach and amongst them nestled the tiny palm-thatched village. The water was vodka-clear and as warm as a bath. The glittering beach was littered with bright shells and here and there a colony of black canoes, like a school of stranded dolphins. As our boat cut its engine and drifted to the shore the entire village erupted and came tumbling down the beach to greet us, clad in every conceivable colour of the rainbow, chanting and playing drums and bamboo valihas. It was like being greeted by a vociferous, melodious flowerbed of people. As soon as we entered the village, it was the lemurs' turn to greet us. They appeared in droves, very cat-like with large fringed ears and chrysanthemum yellow eyes, the females' fur chocolate brown and the males a Satanic black. They rushed in and out of the houses, leapt on our shoulders, clung to our legs, purring and yowling. They found the cameras and tripods fascinating and sat on them in such quantities that we had to bribe them away with a largesse of bananas so that we could get some filming done. Later, when we were partaking of a splendid meal the villagers had cooked us under the palm trees, the lemurs' attentions became too pressing and titbits would disappear like magic from your fork as you were lifting it to your mouth. In the end we had to marshal an army of small boys to chase the thieving lemurs away so that we could eat in peace. Nosy Komba was a ravishing little island and we were sorry to leave it and its happy people and audacious Royal lemurs, but now we were heading south-east to one of the last remaining rainforest areas, at Perinet.

What a fantastic forest it was. Huge chameleons, like polychromatic dinosaurs a foot long, prowled in the bushes, their eyes swivelling like auctioneers', in search of beetles like polished jewels or butterflies like carefully dyed and embroidered lace. On the ground in the leaf-litter, pigmy chameleons that would fit into a matchbox moved slowly about their world of giant leaves, delicately coloured and inscribed with black scribbles and dots so they looked like animated leaves themselves. Around them moved the giant millipedes, magnified to the size of golf balls, decked out in green, bronze and brown livery. But it was the great choir at Perinet that was the most impressive thing. Family groups of the biggest of the lemurs, the Indri, each the size of a six-year-old child, parti-coloured in black and white like a panda, hanging in the trees, marigold-yellow eyes glistening, at intervals bursting into song, a sound so powerful it seemed to make the very ground vibrate and the trees tremble. The first time we saw and heard the Indri choir perform was after a long hot morning when we had been trying to track down a family group without success. Frustrated, we paused in the forest to discuss our strategy in trying to find these elusive beasts, only to discover that there was a whole family in the trees above us, immobile and thus invisible. They suddenly burst into song and nearly deafened us. Stimulated by their vocal efforts, they leapt from tree to tree around us in the most graceful way for such a bulky animal and paused now and then to peer down at us to see how their song was being appreciated. It was a splendid song from a splendid animal, a song so rich and loud it made you feel as if you were locked inside a Steinway grand, on which was being performed one of Beethoven's more complex and ponderous piano concertos.

Filming completed, we came to that happy time in television shows called R and R – rest and relaxation – so Lee and I went to a charming hotel at Mora-mora, north of Tulear, where we had been assured that the reef was 'something special'. We discovered that this was an incredible understatement. The reef was almost indescribable in its beauty. As we climbed out of the boat and hung and drifted like kites in the transparent waters, we saw below us an acre of huge coral flowers; each was bigger than a card table, each sculpted like an old-fashioned tea rose in rich pink. It was as though we were Lilliputians floating over these huge flowers, watching each pink petal alive with multicoloured fish as we drifted from bloom to giant bloom in this enchanted garden. It was a wonderful memory to end the trip with.

It is to be hoped that with the help of wealthier countries Madagascar will be able to save what is left, to save the fabulous forests in which the Indri sings, to save the Didiera forest in which the acrobatic Sifaka live and to save the overwhelmingly beautiful reefs. Madagascar is a miracle of evolution and it behoves us all, Malagasy and foreigner alike, to cherish it as a vitally important part of our world.

Whiffling through Its Tulgey Wood

In the gloom it came along the branches towards me, its round, hypnotic eyes blazing, its spoon-like ears turning to and fro independently like radar dishes, its white whiskers twitching and moving like sensors; its black hands, with their thin, attenuated fingers, the third seeming prodigiously elongated, tapping delicately on the branches as it moved along, like those of a pianist playing a complicated piece by Chopin. It looked like a Walt Disney witch's black cat with a touch of ET thrown in for good measure. If ever a flying saucer came from Mars, you felt that this is what would emerge from it. It was Lewis Carroll's Jabberwocky come to life, whiffling through its tulgey wood.

It lowered itself onto my shoulder, gazed into my face with its huge, hypnotic eyes and ran slender fingers through my beard and hair as gently as any barber. In its underslung jaw, I could see giant chisel-like teeth, teeth which grow constantly, and I sat quite still. It uttered a small, snorting noise like 'humph' and descended to my lap. Here, it inspected my walking stick. Its black fingers played along its length as if the stick were a flute. Then it leant forward and, with alarming accuracy, almost bisected my stick with two bites from its enormous teeth. To its obvious chagrin, it found no beetle larvae there and so it returned to my shoulder. Again, it combed my beard and hair, gentle as a baby breeze.

Then, to my alarm, it discovered my ear. 'Here,' it seemed to say to itself, 'must lurk a beetle larva of royal proportions and of the utmost succulence.' It fondled my ear as a gourmet fondles a menu and then, with great care, it inserted its thin finger. I resigned myself to deafness – move over, Beethoven, I said to myself, here I come. To my astonishment, I could hardly feel the finger as it searched my ear like a radar probe for hidden delicacies. Finding my ear bereft of tasty and fragrant grubs, it uttered another faint 'humph' of annoyance and climbed up into the branches again.

I had had my first encounter with an aye-aye and I decided that this was one of the most incredible creatures I had ever been privileged to meet. Since it needed help, help it we must. To allow such an astonishing and complex creature to become extinct was as unthinkable as burning a Rembrandt, turning the Sistine Chapel into a disco, or pulling down the Acropolis to make way for a Hilton. Yet the aye-aye, this strange creature that has attained near-mythical status on the island of Madagascar, is in danger of vanishing. It is a magical animal, not only biologically speaking, but in the minds of the Malagasy people amongst whom it lives and, unfortunately, perishes.

When this strange beast was first described in 1782, it had such an anatomical jumble of various qualities that for many years scientists could not make up their minds what it was. Obviously, it was not a common or garden lemur and was thought, for a time, to be a rodent, because of its massive teeth. Finally, it was decided that an aye-aye was an aye-aye, one of the lemurs, but a unique inhabitant of the planet, like no other creature. It was dignified with a family of its own and christened with the euphonious name of *Daubentonia madagascariensis*.

Madagascar is an island filled with magic and many taboos, or *fadys* as they are called, which vary from place to place, so it is not surprising that such a weird product of evolution as the aye-aye should be credited with magical powers that vary from village to village, from tribe to tribe. In places, if it is found near a village, it is thought to be a harbinger of death and so must be killed. If it is a small one, then an infant in the village might die. If it is a large, whitish animal, a pale-skinned adult will be in danger and if it is a dark animal, a dark-complexioned human will be in danger.

In other parts of the island, if a villager finds and kills an aye-aye near his house, he thoughtfully removes the bad luck from himself by putting the corpse in his neighbour's back garden. The neighbour, finding this somewhat doubtful gift, makes haste to put it in his neighbour's back garden. So the aye-aye corpse progresses through the village until thrown out onto the road to the alarm of passers-by. It is an aye-aye chain letter: pass this on, or something awful will befall you. In other areas, the animal is killed, its hands and feet bound in raffia and it is hung at the entrance to the village until the corpse starts to rot, when it is fed to the dogs. In other places, its slim third finger is dried and used by the village sorcerer as a magic charm for good or for evil. So the aye-aye, through a quirk of evolution, has become possessed of a magic finger.

At one time, the aye-aye was thought to be extinct, but then it was found that this curious animal was still clinging on in isolated pockets, nearly all of which were threatened by forest destruction. The aye-aye had used its magic to become a survivor of a sort. As its natural habitat diminished, it took to invading what man had replaced it with – coconut plantations, sugar-cane groves and orchards of cloves. With its huge teeth, it trepanned the green coconuts, drank the juice and extracted the jelly-like, unripe fruit by using its thin middle finger like a hook. It disembowelled the sugar cane, leaving the stems looking like some strange, medieval musical instrument. It bisected the clove trees in search of beetle grubs. If you are a villager whose whole livelihood depends on, perhaps, five coconut trees, a tiny patch of sugar cane and half a dozen clove trees, then the aye-aye becomes not a magical menace but a creature that can ruin your income for ever. Therefore, you kill it or starve.

As forest decimation continues unabated, these isolated pockets of aye-aye, leading a bandit-like existence, are doomed. It is to be hoped that new, more intelligent agricultural methods will be soon introduced to replace the destruction. In the meantime, for the sake of the aye-aye, some must be established in captivity to maintain the species: if they vanish in the wild, we will have at least some animals to return to the natural habitat (if, of course, their natural habitat still exists).

PART THREE

More Birds and Beasts

Animals I've Known and Loved

'The man is mad. Invite him to stay and he puts an
eagle in your wine cellar!'

– Lawrence Durrell, c. 1967

*It was a dark day for the planet when man crawled out of his cave
and picked up a rock. Mankind is so used to thinking of himself as
superior that he has eradicated the word 'humble' from his vocabulary. Why do we always have to look at each other and so seldom
consider and learn from our fellow animals?*

*Don't ever think that magic is simply somebody taking a rabbit out of
a hat. Our ancestors believed in magic and were right for the wrong
reasons – for the most part they believed that magic was evil, not
good. But the magic that lies all about you, from your own body to
that of an elephant, to a fly's wing as intricate as anything that lets
the sunlight into Chartres Cathedral, to the great surging sea itself –
that is magic. Anyone who goes through life unastounded by everything
he sees is not alive.*

– Fragments from unpublished autobiography

Gerry had many passions, but high on the list was his obsession with 'mysterious beasts' – animals real or imagined around which a web of myth had been woven, such as the Loch Ness Monster and the Abominable Snowman. He was devoted to and built his conservation reputation on the 'little brown jobs' of the animal kingdom, those drab, obscure and humble species which did not attract much attention from the general public, but which, in his opinion, had as much right to exist as the more charismatic creatures.

The Abominable Snowman

Not long ago that elusive creature the Abominable Snowman was in the news again. Once more those puzzling sets of foot-prints had been found in the snow on the Himalayas, and, once again, argument waxed fierce as to what exactly an Abomin-able Snowman *is*.

This creature looks, according to local reports, like a cross between a bear and an ape, and it has been cropping up in the news ever since 1898, when its tracks were reported for the first time. These footprints are of an animal, apparently walking on its hind legs, with feet that must be almost the circumference of a soup plate. These bi-ped tracks argue a man-like creature of astonishing proportions. In 1925 the Everest Expedition saw some moving objects at a great distance, high above the snow-line, and later they found some of these tracks, but this is the nearest that anyone has come to seeing the Snowman. We know what its footprints look like, but the animal itself remains stubbornly invisible.

A number of people believe that these Snowman tracks are made by some animal already known to science. It is suggested that a monkey is responsible; the size of the tracks is accounted for by the fact that a monkey, bounding along, will sometimes place its hind feet in the same prints as its forefeet, and so, in deep snow, leave a track that would suggest some large animal walking on its hind feet. Other people think that the tracks are evidence of a completely unknown animal, lurking high up in the snow, awaiting capture and a scientific description.

The Abominable Snowman, however, is only one of the many mystery animals that have been reported from various parts of the world at different times. Every continent, it seems, has its own mystery creatures awaiting discovery, and the continent that seems to have more than its fair share is, of course, Africa. Perhaps the most famous – or, one should say, infamous – of Africa's unknown monsters is the so-called Nandi Bear. Like all good criminals it naturally goes under a number of aliases, but Nandi Bear is the commonest. This beast is to Africa what the Snowman is to the Himalayas, but we know a little more about the Nandi Bear than we know about the Snowman: there are many reports of it actually having been seen, and the list of its misdeeds is long. It seems to be a great brownish or yellowish bear-like creature, armed with long claws. Hunting at night it is silent and very ferocious, and has been known to kill pigs, cattle, and even human beings. Its delightful method of killing a man is to rip off the scalp and the top of the head with its great claws. There are cases on record of the Nandi Bear having burrowed through eight-feet-thick walls of thorn bushes, and once it is reported to have jumped over a six-foot-high fence, carrying a sheep in its mouth. Its cry is a loud roaring screaming noise, and both locals and Europeans who have heard it testify that it's a dreadful and frightening sound. Judging by the tracks the beast has left, together with the descriptions of it that various witnesses have reported, it seems to be something unknown to zoologists. Many Europeans who have spent years in Africa, and know the country well and the people well, believe in the existence of the Nandi Bear; it is certainly well known over a great part of Africa, but its favourite haunt seems to be the Nandi country in Kenya. Wherever it is known, the people loathe and fear it, for it has obtained for itself an evil reputation as a killer, and a savage killer at that.

There are European residents in Africa, of course, who refuse to believe in the Nandi Bear, putting the whole thing down to superstition. The various killings, they say, are done by an extra-large Hyena or Leopard. But this attitude of disbelieving anything that is said by locals and dismissing it as mere superstition is rather unwise as has been proved time and time again. During the last seventy years or so there has been discovered an extra-ordinary number of large animals, all new to science, living in the African jungle; the Okapi and the Pigmy Hippo, for example, were only brought to light in the early part of the 1900s, and the Congo Peacock was officially discovered as recently as 1937. Before they were discovered, rumours of all these animals that had reached the outside world were dismissed as native tales, and few people took any notice of them. Yet when they *were* discovered everyone was amazed that such large animals should have escaped notice for so long . . . escaped the notice, that is, of everyone except the locals.

From Tanganyika, next door, as it were, to the Nandi Bear, there come reports of another peculiar creature called the Agogwe, or Little Furry Man. Here again reports are backed by eye-witness accounts from careful and competent observers. Agogwes have been seen several times, sometimes in pairs, sometimes in small family groups. They are shaped like men, but are only four feet high, and covered with a coat of reddish hair. They walk very gracefully, upright, like a man, not on all fours as a monkey does, or crouching and using their knuckles for support as the apes do. But, that they may be in some way related to these animals is suggested by the fact that Agogwes have been seen in company with troupes of monkeys, and neither seemed in the least perturbed by the other's presence. Perhaps the Agogwe, hidden in the forests of East Africa, is a missing link, or a new species of ape.

Africa has its own Loch Ness Monster in the shape of a huge, long-necked beast, like a prehistoric reptile, which is called the Lau. According to eye-witnesses – it has been seen by both natives and Europeans – it seems to be fairly widespread in the great lakes and swamps. In various parts of Africa it is known by various names, but the descriptions tally. It has been seen more than once by the steamers crossing Lake Victoria . . . in fact, on one occasion it swam close to the ship and attempted to seize the look-out from the bows.

Strangely enough, the quickest way to provoke derisive comment about any of these mysterious creatures is to say that it resembles some sort of prehistoric animal. There seems to be a curious belief that no real prehistoric fauna could be found alive today. Actually, there are a great number of animals living in the world today which are, to all intents and purposes, exactly the same as their ancestors were ages ago. But, of course, if you want something *really* prehistoric there is the fish that is called Latimeria, which was caught in 1928 off the coast of South Africa. This strange fish was supposed to have been extinct for several million years, before it turned up, alive and wiggling, in the trawler's nets. You could not get anything more decidedly prehistoric than Latimeria.

There are cases where different animals were thought to be extinct, simply because they had not been seen or shot for a number of years. The Notornis, for example, a curious flightless bird about the size of a turkey, which is found in New Zealand. First, the Notornis was only known from fossil bones, and it was assumed that it was a prehistoric bird that had long since become extinct. Then some living specimens were found in 1884 and the bird, as it were, was brought up to date. From then on nothing more was heard of the bird, and it was believed to have become extinct all over again. In 1948, however, the zoological world was astonished by the discovery of about a hundred Notornis, happily living and breeding on the shores of a lake in New Zealand, unaware that they were supposed to have been extinct for the last fifty years! An even more extra-ordinary case was that of the Cahow, a sea bird peculiar to Bermuda, which was supposed to have been exterminated three hundred years ago. But in 1950 a small number of them were found nesting on a tiny rocky island, just off Bermuda. Now, if these birds can hide themselves away so successfully for such a great number of years, in places as civilised and explored as New Zealand and Bermuda, it makes one wonder if there is any real reason why there shouldn't be a few bear-like or ape-like, or even Loch-Ness-Monster-like creatures to be found in the vast forests and swamps of Africa, or the less explored parts of the Himalayas.

In Australia, where you would think they had enough curi-ous animals to be getting along with, there are reports of a giant kangaroo, a beast which is supposed to stand about fif-teen feet high. It has been seen by gold prospectors and others who travel in the less frequented parts of the interior, but, so far, this is all we know of it. That there should be a kangaroo of such impressive dimensions is not unbelievable, because the forerunners of the present-day Australian fauna included some fantastic giant forms, so large that their present-day counter-parts look like pigmies in comparison. So it is not impossible that there are giant kangaroos in the interior of Australia: all we want now is for someone to go and find them, and bring back concrete evidence of their existence.

There are reports of a strange sea creature from Easter Island, thousands of miles east of Australia. This animal is well known to the inhabitants of the island, and they insist that it is neither a whale nor a shark. They describe it as being about thirty feet long, and very broad. It possesses a pair of arms about four feet long, furnished with claws like hands; when swimming, these arms are stretched behind the monster's neck, but as soon as it sights its prey the arms are shot forward, and the victim is clasped in the claws or hands and drawn towards the tooth-filled mouth. The Easter Islanders are very afraid of these animals as there are a number of cases on record where they have attacked and killed men. They call this creature the Nuihi, but what is apparently the same animal is known from the coast of Queensland, Australia, and there it is called the Moha-Moha. In 1890 an Australian school teacher had the great good fortune to see one of these Moha-Moha or Nuihi, and hers was not a hurried glimpse, for the 'monster turtle-fish', as she called it, let her stand within about five feet of it for about half an hour. She describes it being nearly thirty feet long, with a great dome-shaped body some eight feet across and five feet high. The tail was about twelve feet long. When it eventually got tired of showing itself off to the lady it put its large head and neck into the water and swam off. This creature might well be the one responsible for all the Sea Serpent stories on record. A creature so widespread that it has been seen off the Australian coast as well as Easter Island might well range over a vast area of ocean.

Not to be outdone by the rest of the world, South America has two mystery beasts of her own, and, in many ways, they are perhaps the most interesting of the lot. The first of these is a curious creature, found in the forests of Venezuela, which is supposed to be an ape. In 1928 a French geologist was attacked by two of these animals, and he shot one and killed it while the other made off into the forest. On examining the body of the beast he had killed, the geologist was astonished to find that it was apparently an ape. Now the apes are supposed to be confined

21. Early poster for Jersey Zoo, 1959.

22. Gerald with Trumpy, the trumpeter, Jersey Zoo, 1959.

23. Whiskers, the emperor tamarin, Jersey Zoo, c. 1959.

24. Louisa playing ball with Chumley, Jersey Zoo, c. 1959.

25. Jacquie, Gerald, BBC producer Christopher Parsons and Keeper plan the expedition to Australia in 1962.

26. Gerald with a kaka, a species of parrot, New Zealand, 1962.

27. Gerald with dead wedge-tailed eagles, who had been killed by local farmers for purportedly killing lambs, Australia, 1962.

28. Gerald with N'Pongo, a young gorilla, Jersey Zoo, *c.* 1960.

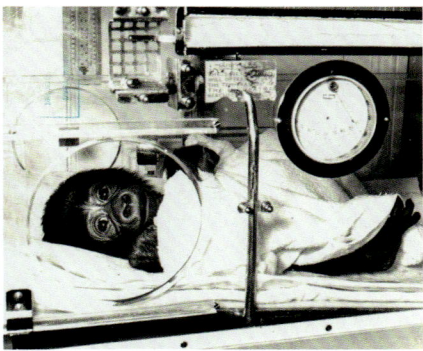

30. Assumbo, first offspring of Jambo and Nandi, Jersey Zoo, 1973.

29. Jambo, the silverback gorilla, Jersey Zoo, 1972.

31. Gerald with fiancé Lee and ring-tailed lemurs, Jersey Zoo, 1978.

32. Lee and Gerald with fossil egg of the elephant bird, *Aepyornis*, which became extinct about 400 years ago, Madagascar, 1981.

33. Gerald with young aye-aye, Jersey Zoo, 1991.

34. Gerald and HRH Princess Anne opening the International Training Centre, Jersey Zoo, 1984.

35. Gerald and Lee with students at the International Training Centre, now Durrell Conservation Academy, Jersey Zoo, 1980s.

36. Golden lion tamarins, Jersey Zoo, early 1980s.

37. Mission stone at the entrance to Jersey Zoo, clearly indicating the mission of the Trust: *saving species from extinction*.

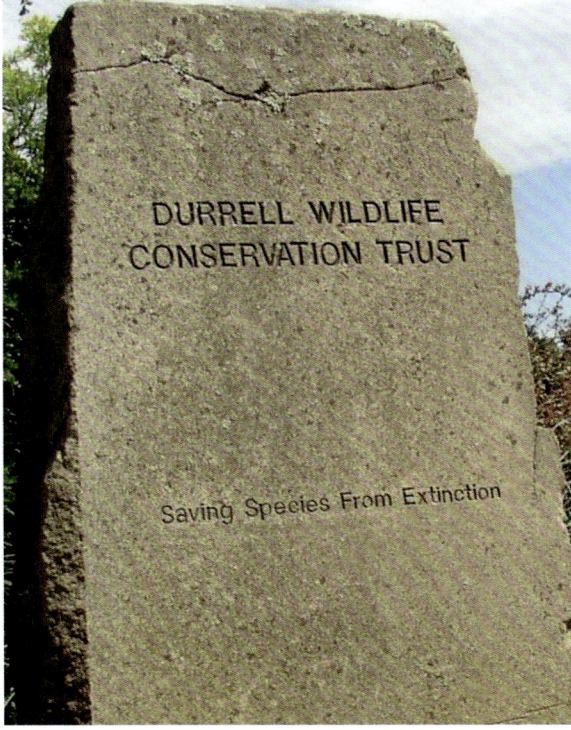

38. Statue of Gerald Durrell by John Doubleday, completed and erected in 1999, at the entrance to Jersey Zoo.

39. Gerald feeding a Mauritius kestrel, newly released to the wild, Mauritius, 1980s.

to Asia and Africa; though rich in monkey life, South America was supposed to be devoid of apes. Realising that he had probably made an important discovery, the Frenchman very wisely wrote a detailed description of the creature, took careful measurements and photographs, and kept its skull. The ape was five feet two inches high, had no tail, and the very small thumb was placed high on the wrist. It was unfortunate that, on the way back to civilisation, the geologist met with an accident, and the most important part of his evidence, the skull, was lost. So all that remains to prove that there is such a thing as a South American ape is a description and one photograph.

The second South American mystery is the Giant Sloth or Mylodon. The mystery about these enormous shaggy animals is not whether they existed, for we know, from all fossil remains, that they lived thousands of years ago in the Southern part of the American Continent. The question is when did they die out? It was believed at first that the Giant Sloth was extinct long before the earliest man invaded the Continent, but various discoveries since then have proved that early man hunted and killed the Sloth for food. However, it seemed certain that the Sloths had become extinct long before America was officially discovered by Europe. There were several species of these Giant Sloths, ranging from one almost the size of an elephant down to one the size of an ox. Some years ago, in a cave in Southern Patagonia, a piece of skin belonging to one of the ox-sized variety was found, but the astonishing thing about it was that, instead of being thousands of years old as it should have been, this bit of skin was fresh! The animal that it had come from could only have been killed quite recently, within the last fifty or hundred years. People began to wonder if the Giant Sloth was extinct after all . . . perhaps they still existed in some remote areas of Patagonia? But it was remembered that the indigenous tribes living in that region talk of a great animal they sometimes see: they said it was the size of a cow, and spent the day sleeping in holes in the ground that it dug for itself with its huge claws. They said that it was quite harmless, but very difficult to kill, for arrows or spears would not penetrate its shaggy hide. Perhaps the most convincing thing about this story is their name for the animal, which in translation means 'the one with the little stones on it'. The Giant Sloth, we know from the fossil remains, had small bony, bean-sized growths fitted like mosaic work into its skin, and so this name would be a very accurate description of it. This would also explain why the natives found it so difficult to kill, for under its long hair the Giant Sloth is armour-plated. So far nothing more has been heard of these curious beasts, but Patagonia is a very large place and maybe somewhere in the area a few of these huge animals have their last sanctuary.

These are only a few of the hundreds of unknown animals reported from various parts of the world. There is supposed to be an animal like an elephant, covered with long red hair, living in the rivers of West Africa; also in West Africa there are reports of a Pigmy Rhinoceros . . . as it is supposed to be found in the same region as the Pigmy Hippo it would not do to be over-sceptical. There is the famous Spotted Lion in Kenya waiting discovery; a great dinosaur-like creature in the vast swamps of Southern Rhodesia and a similar one in New Guinea; a monster that leaves gigantic man-like footprints, said to inhabit the dense jungle of Matto Grosso, might well be a sort of South American cousin to the Abominable Snowman. Even Europe is not lacking in mystery beasts: in the Austrian Alps there is supposed to be a large, short-legged lizard, which is reputedly poisonous. As the only known poisonous lizard is found in America, the Tatzel-wurm, as it is called, might turn out to be a related species.

Of course, the sea has been responsible for the greatest number of animal mysteries, as is only to be expected. Sea Serpents of all shapes and sizes have been reported since the earliest times, from Norway to the Cape of Good Hope, from the Pacific to the Indian Ocean. Nowadays, unfortunately, to say that you have seen a Sea Serpent is considered tantamount to saying that you are a first-class liar. The poor Sea Serpent is treated as a sort of joke, yet there have been so many hundreds of different reports from so many different sources, both reliable and otherwise, that you would think it could be treated in a more serious manner than is usually the case. Perhaps the most famous Sea Serpent was the one seen by H.M. corvette 'Dedalus' in 1848, while on her way home from the East Indies. It was an enormous creature, some sixty feet long, shaped like a snake, and travelling at between 12 and 15 miles an hour. The colour was brownish, with yellowish white on the throat. It kept some four feet of its head and body above the surface while swimming. It was seen by seven members of the ship's company, including the captain. On their return to England, when the matter was reported, the witnesses had to undergo the usual experience of being told that what they saw was a seal, or a piece of seaweed, or something else, but definitely not a Sea Serpent. However, many people believed the story, for it seemed unlikely (to say the least) that the captain and six members of his crew should get together to perpetuate a hoax on the public, and, more particularly, on the Admiralty to whom the matter was reported. To say that the captain and his crew mistook a bit of seaweed or a seal for a serpent-like creature sixty feet long is rather like suggesting that a gamekeeper would mistake a stoat for a fox, or a rabbit for a horse. But in nearly every case of a reported Sea Serpent the witness has been subjected to the same sort of thing. Since the Sea Serpent is treated in this fashion, it is not altogether surprising that reports of mystery animals on land are treated in the same intelligent manner.

In these days of high speed travel the world has become rather a drab place from an explorer's point of view, so it is nice to think that in the few remaining inaccessible parts of the globe there may be animals unknown to science awaiting discovery. It is pleasant to think that the grandeur of the Himalayas shelters an Abominable Snowman, or that in the great swamps of Africa there may be scaly monsters sporting in the waters, as their ancestors did millions of years ago. But it is to be hoped that they occasionally allow themselves to be discovered, if only to confound the sceptics.

Little Brown Jobs

In these days of high-pressure publicity, when even a soap powder is represented as a sort of elixir of life, conservationists are having an uphill struggle in arousing public interest and sustaining it. So the publicity that the abortive Panda marriage has received – which makes that given to the average royal wedding or the extra-marital activities of cabinet ministers pale almost into insignificance – is to be applauded. Although the marriage was never consummated it can be said that Chi Chi and An-An have done their bit towards publicising conservation, and from this point of view alone Chi Chi's flight to Moscow was not a waste of time. The fact of the matter is that of the many hundreds of animal species that are in grave danger of extinction, only a handful of them have the charming and decorative appearance of a Panda and it is awfully difficult to get people worked up over the fate of some obscure, drab and very probably ugly little creature however zoologically important it might be.

Take the Cuban Solenodon for example. Leaving aside its unfortunate name, one has to confess that the thing itself looks like a gigantic rat that has, for a number of years, been addicted to gin; so, although the beast is unique and although it should be preserved at all costs, it is extremely difficult to work out a means of publicising this. What, after all, can one say to arouse public enthusiasm for the protection of such a creature? That it fought against Castro? And yet it is very likely that, in its humble way, the Solenodon possesses an infinitely more attractive character than a Panda. But before the public get worked up over the fate of a creature they demand that that creature should be attractive.

The Koala Bear, for example, quite one of the stupidest animals on earth, arouses everyone's maternal instincts in the same way as the Panda. So, hitherto it has been the fluffy appealing creature that has been winning hands down in the conservation field. They do not really require publicity stunts – they rely on their good looks. The ones who require publicity and who seldom, if ever, get it, are the Solenodons of this world. Tell the average person that say a Long-tailed Sminthopsis has infinitely more personality and charm than half a dozen Koala Bears or a couple of Pandas and he will look at you as though you were mad. This is simply because he has either never seen one or that Koalas and Pandas look cuddly whereas the Long-tailed Sminthopsis probably does not. The difficulties of ramming this home are enormous. How many people would get themselves worked up over the conservation of say snakes or crocodiles? Yet their plight in many parts of the world is just as acute as that of the more cuddly, nursery-type creatures. As you can imagine, the successful mating of a pair of Cuban Solenodons would be lucky to get a three-line mention in any newspaper.

Just telling people that animal life all over the world is in great danger does not seem to be enough. You have to promote the idea like a soap powder or a film star, otherwise people will not take you seriously. The more obvious methods of promotion are out: such headlines as SOLENODONS DEFY THE POPE or PAPA HEMINGWAY – WAS HE A SOLENODON ADDICT? are too far fetched to have a ring of conviction about them. However, in view of the almost morbid interest taken in Chi Chi and An-An's attempts at procreation, there is hope for the more obscure creatures yet. One hopes that Pandas, Koala Bears and similar attractive creatures will act as it were as publicity agents for the fate of the obscurer kinds.

There are many reasons for conservation, quite apart from the feeling that we have no right to exterminate another species. Eventually there will come a time when travel becomes so cheap that people will be able to visit such places as Australia, Africa or South America, and the amount of leisure the two-day week is going to give them will allow them time. One can only hope that by the time this happy state of affairs comes into being there will still be some animals left in the world for people to look at. So I am all for giving publicity to conservation by every means possible. The advertisement of even the commonest every-day product has shown the latitude that we may have with the truth so I feel that conservationists could well start using the same methods for better ends. Chi Chi and An-An have started the ball rolling – let us hope it continues. I for one am delighted to see the newspapers full of speculation about the sexual abilities of Pandas; it makes such a pleasant change. After all, we know how human beings do it.

Although Gerry often declared he did not have a favourite animal ('other than my wife', he would say), the next pieces reveal his particular affection for certain animals.

A Tortoise Called Melville

One way or another, I have been on intimate terms with the tortoise family all my life. On the island of Corfu, where I lived when young, one of my first pets was a tortoise whom I christened Achilles and whose great passion in life was strawberries, for which he would do anything. Unfortunately, he ended up drowned in a well and at his funeral (his mortal remains in a shoe-box) a beautiful piece praising his character and nobility was written and read in a shaking voice by my brother, Lawrence. He was then buried and had a wooden cross on his grave on which I had written: 'Achilles – In Mem-memoriummm', which was a word I could never really get to grips with and still cannot master. On the olive-covered hills surrounding the villas we lived in I watched tortoises, bleary-eyed, emerging from their hibernation. I watched them having fierce mating battles while uttering strange yawping cries, then laying their parchment-like eggs and the subsequent hatching of the fragile soft-shelled young.

I remember at the tender age of ten I was soundly berated by a be-whiskered official at the Natural History Museum in South Kensington for climbing inside the shell of a giant tortoise – unfortunately now extinct – once found in India, in order to see what it was like. I found there was room enough inside for three or four people of my age to have a picnic party. When I explained this to the disgruntled official he displayed no interest in my discovery. He merely said that picnics were not allowed inside the tortoise, which I thought showed a lack of the true scientific approach to the garnering of knowledge.

Once, in Mauritius, I went into a compound containing some 20 or 30 Giant Aldabra tortoises. It was the mating season and so there was a lot of banging and crashing of shells and much grunting and groaning. I was busy taking photographs when a huge male for some reason thought I had designs on the singularly unattractive female he was doing his best to seduce. He left her side and came towards me with astonishing speed like a bulldozer, opening and closing his huge mouth with a fearsome chomping sound reminiscent of a pair of very large hedge-clippers at work. The jaws of these giant reptiles are, of course, razor-sharp and so I took the coward's way out – I fled. He pursued me to the fence and I only just managed to scramble over it in time to avoid getting a nasty bite in the buttocks. Up until then, I had always thought of tortoises as being placid, gentle creatures but apparently, when love fires burn in your veins (even when you are cold-blooded) it brings out the macho instinct in you.

So, with this long career of intimacy with tortoises behind me, I was not overwhelmed with surprise when I and my wife were asked to participate in the opening of a 'tortoise village' near my home in the south of France. The Village des Tortues, as the French have musically called it, sounds like something out of Beatrix Potter with a touch of Enid Blyton but it is, in fact, a very serious, well organised scientific project set up to try and save from extinction France's most endangered reptile, the Hermann's tortoise (*Testudo hermanni hermanni*). This elegant, endearing reptile has been on earth for some 235 million years, and so has an ancient lineage longer than our own. It is encased (without benefit of bank or insurance company) so beautifully in its home, a home so transportable and fitted with all the mod. cons. the tortoise tribe needs. However, in spite of being so well designed, this tortoise is now urgently in need of protection like all endangered animal species in the world, of which there are far too many. In human terms they are voiceless, voteless and helpless and need our assistance.

The Tortoise Village is not a gimmick for it represents a new type of conservation which – if I may be immodest – my Wildlife Preservation Trust in Jersey has for the last 25 years helped to pioneer. The idea is simply the captive breeding of animals who are in danger as an insurance policy against their extinction in the wild. When the numbers of an animal species plummet (generally through habitat destruction among other things) they can no longer cope with the normal hazards of existence, such as predators, drought or sudden falling off of food supply, let alone the direct interference of man. Captive breeding is an important conservation tool and has, even in these early stages, proved its value. The Père David's deer, for example, extinct in China since the middle of this century, has now been returned to the wild from captive bred stock. The Arabian oryx, the Scimitar-horned oryx and the Addax – all bred in zoos – have been returned to their countries of origin. We in Jersey are involved with or have instigated similar undertakings for the Pink pigeon of Mauritius, the Golden lion tamarin of Brazil, the Thick-billed parrot of North America, the Jamaican hutia and the Bali starling. At one time (when I founded my Trust) the idea of captive breeding was anathema to dyed-in-the-wool conservationists. However, now twenty-five years later, they are beginning to realise the importance of it. Hence the creation of Tortoise Village.

Here in the Village the baby chelonians – offspring of pets that people have donated to the project – are protected from predators and given an unfailing food supply, and some of the pets themselves undergo a 'rehabilitation' programme. Then, when the tortoises are old or strong enough, they are released into the low thyme and oak covered hills that rise behind the Village, the Massif des Maures, which is the only area in France now where wild Hermann's tortoises can be found. Their progress is carefully monitored by the project's scientific team, who are also studying the distribution and ecology of wild tortoises and are lobbying for protection of the Massif des Maures. The Village is now open to the public for a nominal charge. There are pathways through naturalistic settings leading to tortoise nurseries and rearing enclosures, each with a superb educational display. There is also a small veterinary and research building and, of course, a gift shop where tortoise-y items are on sale, the proceeds from which are put back into the project.

At the inauguration of Tortoise Village, I was handed, as a prop, a young Hermann's tortoise of great beauty. Naturally, I mentally christened him Melville – what else? He was gleaming as though freshly polished and had an intelligent glint in his eye. I felt he would add lustre to the short speech I was to make. I said a lot of time and money was spent on preserving man-made things, and quite rightly. However, great works of art, architecture and sculpture were, after all, man-created and it was conceivable that the genius who wrought these things could be born again. We might have another Rembrandt, another Rodin, another Mozart or a Christopher Wren, but when an animal species – which is nature's work of art – vanishes, there is no technology, no human genius, that can re-create it. We cannot re-create the song of the nightingale, we cannot re-create the intricate beauty of a tortoise. Here, I held up Herman Melville.

"This tortoise," I said to the assembled company, which included newspaper reporters from as far afield as Paris and

London, "is a work of art as important as anything produced by man."

Apparently, Herman Melville took this as his cue. He suddenly urinated copiously down the front of the new suit I had donned for the occasion and then deposited on the toe of my expensive Italian shoe a huge and extremely smelly faecal sample of a livid green hue.

The Fauna and Flora Preservation Society (now Fauna and Flora International) helped to create Tortoise Village. I, in my capacity as one of their Vice-Chairmen, was asked to attend this function. I am therefore sending them the bill for a new suit and a pair of shoes. I hope they will pay it. I feel it is the least they can do for the preservation of a Vice-Chairman.

Nevertheless, I still love tortoises, and so should everyone else.

The Art of Birdwatching

The English have always prided themselves on being slightly eccentric lovers of nature, as indeed, if you look into the history of natural history, you will find that they are, from people like Waterton, who rode on the back of a caiman, to Darwin, who observed with grave interest the fact that his red waistcoat glowed with phosphorescence during a thunderstorm in Patagonia. But there is one thing, however, that has probably more eccentric adherence than any other pastime and that is the art of birdwatching.

One is constantly surprised to come across little old ladies in roll-top pullovers and grey flannel slacks, frantically ticking off birds they see on huge lists with all the reverence of someone checking their football pools. You suddenly and rather startlingly stumble over elderly clergymen with telescopes lying in damp ditches, or portly brigadiers swaying dangerously up in oak or pine trees, trying to photograph some rarity. Or you may bump into earnest bespectacled bank clerks, weighed down with a recording machine and parabolic reflector, their eyes gleaming fanatically as they pursue the nightingale to its lair. Everyone, from earls to engine drivers, joins in this sport and I sometimes think that there must be more bird watchers than there are birds.

I must confess that I have been more than privileged in my association with this hobby. I have stood among approximately a thousand penguins, many of whom attacked my legs with vigour, while I marvelled at the fact that in this gigantic megalopolis of birds each parent, coming back from a long and arduous fishing task and walking over immense sand dunes, could unerringly pick out their own offspring from the hundreds of clamouring babies that surrounded them. I have been privileged, in Australia, to see bright blue Fairy Wrens (minute birds that look as though they had been designed by Walt Disney) bathing in the cups of magnolia flowers in the early morning dew and, quite recently, in Costa Rica, I was privileged to look into a sunlit valley and watch a male Quetzal fly across it, trailing his tail like some splendid medieval banner as he flew to his nest, glittering golden-green like a dragon.

I have, in the course of my bird watching experiences, of course come into contact with a number of eccentric people who love to watch birds. James Fisher, for example, was a magnificent man who was a great friend of mine and it was he, with his puckish sense of humour, who told me the story of an ornithological conference that took place in Finland, where a great mass of brilliant ornithologists, including James, packed themselves into a car between sessions and drove off to do a little bird watching. It was icy cold, with a grey sky, and so it was some considerable time before they discovered any avian life at all and this was a small bird sitting on a telegraph wire by the side of the road. The car screeched to a halt and all the world's most famous ornithologists got out and stood in a row, huddled in their duffle coats peering at this tiny bird on the wire above them. There was a prolonged silence and then somebody said, "Yes, h'm, most interesting," and then another eminent ornithologist said, "H'm, yes, extraordinary," and James Fisher said to me, "There we had at the side of the road all the most professional ornithologists in the world and not one of them knew what the bloody bird was."

In the Scilly Isles once, I met a marvellous lady who had

lived there for many years and studied the birds with great care and I called upon her so that she should give me guidance as to what I should see and where. It was unfortunate that she opened up a bottle of cowslip wine before we got down to all the finer details of my survey of these enchanting islands and I had never realised until then what an effect cowslip wine could have on one. When we did get to the end of the bottle she opened another one, getting more and more enthusiastic about the avifauna of the Scilly Isles, and presently, rather unsteadily, she led me to the window which overlooked a beach on which both she and I, carefully and with incredible scientific pomposity, mis-identified more British birds than are on the British list.

However, we are all, even with our foibles, imbued with this love of birds and born out of this love and interest in birds comes a fascinating book by Viscount Grey, one of the forerunners of many bird books that have been published since, but it is probably one of the best for not only does it contain accurate and well-written accounts of birds' lives but the observations cover a long period of time which makes it doubly interesting to me. The author in his introduction starts by saying bluntly and humbly, "This book will have no scientific value." Equally bluntly, I can say, "Do not believe him." If every one of us who admires and enjoys nature around us had written a book like this we could be very proud. Beautifully written, it contains a wealth of meticulous and fascinating observations of a host of different birds. The author is a careful and thoughtful observer and the result is an ornithological tour de force, a book that should stand beside the works of Hudson, Gilbert White or any of the other great British naturalists who have written about the English countryside. Speaking of the woodlark, for example, he has this to say, and it is worthy of the great Gilbert White at his best:

I have never lived in the company of woodlarks, and my acquaint-ance with them is confined to one or two expeditions, made to places where woodlarks were known to be, for the purpose of hearing their song. They are therefore to me like celebrities to whom one has once or twice paid a visit of ceremony, and I cannot speak of them with intimacy. As I saw the bird it sang on the wing, and the flight was less clearly a joy-flight than that of the skylark. The bird did not soar; it flew as if the flight might have some other object, such as change of place, combined with that of song; but song was evidently part of the object, though the bird also sang when perched on a tree. There were notes of finer quality than any that the skylark has; the shortness of the tail recalled the appearance of a bat in flight. The quality and sweetness of the notes and the manners of the bird were very pleasing, and I regret that it has not been my good fortune to live in company with woodlarks.

It takes a person with a keen appreciation of the world around him to spot and enjoy the minute but perceptible contribution that all living creatures give to you if you use your senses. It was Sherlock Holmes who said of someone: "You see but you do not observe." This applies to so many of us. We should be thankful for writers like Viscount Grey who can, through their sensitivity and skill, hone our own senses.

Dogs in My Life

Of all the domestic animals, I think what man has achieved in the creation of different types of dog has almost excelled nature. From the wolf (or maybe the Cape Hunting dog, depending on where you think man originated) we have, by careful manipulation, evolved such diverse types as the Great Dane and the Chihuahua, the Bloodhound and the Bulldog, the Whippet and the Irish Wolfhound. Thus man's best friend comes to you in a bewildering assortment of colours and sizes, and with an extraordinary assortment of decorations in the shape of wrinkles, jowls, ears and tails. In my less intelligent moments, I dream of owning a huge property and having one of every known breed of dog, but then I fear I would have to change my name to Crufts by deed poll, and earn considerably more money than I do now.

I have been involved with dogs all my life. My very first acquisition, at the age of six, was a honey-coloured Cocker spaniel called Simon. He was a sweet-natured creature with limpid eyes and a great desire to please. He once spent a long and hot afternoon digging up my mother's herbaceous border under the impression that he was helping. He had seen mother digging and weeding and occasionally bemoaning her lot and he, not unnaturally, came to the conclusion that it was the plants that distressed mother, so what could be more natural than for him to help by digging them up. My mother was not amused by his horticultural achievements.

Simon had one distressing trait in his otherwise impeccable

character; he was the biggest coward I had ever seen. To Simon, the world was populated by a vast array of things which had been invented solely for the purpose of doing him evil. The flushing of a toilet meant that he was being pursued inexorably by a sort of giant Niagara, Hell bent on dragging him to a watery grave. The slamming of a door would make him leap in the air as if shot, before burrowing underneath the nearest piece of furniture for protection. High days and holidays were made difficult, for on Guy Fawkes night the curtains had to be drawn and a heavy sedative administered so that he could survive the fireworks, and at Christmas time the tree had to be inserted into the drawing room and decorated by degrees to save his nerves from injury. He once went into a nervous decline lasting several days when he came unexpectedly upon a snowman I had constructed without telling him. To him, a garden hose was as deadly as any Spitting Cobra, a lawn mower as fearsome and potentially deathdealing as a Sherman tank, and a bicycle as lethal as an Exocet carrying a small hydrogen bomb. It was Simon's cowardice that was his ultimate undoing. A sweep came to clean the chimneys and he arrived carrying the tools of his trade in a motorbike and sidecar. Simon was asleep upstairs in my bedroom, so unaware of this horrid invasion. When he woke, he came downstairs and went out to the front of the house to attend to nature. As he was in the middle of this delicate operation the sweep left, starting up his vehicle with an overpowering clatter and roar. Simon stared, petrified. This was the ultimate horror – this was the monster that he always knew was waiting for him. He turned and fled out of the gate and on to the road where a car, unable to brake in time, neatly crushed Simon's skull, killing him instantly.

It took me some time to get over Simon's death, but one day as my birthday was approaching, I added to my list of wants (which included a new white mouse cage, a mate for my hamster, a bigger aquarium for my sticklebacks and a proper vivarium for my grass snakes) one puppy. My mother, glad to see I had recovered from Simon's demise, and keen to cheer me up after my traumatic experience at Witchwood, accepted this idea with enthusiasm. We went down to the pet shop and there in the window was a sprawl of puppies with pot bellies and covered with black curls. They were all irresistible and the difficulty was to choose one out of the litter. After much cogitation, I chose the smallest and weakest looking one, as the others were bullying him and he kept casting soulful glances at me from his large brown eyes. So, for the astronomical price of ten shillings and sixpence, he became mine and was christened, for no particular reason, Roger. He became my stalwart companion for the next eight years, and a more intelligent and brave dog I never possessed. He was, of course, a mongrel, but to me a mongrel of pedigree. As far as we could make out, as he grew, he must have been a first cross between a Kerry Blue and an Airedale, the latter predominating. Having house trained him – a job quickly accomplished as he was so intelligent – Roger took to living with us in a big way. He recognised the family as the pack and would leap to their defence, but he realised that I was his immediate boss and should therefore have special treatment. He took his duties in guarding us very seriously and looked after us as assiduously as if we were a flock of dim sheep.

I remember the first afternoon that we left him on his own. He was just able, in a very wobbly way, to clamber up the stairs like a slightly inebriated mountain climber, and when we got back we found him sitting mournfully on the landing, looking down at us. He had been into our bedrooms and draped down the staircase was one item of clothing belonging to each member of the family. As a protest it made its point.

When Roger was about a year old we left the damp, grey English summer and migrated to the Greek island of Corfu. The contrast could not have been greater. To move from the dankness of England to a place drenched in sunshine and with a blue sea warm enough to bathe in even on Christmas Day was unbelievable. To Roger, of course, it was a cornucopia of new scents and smells. Now, no longer confined to the limits of a suburban garden, he had a whole island at his disposal, and he took full advantage of it. To me, also, the island was a paradise. The vast olive groves, sizzling with the cries of cicadas, were full of strange creatures I had never seen before – a vast array of snakes, water and land tortoises, huge dormice and shiny black rats, toads and frogs like jewels, and birds ranging from Goldcrests smaller than your thumb to Eagle owls two feet high and capable of killing a new-born lamb. All these, of course, had to be captured and added to my ever growing menagerie, to the alarm and despondency of my family.

Roger and I spent every day exploring and though he got a bit bored if I spent too long watching to see how a spider made its web, or how a Praying Mantis stalked its prey, he was very good natured about my natural history studies. He was also very useful, for he would run ahead, fossicking in the myrtle bushes and the beds of wild thyme and as soon as he found anything he thought would interest me a torrent of deep throated barks would apprise me of the fact and I would hurry towards him to find he had encountered a snake, or a tortoise, or a toad, or sometimes an exceptionally huge spider.

We would spend all day exploring, but at noon we would make our way down to the coast and the glittering blue sea, to bathe, eat the provender we had brought with us (Roger had a passion for grapes and tangerines) and then, while I dozed in the shade of the giant olives, Roger would go fishing. To be more accurate, he would attempt to go fishing. The fact that he never caught anything did not deter him the least, any more than it deters a human fisherman. He would enter the shallow waters, as clear as gin, and pace slowly along, head down, the picture of concentration. Suddenly, from under his woolly feet, a crab or a small fish would dart. Roger would plunge his head into the water, his jaws would clop together and he would come up sneezing and coughing – for he never learnt to hold his breath – and with no crab or fish to show for it. Undaunted, he would set off again and get another noseful of sea water. He never tired of this game and would pace in the shallows for hours at a time. When we moved to a villa very close to the sea and Roger was missing, I always knew where to find him – he'd gone fishing.

On my thirteenth birthday a peasant family I knew presented me with two puppies. They were typical Corfu mongrels, with smooth sleek coats, tufted legs, flop ears and a curved plume-like tail. They came in a variety of colours (in this case one was a ginger and white skewbald and the other was black with brown legs and belly) but they both had the distinguishing mark of the Corfu dog, large bright ginger eyebrows like thumbprints. They were like the sort of eyebrows which clowns paint on themselves. Busy with my party, I gave these puppies a large plate of party goodies and locked them in the dining room until I could deal with them properly. When we came to use the dining room to feed our guests I found, to my horror, that the puppies had eaten and drunk unwisely and too well. The state of the dining room closely resembled a cross between a midden, a pig sty and a public convenience of the less functional kind. My elder brother, viewing the mess, suggested that the puppies be called Widdle and Puke. My mother immediately vetoed this on the grounds of vulgarity, but the names stuck and Widdle and Puke they remained.

Roger was very benign about their invasion of his domain and would play with them in an avuncular fashion. As they grew older he occasionally gave them a warning nip when they became too swaggeringly over-confident, just to show where the real power lay, but by and large they settled down amicably enough. For my birthday my second brother had built me a boat of my own as a surprise, and surprise it was. Almost completely circular, flat bottomed, painted in orange and green stripes, she was christened – in spite of my mother's protests – the Bootle Bumtrinket and in her I used to put to sea and travel up and down the coast, searching for such exciting things as sea anemones, sea horses, spider crabs and pipe fish to add to my menagerie. My crew, of course, consisted of the three dogs (Puke was a bad sailor and lived up to his name, but did not want to be left behind) and we were frequently accompanied by my Scops owl, Ulysses, and my pigeon, Quasimodo. Some of my happiest recollections are of my voyages in the Bootle Bumtrinket, rowing along on the placid sea, my jars filling up with the multi-coloured and bizarre sea fauna. Roger would stare down into the jars knowingly, looking like a black furry marine biologist. Widdle would be sleeping quietly, twitching in and out of dreams, while Puke, his head over the side, would vomit quietly at regular intervals. This is more years ago than I want to remember but I am glad to say that my trio of canine friends lived long lives and died peacefully.

My most recent dog was a Boxer, a breed for which I have a great love. He came to me fully grown and his name was Keeper – Keeper of the Keys – which was singularly appropriate since he was coming to live in my zoo on the island of

Jersey, one of the Channel Islands. He was a very large dog with his ears fortunately uncropped and a massive blunt tail which he never ceased wagging. His prominent brown eyes were capable of more different expressions than any other dog I owned. I viewed with a certain trepidation the introduction into a zoo of a two year old dog who had – according to his owners – never seen another animal apart from a dog – not even a cow. However, Keeper, oozing good will, shambled his way into everyone's hearts and was an immediate success. His day would start with him visiting all his friends, exchanging kisses through the wire with the Tapirs, saying goodday to the Peccaries and being greeted by a clatter of tusks, for these pigs were not fond of him. He would go and say hello to the Spectacled Bears and the Gorillas and Orangs, have a limbering-up race with the Cheetah, say good morning and give a quick lick to the zoo cat, Mimi, and to Trumpy our Trumpeter Bird, who stalked the zoo like the Squire of the Manor. Having done all this exuding of good will, it was time to go and meet his friend, Dick, the big Labrador from next door, and after much kissing they would set off shoulder to shoulder, a formidable but harmless pair, to see how the world wagged. Keeper lived with me for eight years and not once in that time did he show anything but extreme benevolence to any of the vast array of strange animals he was to come into contact with. I think this was pretty extraordinary for a dog who, until he was two, had never even seen a cow.

I think dogs are an important part of life and I feel strongly that no child should be brought up without the companionship of one, whether it is a mongrel whose ancestry is a tangled web of blood lines, or a dog who has a pedigree to compare with a Crown prince, and is, in some cases, better, depending on the Crown Prince.

All over the world there are various species of wild dog, some of which are the ancestors of our domestic breeds and most of these wild species are in danger of extinction today, due to persecution, and to the destruction of their habitat. In a few years they will have vanished unless we do something urgently. They need help. The tiny little Corgi-like Bush Dog from the Amazon Rainforest, the lanky red Maned Wolf from Argentina, the Red Wolf of North America, the various delicate and beautiful foxes, the Dhole of India and the Hunting Dog of Africa. The Jersey Wildlife Preservation Trust which I founded, and its sister organisation in Canada, is doing the best it can for these lovely canines, but what we want is the help of dog lovers all over the world. Dogs, over the years, have given you all pleasure and, in some cases, are your livelihood. Surely it is up to us to help the wild breeds of these wonderful animals? To my mind a home without a dog is like a house without a fire, and it is up to us all to help these important animals wherever and in whatever guise we find them.

The two pieces that follow show the range of Gerry's views on animals, small and large. He was deeply influenced by the lessons learned from the great French naturalist, Jean Henri Fabre, and deeply offended by modern 'panda politics'.

An Explorer in Lilliput

Jean Henri Fabre has played an important part in my life since I was eight years old. At that time I was having a wonderful childhood on the island of Corfu, and the island was for me a magical place because there were so many animals living there which I had never seen before. I was particularly fascinated by the insects which – in the days before D.D.T. and other noxious sprays – were to be found in great abundance. However, it was a frustrating time for me as well. Deeply interested in the insect life around me, I had no books to tell me what the insects were or what they did. This was because my family were not zoologically orientated and so they had no idea of the sort of books I needed. So I watched the insects with irritated ignorance. Why did a large and obviously predatory wasp sting spiders and then carry them off – why not eat them on the spot? Where did they carry them to? How did cicadas make that thrumming noise that trepanned your skull on hot afternoons? Why did scarab beetles collect dung, roll it into balls and then take it into tunnels? These and myriad other questions surrounded me and I had no means of answering them. I was surrounded on every side by the word *why*.

Then, one day, my elder brother – who had obviously been giving the problem some thought – presented me with the collected works of J.H. Fabre. If someone had presented me with the touchstone that turns everything to gold I could not have been more delighted. From that moment Fabre became my personal friend. He wrote for me in simple but poetic language and in his gentle, enthusiastic voice (which I could hear whispering in my brain) he unravelled the many mysteries that surrounded me and showed me miracles and how they were performed. Through his entrancing prose I became the hunting wasp, the paralysed spider, the cicada, the burly, burnished scarab beetle, and a host of other creatures as well.

Fabre was an extraordinary man, every bit as exciting as people who explored the mighty Amazon, or plunged into what was then called Darkest Africa. He was an explorer in Lilliput, the vast world that lies under our shoes and which we so seldom notice. He did more than that. He stepped outside the museum. Anyone interested in animals has, at one time or another, visited the strange backwaters of a natural history museum, catacombs smelling of camphor, ether, formaldehyde, of fur and feather and chiton. Here the mammals and birds lie in serried ranks, each with a label attached to its leg, like humans in a mortuary; snakes and frogs floating immobile in bottles of spirit, insects carefully crucified on cork.

There are three vital questions to be asked about the living world around us: what? where? and why? Museums answer the first two queries but not the third, and certainly in Fabre's day they were still busy with the 'what?' and 'where?' questions, so the enquiry 'why?' was getting scant attention. It was Fabre who took us from the dim recesses of the museums, redolent of death, out into the brilliant countryside, there to point out to us his beloved insects and pose the questions 'why?'. Why did Pine Processionary caterpillars walk, head to tail, in long caravans? Why, if you attached the leader to the hindmost caterpillar, would they walk in a circle until they died of starvation? Were cicadas, noisiest of the insects in his area of France, deaf? To try and find out, he dragged the village cannon into his garden and fired off a salvo which did not prevent the cicadas from continuing their monotonous song. It proved, at least, that cicadas were not affected by cannon fire.

Fabre's pursuit of the truth was insatiable. He would lie in a ditch in the stunning sunshine of Provence, watching and recording the lives of ants, beetles, wasps and a myriad other tiny inhabitants of the region and then write about their fascinating lives so enthusiastically, so poetically, that even someone not interested in insects became entranced. If these people were entranced, you can imagine the magical effect the discovery of Fabre had on a budding eight-year-old naturalist.

When I acquired a house in Provence, it was within easy reach of Fabre's old home, now a museum. On my first visit I was overwhelmed. The main rooms of the house were as he had left them, his workroom looking exactly as I imagined and as though he had only that moment slipped out to interview a beetle. The garden was peaceful and delightful, planted with aromatic herbs like thyme, lavender and rosemary to attract the insects, and a round deep pond full of water lilies and frogs, where the insects could come and drink and gather moisture for their multifarious building operations.

I was reluctant to make my way to the tiny village cemetery where Fabre was buried, for I feared I would find that his small, frail body had been interred beneath one of those tombstones beloved by the French and Italians, the ones that look like a gigantic vulgar wedding cake that has been left out in a torrential thunderstorm. But to my relief the gravestone was a simple slab, decorated only with a granite urn. It was a tasteful grave worthy of the man. Then I saw, to my delight, that a Mason wasp had built its little grey, multi-celled mud nest under one of the handles of the urn. What better tribute to the great man could there be? No plastic flowers under plastic domes, but the nursery of one of the insects he loved. He would have been enchanted.

Panda Politics

I met my first Giant Panda, called Ming, at London Zoo in 1939. Everyone was Panda-mad and if you had not seen Ming it was like confessing to the fact that you could not read or write. You were a social outcast. So I went to see Ming out of curiosity, to find out what all the fuss was about. I found what looked like a medium-sized bear with curious camouflage markings, that's all. But the Panda craze stuck and replaced poor old Winnie-the-Pooh in people's imaginations. I met Ming again briefly at the end of the war at Whipsnade, where she had been evacuated. I had become a keeper there, and still found her dull as an animal.

But most people think Pandas look cute and cuddly, symbolic of the Teddy Bears of our childhood. In the sixties the public adored Chi Chi, another London Zoo Panda, for she represented a fairytale animal come miraculously to life.

To the hard-headed accountants, however, Chi Chi represented hard cash and was exploited in the same cold, clinical way a pimp manipulates a prostitute. She was simply a star attraction, nothing more. The cries of horror that went up from this pin-striped gang of figure manipulators when it was suggested that she be sent to Moscow to breed can be imagined. To deliver such a golden asset into the untrustworthy hands of the Russians would be madness, they said, and only changed their tune and allowed it when it was craftily pointed out how much more of an asset she would be if she returned with a tiny, cuddly replica of herself. Only a few far-sighted people were considering the idea of captive breeding for the conservation of biodiversity, for this was in the days before zoos woke up to the fact that they had an important role to play in world conservation, and they were still behaving like circus owners, forever pursuing the Fattest Lady on Earth or praying for another Elephant Man to send their receipts soaring.

In the 1980s, we were treated to the disgusting display of Rent-a-Panda. I have no idea who thought this up (possibly the Chinese themselves) but the unfortunate animals were shunted around from zoo to zoo simply as crowd pullers. Again, no thought of captive breeding for conservation sullied the minds of these zoo directors. The Pandas, to them, were simply fur-covered dollar signs. It was said that part of the money thus raised was to be used for Panda conservation, but money with no strings attached has an ephemeral quality about it and the wild Pandas did not benefit.

Somewhat unwisely, the World Wildlife Fund (as it was then) had adopted the Panda as its logo. When it was discovered that the breeding success of the Panda in captivity was virtually nil, and that its numbers in the wild were decreasing alarmingly for a variety of reasons, the W.W.F. were worried. To lose the Giant Panda would be bad enough, but to lose the Giant Panda and one's logo in one fell swoop would be unthinkable. So money was poured into China and, among other things, extremely expensive captive breeding facilities were constructed. The Panda numbers in the wild continued to plummet and only one Panda baby was produced in the one-million-pound nursery. Years passed. The Chinese looked inscrutable, the Europeans and Americans beat their breasts and the peasantry of over-populated China continued to chop down the Panda reserves and kill Pandas for their skins. Now, however, after many committees have been formed and become extinct, a new plan has been formulated which, if successful, may save our black and white friend. It will, however, cost 50 million pounds and there are some who might say that the money would be better spent on a nuclear submarine.

All this current co-operation, of course, should have been done in the days of Chi Chi but, with the cold war in full swing, cooperation over an animal was unthinkable and so, as usual, politics got in the way of conservation, as it is still doing all over the world. It is to be hoped that the gigantic Earth Summit in Brazil in June will at long last persuade politicians that it is more important to save Pandas and their habitat than to squabble over frontiers and ideologies, like mariners on a sinking ship quarrelling about whether to have tea or coffee and a breakfast which may never materialise.

PART FOUR

On the Ark

Notes on Conservation

'The man is mad, wanting to have a zoo!'

– Lawrence Durrell, c. 1958

The task of conservation of the planet is highly complex and multi-faceted. The world is like a mammoth jigsaw puzzle of a billion or more pieces with no overall picture to guide you. To make matters worse, while the scientists are trying to find pieces to complete the picture, other Homo sapiens are throwing pieces away which may be of inestimable value in the future. Conservation is of immense importance to us all. Whoever invented that disgusting phrase 'third world' ought to be ashamed. There is only one world and it belongs to all of us.

– Fragments from unpublished autobiography

From childhood Gerry had always wanted to own his own zoo. He'd had experience in Corfu looking after small creatures, which stood him in good stead in his first real job – an assistant in a pet shop in London where he earned the admiration of the owner for creating natural environments and appropriate diets for the animals – but he needed to learn about the larger animals more frequently found in zoos. He was taken on at Whipsnade Zoo as a relief keeper, otherwise known as the 'odd-beast boy', who would be deployed wherever he was needed on any and all sections of the zoo. It was a steep learning curve, but it prepared him well for the next phase of his career – as an animal collector for zoos.

First Job

Towards the end of 1939, when it looked as though war was inevitable, my family uprooted itself from Corfu and came back to England. We settled for a time in a flat in London while my mother made repeated forays into different parts of the English countryside in search of a house. And while she was doing this I was free to explore London. Although I have never been a lover of big cities I found London, at that time, fascinating. After all, the biggest metropolis I was used to was the town of Corfu, which was about the size of a small English market town, and so the great sprawling mass of London had hundreds of exciting secrets for me to discover. There was, of course, the Natural History Museum, and the inevitable visits to the Zoo, where I got on quite intimate terms with some of the keepers. This only strengthened my belief that working in a zoo was the only real vocation for anyone, and confirmed me in my desire to possess a zoo of my own.

Quite close to the flat where we were staying was a shop which always had my undivided attention. It was a place called 'The Aquarium', and its window was full of great tanks full of brightly coloured fish and, what was even more interesting, rows of glass-fronted boxes that contained grass snakes, pine snakes, great green lizards and bulbous-eyed toads. I used to gaze longingly in the window at these beautiful creatures and I had a great desire to possess them. But as I already had a whole host of birds, two magpies and a marmoset in the flat, I felt that the introduction of any other livestock of any shape or form would bring down the wrath of the family upon me, and so I could only gaze longingly at these lovely reptiles.

Then, one morning, when I happened to pass the shop, my attention was riveted by a notice that was leaning up against an aquarium. It said, 'Wanted: Young, reliable assistant'. I went back to the flat and thought about it for some time.

'They've got a job going in that pet shop down the road,' I said to my mother.

'Have they, dear?' she said, not really taking any notice.

'Yes. They say they want a young, reliable assistant. I . . . I thought of applying for it,' I said carelessly.

'What a good idea,' said Larry 'Then, perhaps, you could take all your animals there.'

'I don't think they'd let him do that, dear,' said my mother.

'How much do you think they'd pay for a job like that?' I asked.

'Not very much, I shouldn't think,' said Larry. 'I doubt that you are what they mean by reliable.'

'Anyway, they'd have to pay me something, wouldn't they?' I said.

'Are you old enough to be employed?' inquired Larry.

'Well, I'm almost sixteen,' I said.

'Well, go and have a shot at it,' he suggested.

So the following morning I went down to the pet shop and opened the door and went in. A short, slender, dark man with very large horn-rimmed spectacles danced across the floor towards me.

'Good morning! Good morning! Good morning, sir!' he said. 'What can I do for you?'

'You, um . . . you want an assistant . . .' I said.

He cocked his head on one side and his eyes grew large behind his spectacles.

'An assistant,' he said. 'Do you mean to say you want the job?'

'Er . . . yes,' I said.

'Have you had any experience?' be inquired doubtfully.

'Oh, I've had plenty of experience,' I said. 'I've always kept reptiles and fish and things like that. I've got a whole flatful of things now.'

The little man looked at me.

'How old are you?' he asked.

'Sixteen . . . nearly seventeen,' I lied.

'Well,' he said, 'we can't afford to pay very much, you know. The overheads on this shop are something extraordinary. But I could start you off at one pound ten.'

'That's alright,' I said. 'When do I start?'

'You'd better start on Monday,' he said. 'I think on Monday because then I can get all your cards stamped up and straight. Otherwise we get in such a muddle, don't we? Now, my name's Mr Romilly.'

I told him my name and we shook hands rather formally, and then we stood looking at each other. It was obvious that Mr Romilly had never employed anybody before and did not know quite what the form was. I thought perhaps I ought to help him out.

'Perhaps you could just show me round,' I suggested, 'and tell me a few things that you will want me to do.'

'Oh, what an excellent idea,' said Mr Romilly. 'An excellent idea!'

He danced round the shop waving his hands like butterfly wings and showed me how to clean out a fish tank, how to drop the mealworms into the cages of frogs and toads, and where the brush and broom were kept that we swept the floor with. Under the shop was a large cellar where various fish foods, nets and other things were kept, and it included a constantly running tap that dripped into a large bowl containing what at first glance appeared to be a raw sheep's heart. This, on close inspection, turned out to be a closely knitted ball of threadlike tubifex worms. These bright red worms were a favourite food of all the fish and some of the amphibians and reptiles as well. I discovered that as well as the delightful things in the window there were hosts of other creatures in the shop besides – cases full of lizards, toads, tortoises and treacle shiny snakes, tanks full of moist, gulping frogs, and newts with frilled tails like pennants. After having spent so many months in dry, dusty and desiccated London, the shop was, as far as I was concerned, a Garden of Eden.

'Now,' said Mr Romilly, when he had shown me everything, 'you start on Monday, hm? Nine o'clock sharp. Don't be late, will you?'

I did not tell Mr Romilly that nothing short of death would have prevented me from being there at nine o'clock on Monday.

So at ten to nine on Monday morning I paced the pavement outside the shop and eventually Mr Romilly appeared, clad in a long black coat and a black Homburg hat, waving his bunch of keys musically.

'Good morning, good morning,' he trilled. 'I'm glad to see you're on time. What a good start.'

So we went into the shop and I started on the first chores of the day, which were to sweep the comparatively spotless floor clean and then to go round feeding little knots of wriggling tubifex to the fishes.

I very soon discovered that Mr Romilly, though a kindly man, had little or no knowledge of the creatures in his care. Most of the cages were most unsuitably decorated for the occupants' comfort and, indeed, so were the fish tanks. Also, Mr Romilly worked on the theory that if you got an animal to eat one thing, you then went on feeding it with that thing incessantly. I decided that I would have to take a hand both in the cage decoration and also in brightening up the lives of our charges, but I knew I would have to move cautiously for Mr Romilly was nothing if not conservative.

'Don't you think the lizards and toads and things would like a change from mealworms, Mr Romilly?' I said one day.

'A change?' said Mr Romilly, his eyes widening behind his spectacles. 'What sort of a change?'

'Well,' I said, 'how about wood lice? I always used to feed my reptiles on wood lice.'

'Are you sure?' said Mr Romilly.

'Quite sure,' I said.

'It won't do them any harm, will it?' he asked anxiously.

'No,' I said, 'they love wood lice. It gives them a bit of variety in their diet.'

'But where are we going to get them?' asked Mr Romilly despondently.

'Well, I expect there are plenty in the parks,' I said. 'I'll see if I can get some, shall I?'

'Very well,' said Mr Romilly reluctantly, 'if you're quite sure they won't do them any harm.'

So I spent one afternoon in the park and collected a very large tin full of wood lice, which I kept in decaying leaves down in the cellar, and when I thought that the frogs and the toads and the lizards had got a bit bored with the mealworms, I would try them on some mealworm beetles, and then, when they had had a surfeit of those, I would give them some wood lice. At first, Mr Romilly used to peer into the cages with a fearful look on his face, as though he expected to see all the reptiles and amphibians dead. But when he found that they not only thrived on this new mixture but even started to croak in their cages, his enthusiasm knew no bounds.

My next little effort concerned two very large and benign Leopard toads which came from North Africa. Now, Mr Romilly's idea of North Africa was an endless desert where the sun shone day and night and where the temperature was never anything less than about a hundred and ninety in the shade, if indeed any shade was to be found. So in consequence he had incarcerated these two poor toads in a small, glass-fronted cage with a couple of brilliant electric light bulbs above them. They sat on a pile of plain white sand, they had no rocks to hide under to get away from the glare, and the only time the temperature dropped at all was at night when we switched off the light in the shop. In consequence, their eyes had become milky and looked almost as though they were suffering from cataract, their skins had become dry and flaky, and the soles of their feet were raw.

I knew that suggesting to Mr Romilly anything so drastic as putting them into a new cage with some damp moss would horrify him beyond all bounds, so I started surreptitiously to try and give the toads a slightly happier existence. I pinched some olive oil from my mother's kitchen for a start, and when Mr Romilly went out to have his lunch hour, I massaged the oil into the skin of both toads. This improved the flakiness. I then got some ointment from the chemist, having explained – to his amusement – why I wanted it, and anointed their feet with it. This helped, but it did not clear up the foot condition completely. I also got some Golden Eye Ointment, which one normally used for dogs, and applied it to their eyes with miraculous results. Then, every time Mr Romilly had his lunch hour I would give them a warm spray and this they loved. They would sit there, gulping benignly, blinking their eyes and, if I moved the spray a little, they would shuffle across the floor of their cage to get under it again. One day I put a small section of moss in the cage and both toads immediately burrowed under it.

'Oh, look, Mr Romilly,' I said with well-simulated surprise, 'I put a bit of moss in the toads' cage by mistake, and they seem to like it.'

'Moss?' said Mr Romilly. 'Moss? But they live in the desert.'

'Well, I think some parts of the desert have got a little bit of vegetation,' I said.

'I thought it was all sand,' said Mr Romilly. 'All sand. As far as the eye could see.'

'No, er . . . I think they've got some small cactuses and things,' I said. 'Anyway, they seem to like it, don't they?'

'They certainly do,' said Mr Romilly. 'Do you think we ought to leave it in?'

'Yes,' I said. 'Shall we put a little more in, too?'

'I don't suppose it could do any harm. They can't eat it and strangle themselves with it, can they?' he asked anxiously.

'I don't think they will,' I said reassuringly.

So from then onwards my two lovely toads had a bit of moss to hide under and, what was more important, a bed of moss to sit on, and their feet soon cleared up.

I next turned my attention to the fish, for although they loved tubifex dearly I felt that they, too, should have a little variety in their diet.

'Wouldn't it be possible,' I suggested to Mr Romilly in a tentative sort of way, 'to give the fish some daphnia?'

Now, daphnia were the little water fleas that we used to get sent up from the farm that supplied the shop with all its produce, like waterweed and water snails and the freshwater fish that we sold. And the daphnia we used to sell in little pots to fish lovers to feed their fish with.

'Daphnia?' said Mr Romilly. 'Feed them on daphnia? But they wouldn't eat it, would they?'

'Well if they won't eat it, why do we sell it to people to feed their fish?' I inquired.

Mr Romilly was powerfully struck by this piece of logic.

'You're right, you know,' he said. 'You're right. There's a little left over down in the cellar now. The new supply comes tomorrow. Try some on them and see.'

So I dropped about a tablespoonful of daphnia into each tank and the fish went as mad over them as the toads and frogs had gone over the wood lice.

The next thing I wanted to do, but I had to do it more cautiously, was to try and decorate the cages and tanks to make them look more attractive. Now, this was a task that Mr Romilly always undertook himself, and he did it with a dogged persistence. I do not think he really enjoyed it, but he felt that, as the senior member of the firm, as it were, it was his duty to do.

'Mr Romilly,' I said one day. 'I've got nothing to do at the moment, and there are no customers. You wouldn't let me decorate a fish tank, would you? I'd love to learn how to do them as well as you do.'

'Well, now,' said Mr Romilly, blushing. 'Well, now. I wouldn't say I was all that good . . .'

'Oh, I think you do it beautifully,' I said. 'And I'd like to learn.'

'Well, perhaps just a small one,' said Mr Romilly. 'And I can give you some tips as you go along. Now, let's see . . . let's see . . . Yes, now, that mollies' tank over there. They need clearing out. Now, if you can move them to the spare tank, and then empty it and give it a good scrub, and then we'll start from scratch, shall we?'

And so, with the aid of a little net, I moved all the black

mollies, as dark and glistening as little olives, out of their tank and into the spare one. Then I emptied their tank and scrubbed it out and called Mr Romilly.

'Now,' he said. 'You put some sand at the bottom and . . . um . . . a couple of stones, and then perhaps er . . . Vallisneria, I would say, probably in that corner there, wouldn't you?'

'Could I just try it on my own?' I asked. 'I, er . . . I think I'd learn better that way – if I could do it on my own. And then, when I'm finished you could criticise it and tell me where I've gone wrong.'

'Very good idea,' said Mr Romilly. And so he pottered off to do his petty cash and left me in peace.

It was only a small tank but I worked hard on it. I piled up the silver sand in great dunes. I built little cliffs. I planted forests of Vallisneria through which the mollies could drift in shoals. Then I filled it carefully with water, and when it was the right temperature I put the mollies back in it and called Mr Romilly to see my handiwork.

'By Jove!' he said, looking at it. 'By Jove!'

He glanced at me and it was almost as though he was disappointed that I had done so well. I could see that I was on dangerous ground.

'Do . . . do you like it?' I inquired.

'It . . . it's remarkable! Remarkable! I can't think how you . . . how you managed it?'

'Well, I only managed it by watching you, Mr Romilly,' I said. 'If it hadn't been for you teaching me how to do it I could never have done it.'

'Well, now. Well, now,' said Mr Romilly, going pink. 'But I see you've added one or two little touches of your own.'

'Well, they were just ideas I'd picked up from watching you,' I said.

'Hmmm . . . Most commendable. Most commendable,' said Mr Romilly.

The next day he asked me whether I would like to decorate another fish tank and I knew that I had won the battle without hurting his feelings.

The tank that I really desperately wanted to do was the enormous one that we had in the window. It was some four and a half feet long and about two foot six deep, and in it we had a great colourful mixed collection of fish. But I knew that I must not overstep the bounds of propriety at this stage. So I did several small fish tanks first, and when Mr Romilly had got thoroughly used to the idea of my doing them, I broached the subject of our big show tank in the window.

'Could I try my hand at that, Mr Romilly?' I asked.

'What? Our show piece?' he said.

'Yes,' I said. 'It's . . . it's in need of . . . of a clean, anyway. So I thought, perhaps, I could try my hand at redecorating it.'

'Well, I don't know . . .' said Mr Romilly doubtfully. 'I don't know. It's a most important piece that, you know. It's the centre-piece of the window. It's the one that attracts all the customers.'

He was quite right, but the customers were attracted by the flickering shoals of multicoloured fish. They certainly were not attracted by Mr Romilly's attempts at decoration, which made it look rather like a blasted heath.

'Well, could I just try?' I said. 'And if it's no good, I'll do it all over again. I'll even . . . I'll even spend my half day doing it.'

'Oh, I'm sure that won't be necessary,' said Mr Romilly, shocked. 'You don't want to spend all your days shut up in the shop, you know. A young boy like you . . . you want to be out and about . . . Well, alright, you try your hand at it, and see what happens.'

It took me the better part of a day to do, because in between times I had to attend to the various customers who came to buy tubifex or daphnia or buy a tree frog for their garden pond or something similar. I worked on that giant tank with all the dedication of a marine Capability Brown. I built rolling sand dunes and great towering cliffs of lovely granite. And then, through the valleys between the granite mountains, I planted forests of Vallisneria and other, more delicate, weedy ferns. And on the surface of the water I floated the tiny little white flowers that look so like miniature waterlilies. With the aid of sand and rocks I concealed the heater and thermostat and also the aerator, none of which were attractive to look at. When I had finally finished it and replaced the brilliant scarlet sword-tails, the shiny black mollies, the silver hatchet fish, and the brilliant Piccadilly-like neon-tetras, and stepped back to observe my handiwork, I found myself deeply impressed by my own genius. Mr Romilly, to my delight, was ecstatic about the whole thing.

'Exquisite! Exquisite!' he exclaimed. 'Simply exquisite.'

'Well, you know what they say, Mr Romilly,' I said. 'That a good pupil needs a good master.'

'Oh, you flatter me, you flatter me,' he said, wagging his finger at me playfully. 'This is a case where the pupil has sur-passed the master.'

'Oh, I don't think that,' I said. 'But I do think that I'm getting almost as good as you.'

After that, I was allowed to decorate all the tanks and all the cages.

Student Keeper

When I was a child I was lucky enough to be brought up on the Greek island of Corfu. In those days – before the introduction of the detrimental insecticides and the all-destroying tourist book – this enchanted island was a paradise for wildlife and so I caught and kept a menagerie of creatures. I made valiant attempts to confine these to my bedroom, but on more than one occasion they escaped and caused havoc, for my family were not as zoologically orientated as I was, and so the scattering of a matchbox full of scorpions among them as they sat at a meal had an electric effect.

But my bedroom teemed with strange creatures, praying mantis with their prim, evil little faces and bulbous eyes, tree frogs that looked as if carved out of jade, huge warty toads with great golden eyes, Squirrel dormice, shrews, sea horses and slugs, and outside in the garden a host of birds such as hoopoes, kestrels, magpies and seagulls, to say nothing of my three dogs and a donkey. I had, by that time, decided what I wanted to do in life. I wanted to travel the world collecting animals for zoos and, later, to establish a zoo of my own.

When we returned to England I realised that, if I was to achieve my ambitions, it was necessary for me to have experience with creatures larger than scorpions and sea horses, so I applied for and, to my astonishment, got a job at Whipsnade. I was the lowest of the low, the relief keeper. It was Geoffrey Vevers, then Superintendent of London Zoo, who, when he gave me my final reference, thought up the grandiose title of

'Student Keeper'. However, being the relief keeper suited me very well, for I went on the various sections to help out when people had their days off or sick leave. Thus, one minute I would be helping to deal with lions and tigers and the next day perhaps zebra and gnus or cranes and geese or – best of all – the creature I fell irrevocably in love with, the giraffe. Its enormous but elegant body, its strange silence, its huge liquid eyes, with eyelashes as thick as an Astrakhan rug, and its long blue tongue, all went to make one of the strangest and most beautiful animals on earth, whose disappearance from this planet would be more terrible than losing a Rembrandt or the Acropolis. So my time at Whipsnade was, from my point of view, very well spent and stood me in good stead in the future.

A pioneer of its kind in a zoo world full of bars and concrete, Whipsnade showed the way animals could and should be kept, and what all zoos should endeavour to emulate. Long may it prosper.

An inheritance from his father allowed Gerry to fulfil the first of his dreams – to travel the world collecting animals for zoos. He spent ten years in the wilds of Africa and South America catching and caring for animals great and small until he reluctantly had to hand them over to the buyers, the zoos of the day which were hardly more than menageries with little knowledge of looking after wild animals. He began writing up his experiences and was astonished to discover he could actually earn a living from writing. This emboldened him to embark on his next dream – establishing his own zoo. But he needed more money, as he tells his brother Lawrence in the following letter.

'Who do you know that is stinking rich . . .'

Dear Larry,

I am sorry to have been so long in writing to you, but you know how it is. Mother keeps pestering me to write you a long boastful letter about my achievements, and so, if this is full of figures and percentages, you have only her to blame.

First of all, *The Overloaded Ark*: that was quite a success over here, although Fabers did not push it as much as they should have done. In all, including 15,000 taken by the Book Society, we have sold 27,000 copies and about 10,000 of the American edition. Out of *The Ark* I have made so far about £3,000, most of which, of course, was spent on our trip to the Argentine. The second epic *Three Singles to Adventure*, which mother has just sent off to you, did not do so well. It only sold 10,000 copies and brought in about £500. The third book, *The Bafut Beagles*, which has just been published, has sold about 10,000 before publication, so I am hoping for a nice little scoop with it. I have sent you off a copy by sea, together with some of the first crits and you should get it in about three weeks. All these books, of course, are being published in America, and are also being translated into about six or seven European languages. *The Ark* and this last book were serialised in *Harper's Magazine* in America and *Lilliput* over here, and I also had a portion in the *Reader's Digest*. At the moment, I feel quite happy about things, but the only thing that worries me is how long is the great British Public going to continue to read this sort of slush without getting bored by it. Hart-Davis seemed to think that I can do several more without spoiling my market, but I think it might be a good idea if I interspersed them with something of a different type. At present I am doing a children's book for Collins, for which they are paying very well, and I am working on my Argentinian epic, which I hope will be published next Spring. On top of this, I am doing TV and script-writing and talks for the BBC, and I am also lecturing at the Festival Hall on 13th November and showing the colour film I made in Argentina and Paraguay. I enclose also an advertisement for it, so if you know any rich people that are going to be in England by then, don't hesitate to show them.

I think that this is all the news about my 'literary' achievement to date.

Now I wish to propound an idea to you, on which I should like your help and co-operation. I am now, I think, sufficiently well known to attempt something which I have had in mind for a number of years. To you, no doubt, it will sound completely mad and a lot of rubbish. I want to start a Trust or organisation, with land in somewhere like the West Indies, for the breeding of those forms of animal life which are on the borders of extinction, and which without help of this sort cannot survive. I had always privately thought that such a scheme would be too harebrained to have very much of success, but when I met Julian Huxley (who wrote me a very nice crit on *The Ark*) I put my idea to him and he agreed that it was very necessary and an excellent idea all round, but as he pointed out that while I could get nearly every well known zoologist on my side in such a scheme, very few of them have sufficient funds to be able to help financially, though they would be only too willing to lend their names if these carried any weight. What I should like to know from you is, who do you know that is stinking rich. If I could find three or four people who would be willing between them to put up £10,000, I could get the whole thing started.

Gerry

Gerry had the animals to start a zoo, only needing to find a place, which was easier said than done. Meanwhile, he kept his animals in his sister's garden in Bournemouth, much to the annoyance of the neighbours.

A Zoo in My Luggage

Postcard

Yes, bring the animals here. Don't know what the neighbours will say, but never mind. Mother very anxious to see chimps so hope you are bringing them as well. See you all soon. Much love from us all. Margo

Most people who lived in this suburban road in Bournemouth could look out on their back gardens with pride, for each one resembled its neighbours. There were minor differences, of course: some preferred pansies to sweet peas, or hyacinths to lupins, but basically they were all the same. But anyone looking out at my sister's back garden would have been forced to admit that it was, to say the least, unconventional. In one corner stood a huge marquee, from inside which came a curious chorus of squeaks, whistles, grunts and growls. Alongside it stretched a line of Dexion cages from which glowered eagles, vultures, owls and hawks. Next to them was a large cage containing Minnie, the Chimp. On the remains of what had once been a lawn, fourteen monkeys rolled and played on long leashes, while in the garage frogs croaked, touracos called throatily, and squirrels gnawed loudly on hazelnut shells. At all hours of the day the fascinated, horrified neighbours stood trembling behind their lace curtains and watched as my sister, my mother, Sophie, Jacquie and I trotted to and fro through the shambles of the garden, carrying little pots of bread and milk, plates of chopped fruit or, what was worse, great hunks of gory meat or dead rats. We had, the neighbours felt, taken an unfair advantage of them. If it had been a matter of a crowing cockerel, or a barking dog, or our cat having kittens in their best flower-bed, they would have been able to cope with the situation. But the action of suddenly planting what amounted to a sizeable zoo in their midst was so unprecedented and unnerving that it took their breath away, and it was some time before they managed to rally their forces and start to complain.

In the meantime I had started on my search for a zoo in which to put my animals. The simplest thing to do, it occurred to me, was to go to the local council, inform them that I had the contents of a fine little zoo and wanted them to let me rent or purchase a suitable site for it. Since I already had the animals, it seemed to me in my innocence that they would be delighted to help. It would cost them nothing, and they would be getting what was, after all, another amenity for the town. But the Powers-that-Be had other ideas. Bournemouth is nothing if not conservative. There had never been a zoo in the town, so they did not see why there should be one now. This is what is known by local councils as progress. Firstly, they said that the animals would be dangerous; then they said they would smell; and then, searching their minds wildly for ideas, they said they had not got any land anyway.

I began to get a trifle irritable. I am never at my best when dealing with the pompous illogicalities of the official mind. But I was beginning to grow worried in the face of such complete lack of co-operation. The animals were sitting in the back garden, eating their heads off and costing me a small fortune weekly in meat and fruit. The neighbours, now thoroughly indignant that we were not conforming to pattern, kept bombarding the local health authorities with complaints, so that on an average twice a week the poor inspector was forced to come up to the house, whether he wanted to or not. The fact that he could find absolutely nothing to substantiate the wild claims of the neighbours made no difference: if he received a complaint he had to come and investigate. We always gave the poor man a cup of tea, and he grew quite fond of some of the animals, even bringing his little daughter to see them. But I was chiefly worried by the fact that winter was nearly upon us, and the animals could not be expected to survive its rigours in an unheated marquee. Then Jacquie had a brilliant idea.

'Why not let's offer them to one of the big stores in town as a Christmas show?' she suggested.

So I rang every big store in town. All of them were charming but unhelpful; they simply had not the space for such a show, however desirable. Then I telephoned the last on my list, the huge emporium owned by J. J. Allen. They, to my delight, expressed great interest and asked me to go and discuss it with them. And 'Durrell's Menagerie' came into being.

A large section of one of their basements was set aside, roomy cages were built with tastefully painted murals on the walls depicting a riot of tropical foliage, and the animals were moved out of the cold and damp, which had already started, into the luxury of brilliant electric light and a constant temperature. The charge for admission just covered the food bills, and so the animals were warm, comfortable and well fed without being a drain on my resources. With this worry off my mind I could turn my attention once more to the problem of getting my zoo.

It would be wearisome to go into all the details of frustration during this period, or to make a catalogue of the number of mayors, town councillors, parks superintendents and sanitary officers I met and argued with. Suffice it to say that I felt my brain creaking at times with the effort of trying to persuade supposedly intelligent people that a zoo in any town should be considered an attraction rather than anything else. To judge by the way they reacted one would have thought I wanted to set off an atomic bomb on one of the piers.

In the meantime the animals, unaware that their fate hung in the balance, did their best to make life exciting for us. There was, for example, the day that Georgina the baboon decided that she wanted to see a little more of Bournemouth than the inside of J. J. Allen's basement. Fortunately it was a Sunday morning, so there was no one in the store: otherwise I dread to think what would have happened.

I was sipping a cup of tea, just before going down to the store and cleaning and feeding the animals, when the telephone rang. Without a care in the world I answered it.

'Is that Mr Durrell?' inquired a deep, lugubrious voice.

'Yes, speaking.'

'This is the Police 'ere, sir. One of them monkeys of yours 'as got out, and I thought I'd better let you know.'

'Good God, which one is it?' I asked.

'I don't know, sir, really. It's a big brown one. Only it looks rather fierce, sir, so I thought I'd let you know.'

'Yes, thanks very much. Where is it?'

'Well, it's in one of the windows at the moment. But I don't see as 'ow it'll stay there very long. Is it liable to bite, sir?'

'Well, it may do. Don't go near it. I'll be right down,' I said, slamming down the receiver.

I grabbed a taxi and we roared down to the centre of the town, ignoring all speed limits. After all, I reflected, we were on police business of a sort. As I paid off the taxi the first thing that greeted my eyes was the chaos in one of the big display windows of Allen's. The window had been carefully set out to exhibit some articles of bedroom furniture. There was a large bed, made up, a tall bedside light and several eiderdowns taste-fully spread over the floor. At least, that was how it had been when the window dresser had finished it. Now it looked as if a tornado had hit it. The light had been overturned and had burned a large hole in one of the eiderdowns; the bedclothes had been stripped off the bed and the pillow and sheets were covered with a tasteful pattern of paw marks. On the bed itself sat Georgina, bouncing up and down happily, and making fer-ocious faces at a crowd of scandalized churchgoers who had gathered on the pavement outside the window. I went into the store and found two enormous constables lying in ambush behind a barricade of turkish towelling.

'Ah!' said one with relief, 'there you are, sir. We didn't like to try and catch it, see, because it didn't know us, and we thought it might make it worse, like.'

'I don't think anything could make that animal worse,' I said bitterly. 'Actually she's harmless, but she makes a hell of a row and looks fierce . . . it's all bluff, really.'

'Really?' said one of the constables, polite but unconvinced.

'I'll try and get her in the window there if I can, but if she breaks away I want you two to head her off. Don't, for the love of Allah, let her get into the china department.'

'She came through the china department already,' said one of the constables with gloomy satisfaction.

'Did she break anything?' I asked faintly.

'No, sir, luckily; she just galloped straight through. Me and Bill was chasing 'er, of course, so she didn't stop.'

'Well, don't let's let her get back in there. We may not be so lucky next time.'

By this time Jacquie and my sister Margo had arrived in another taxi, so our ranks had now swelled to five. We should,

I thought, be able to cope with Georgina between us. I stationed the two constables, my sister and wife at suitable points guarding the entrance to the china department, and then went round and entered the window in which Georgina was still bouncing up and down on the ruined bed, making obscene faces at the crowd.

'Georgina,' I said in a quiet but soothing voice, 'come along then, come to Dad.'

Georgina glanced over her shoulder in surprise. She studied my face as I moved towards her, and decided that my expression belied my honeyed accents. She gathered herself and leapt through the air, over the still smouldering eiderdown, and grabbed at the top of the great rampart of turkish towelling that formed the background of the window display. This, not having been constructed to take the weight of a large baboon hurtling through the air, immediately collapsed, and Georgina fell to the ground under a cascade of many-hued towelling. She struggled madly to free herself, and just succeeded in doing so as I flung myself forward to catch her. She gave a hysterical squawk and fled out of the window into the interior of the shop. I unravelled myself from the towelling and followed her. A piercing shriek from my sister told me of Georgina's whereabouts; my sister always tends to go off like a locomotive in moments of crisis. Georgina had slipped past her and was now perched on a counter, surveying us with glittering eyes, thoroughly enjoying the game. We approached her in a grim-faced body. At the end of the counter, suspended from the ceiling, hung a Christmas decoration made out of holly, tinsel and cardboard stars. It was shaped somewhat like a chandelier, and looked, as far as Georgina was concerned, ideal for swinging. She poised herself on the end of the counter and as we ran forward she leaped up and grabbed at the decoration in a manner vaguely reminiscent of the elder Fairbanks. The decoration promptly gave way, and Georgina fell to the ground, leapt to her feet and galloped off wearing a piece of tinsel over one ear.

For the next half-hour we thundered to and fro through the deserted store, always with Georgina one jump ahead of us, as it were. She knocked down a huge pile of account books in the stationery department, paused to see if a pile of lace doilies was edible, and made a large and decorative puddle at the foot of the main staircase. Then, just as the constables were beginning to breathe rather stertorously and I was beginning to despair of ever catching the wretched animal, Georgina made a miscalculation. Loping easily ahead of us she came upon what looked like the perfect hiding-place constructed of rolls of linoleum arranged on end. She fled between the rolls and was lost, for the rolls had been arranged in the form of a hollow square, a three-sided trap from which there was no escape. Quickly we closed in and blocked the entrance to the linoleum trap. I advanced towards her, grim-faced, and she sat there and screamed wildly, begging for mercy. As I made a lunge to grab her she ducked under my hand, and as I swung round to prevent her escape I bumped into one of the massive rolls of linoleum. Before I could stop it this toppled forward like a gigantic truncheon and hit one of the constables accurately on the top of his helmet. As the poor man staggered backwards, Georgina took one look at my face and decided that she was in need of police protection. She rushed to the still swaying constable and wrapped her arms tightly round his legs, looking over her shoulder at me and screaming. I jumped forward and grabbed her by her hairy legs and the scruff of her neck, and dragged her away from the constable's legs.

'Cor!' said the constable, in a voice of deep emotion, 'I thought I'd 'ad me chips that time.'

'Oh, she wouldn't have bitten you,' I explained, raising my voice above Georgina's harsh screams. 'She wanted you to protect her from me.'

'Cor!' said the constable again. 'Well, I'm glad that's over.'

We put Georgina back in her cage, thanked the constables, cleared up the mess, cleaned and fed the animals and then went home to a well-earned rest. But for the rest of that day, every time the telephone rang I nearly jumped out of my skin.

In the meantime I was still continuing my struggle to find my zoo, but my chance of success seemed to recede farther and farther each day. The collection had to be moved from J. J. Allen's, of course, but here Paignton Zoo came to my rescue. With extreme kindness they allowed me to board my collection with them, on deposit, until such time as I could find a place of my own. But this, as I say, began to seem more and more unlikely. It was the old story. In the initial stages of a project, when you need people's help most, it is never forthcoming. The only solution, if at all possible, is to go ahead and accomplish it by yourself. Then, when you have made a success of it, all the people who would not help you launch it gather round, slap you on the back and offer their assistance.

'There must be an intelligent local council somewhere,' said Jacquie one evening, as we pored over a map of the British Isles.

'I doubt it,' I said gloomily, 'and anyway I doubt whether I have the mental strength to cope with another round of mayors and town clerks. No, we'll just have to get a place and do it ourselves.'

'But you'll have to get their sanction,' Jacquie pointed out, 'and then there's Town and Country Planning and all that.'

I shuddered. 'What we should really do is to go to some remote island in the West Indies, or somewhere,' I said, 'where they're sensible enough not to clutter their lives with all this incredible red tape.'

Jacquie moved Cholmondely St John, our chimpanzee, from the portion of the map on which he was squatting.

'What about the Channel Isles?' she asked suddenly.

'What about them?'

'Well, they're a very popular holiday resort, and they've got a wonderful climate.'

'Yes, it would be an excellent place, but we don't know anyone there,' I objected, 'and you need someone on the spot to give you advice in this sort of thing.'

'Yes,' said Jacquie, reluctantly, 'I suppose you're right.'

So, reluctantly (for the idea of starting my zoo on an island had a very strong appeal for me) we forgot about the Channel Islands. It was not until a few weeks later that I happened to be in London and was discussing my zoo project with Rupert Hart-Davis that a gleam of daylight started to appear. I confessed to Rupert that my chances of having my own zoo now seemed so slight that I was on the verge of giving up the idea altogether. I said that we had thought of the Channel Islands, but that we had no contact there to help us. Rupert sat up, and with an air of a conjurer performing a minor miracle, said he had a perfectly good contact in the Channel Islands (if only he was asked) and a man moreover who had spent his whole life in the islands and would be only too willing to help us in any way. His name was Major Fraser, and that evening I telephoned him. He did not seem to find it at all unusual that a complete stranger should ring him up and ask his advice about starting a zoo, which made me warm to him from the start. He suggested that Jacquie and I should fly across to Jersey and he would show us round the island, and give us any information he could. And this accordingly we arranged to do.

So we flew to Jersey. As the plane came in to land the island seemed like a toy continent, a patchwork of tiny fields, set in a vivid blue sea. A pleasantly carunculated rocky coastline was broken here and there with smooth stretches of beach, along which the sea creamed in ribbons. As we stepped out on to the tarmac the air seemed warmer, and the sun a little more brilliant. I felt my spirits rising.

In the car park Hugh Fraser awaited us. He was a tall, slim man, wearing a narrow-brimmed trilby tilted so far forward that the brim almost rested on his aquiline nose. His blue eyes twinkled humorously as he shepherded us into his car and drove us away from the airport. We drove through St Helier, the capital of the island, which reminded me of a sizeable English market town; it was something of a surprise to find, at a cross-roads, a policeman in a white coat and white helmet, directing the traffic. It suddenly gave the place a faintly tropical atmosphere. We drove through the town and then out along narrow roads with steep banks, where the trees leaned over and entwined branches, turning it into a green tunnel. The landscape, with its red earth and rich green grass, reminded me very much of Devon, but the landscape was a miniature one, with tiny fields, narrow valleys stuffed with trees, and small farmhouses built of the beautiful Jersey granite, which contains a million autumn tints in its surface where the sun touches it. Then we turned off the road, drove down a long drive and suddenly, before us, was Hugh's home, Les Augres Manor.

The Manor was built like an E without the centre bar; the main building was in the upright of the E, while the two cross pieces were wings of the house, ending in two massive stone arches which allowed access to the courtyard. These beautiful arches were built in about 1660 and, like the rest of the building, were of the lovely local granite. Hugh showed us round his home with obvious pride, the old granite cider-press and cow-sheds, the huge walled garden, the small lake with its tattered fringe of bulrushes, the sunken water-meadows with the tiny streams trickling through them. At last we walked slowly back under the beautiful archways and into the courtyard, flooded with sunshine.

'You know, Hugh, you've got a wonderful place here,' I said.

'Yes, it is lovely . . . I think one of the loveliest Manors on the island,' said Hugh.

I turned to Jacquie. 'Wouldn't it make a wonderful place for our zoo?' I remarked.

'Yes, it would,' agreed Jacquie.

Hugh eyed me for a moment. 'Are you serious?' he inquired.

'Well, I was joking, but it would make a wonderful site for a zoo. Why?' I asked.

'Well,' said Hugh thoughtfully, 'I'm finding the upkeep too much for my resources, and I want to move to the mainland. Would you be interested in renting the place?'

'Would I?' I said. 'Just give me the chance.'

'Come inside, dear boy, and we'll discuss it,' said Hugh, leading the way across the courtyard.

So, after a frustrating year of struggling with councils and other local authorities, I had gone to Jersey, and within an hour of landing at the airport I had found my zoo.

Gerry's strong convictions on what a zoo should be and why were kindled in Corfu and took shape during the ten years he spent on animal-collecting expeditions. They were radically different from the conventional view that prevailed until recently and persists in some quarters today. He expresses his views in a pioneering book, The Stationary Ark, *very clearly.*

A Zoo that is More than a Zoo

It was while I was at Whipsnade and during my first four expeditions that I began to have doubts about zoos. Not doubts about the necessity for having them, for I believed (and still believe) that zoos are very important institutions. My doubts were about the way that some zoos were run and the way that the majority of them were orientated. Until I had gone to Whipsnade, zoomaniac that I was, I felt that to criticize any zoo, however lightly, was asking to be struck down by a bolt of lightning straight from heaven. But my experiences at Whipsnade and later, in collecting animals for zoos (thus visiting a great many of them), gave me an ever-growing sense of disquiet. As my experience grew, I came to the conclusion that there was a great deal to be criticized in the average zoo and, indeed, a lot that needed to be criticized if zoos, as the valuable institutions that I felt them to be, were to progress out of the stagnant state into which the greater majority appeared to have fallen, or from which they had never succeeded in emerging since their inception. However, it is simplicity itself to criticize a tightrope walker if you have never been aloft yourself and so I became even more determined to start my own zoo.

The low ebb to which zoos had allowed themselves to fall in public estimation was made apparent by the reactions I got when people found out what I intended to do. If I had informed them that I was going to start a plastic bottle factory, a pop group, a strip club or something else of such obvious benefit to mankind, they would doubtless have been deeply sympathetic.

But a zoo? A place where you reluctantly took the children to ride on an elephant and get sick on ice cream? A place where animals were imprisoned? Surely I could not be serious? Why a zoo, of all things, they asked?

To a certain extent I understood and even sympathized with their views. Theirs was a difficult question to answer, for their conception of a zoo and mine were totally different. The core of the problem lay in the fact that in the past – and even today – few people, scientists or laymen, properly appreciate the value of a good zoological garden. As scientific institutions, they are simply not taken seriously and there is too little recognition of the fact that they can provide the opportunity for an enormous amount of valuable work in research, conservation and education. To a large extent, this ignorance has been promoted by the zoos themselves, for far too many of them seem totally unaware of their own potentialities, scientifically speaking, and continue to encourage everyone to look upon them as mere places of amusement. It is therefore not altogether surprising that both the public and the scientific fraternity regard zoos as places of entertainment, something less mobile and transitory than a circus but of much the same level of scientific importance. Zoos have, in the main, encouraged this, for to be considered scientific is, to most people, synonymous with being dull and this is not box-office.

A zoological garden can offer facilities that no other similar institution can emulate. At its best, it should be a complex laboratory, educational establishment and conservation unit. Our biological knowledge of even some of the commonest animals is embarrassingly slight and it is here that zoos can be of inestimable value in amassing information. That this can only help the ultimate conservation of an animal in the wild state is obvious, for you cannot begin to talk about conservation of a species unless you have some knowledge of how it functions. A well-run zoological garden should provide you with the facilities for just such work.

While it is obviously more desirable to study animals in the wild state, there are many aspects of animal biology which can be more easily studied in zoos and, indeed, there are certain aspects that can only be studied conveniently when the animal is in a controlled environment, such as a zoo. For example, it is almost impossible to work out accurate gestation periods for animals in the wild or follow the day-to-day growth and development of the young and so on. All this can be studied in a zoo. Therefore zoological gardens – properly run zoological gardens – are enormous reservoirs of valuable data, if the animals in them are studied properly and the results recorded accurately.

Educationally, too, zoos have a most important role to play. Now that we have invented the megalopolis, we are spawning a new generation, reared without benefit of dog, cat, goldfish or budgerigar, in the upright coffins of the high-rise flats; a generation that will believe that milk comes from a bottle, without benefit of grass or cow or the intricate process between the two. This generation or its future offspring might have only the zoo to show them that creatures, other than their own kind, are trying to inhabit the earth as well.

Finally, zoos can be of immense importance in the field of conservation. Firstly, they should endeavour to breed as many of the animals in their care as possible, thus lessening the drain upon wild stocks. More important still, they can build up viable breeding groups of those species whose numbers in the wild state have dropped to an alarmingly low level. Many zoos have done, and are doing this successfully. Out of the thousand or so species of animal that are currently in danger of extinction, a great number have populations that have dropped so low in terms of individual specimens that it is imperative that a controlled breeding programme should be set up for them, as well as the more conventional methods of protection. Over the years, people I have talked to (including zoo directors) seem to have only the vaguest idea as to the scope and importance of controlled breeding as a conservation tool and little idea of the necessity for it. In recent years, however, more progressive zoos and the more realistic conservationists have been talking in terms of zoo banks for certain species. Let us call them low-ebb species. This means that when the numbers of a creature drop to a certain level, all efforts should be made to maintain it in the wild state but, as a precautionary measure, a viable breeding group should be set up in a zoo, or, better still, a breeding centre created specially for the purpose. Thus, whatever happens in the wilds, your species is safe. Moreover, should it become extinct in the wild, you still have a breeding nucleus and from this you can, at some future date, try to reintroduce it into safe areas of its previous range.

This sort of captive breeding has already helped – and in some cases saved – such species as the Père David's deer, the European bison, the bontebok, the Nene goose and so on, but the zoos undertaking this work were in the minority and the help was given to only a handful of species. The list of animals that needed this sort of assistance for survival was increasing with alarming rapidity. It was apparent to me that unless more attention was paid to this particular form of conservation, a whole host of species was in danger of vanishing.

I felt that this most urgent work was one that the zoos already in existence should be concentrating on to a much greater degree than they were. Any new zoo that came into being should have it as its major objective. What was wanted, in fact, was not more large, comprehensive zoos, but smaller specialist ones, which could concentrate their efforts and devote the time and the trouble to the controlled breeding of species in urgent need of this type of help. Such a place would, moreover, be able to help some of the more obscure and unattractive animals, which generally tended to get neglected because they were not 'box-office'; it would concentrate on building up and maintaining (at least until they were numerically out of danger) viable breeding groups of threatened species, and the whole organization would act not only as a sanctuary, but as a research station and, most important, as a training ground. Keeping and breeding animals, particularly rare and delicate animals, is an art that has to be taught and learnt. Unfortunately, in the past (and in many zoos this is still the case) the people employed to look after the animals would be far better employing their minuscule talents elsewhere.

While the urgent need for the sort of place I wished to create seemed patently obvious to me, one had still, in those days (and to a lesser extent today), considerable opposition from what one could describe as hard-core conservationists. It was difficult to get them to see that controlled breeding was a desirable and necessary second line of defence to the conventional method of conservation, such as the creation of reserves, parks and so on. For many years, if you mentioned the subject in any august body of conservationists, they tended to look at you as if you had confessed to the belief that necrophilia was an ideal form of population control.

So ingrained was the idea that zoos were nothing more than Victorian menageries that it was almost impossible to get anyone to believe that a zoo could have a purpose more serious. The basic argument was that all zoos were badly run and few, if any, had shown any ability or desire to assist in conservation by controlled breeding programmes. Rather, by their cavalier attitude of 'there's plenty more where that came from', zoos had been a drain on wild stocks, depleting animal populations to replace the ones in their collections, lost through bad luck or carelessness, or both. There were too many zoos (so the conservationists argued) paying vociferous lip service to conservation, without doing anything worthwhile; too many zoos who only thought of a rare animal in terms of gate money and publicity and not of its importance from a conservation point of view; too many zoos whose much publicized 'conservation efforts' bore about as much resemblance to intelligent conservation work as a window-box does to a reafforestation programme.

It is unfortunate that these criticisms, to a large extent, were, and still are, valid. My plea that what was wanted now was not more normal zoos, but specialist ones, with carefully worked out conservation breeding programmes, fell on deaf ears. In this atmosphere, it required a certain amount of resolve to start yet another zoo, even if one intended that it should grow into something quite different from most of the others already in existence. I felt, however, that it was useless waiting for the approbation of the conservationists. The only thing to do was to start a specialist zoo of my own and see if it worked.

Jersey welcomed Gerry and his zoo with open arms. He always said it was 'Durrell's Luck' to have ended up on that beautiful island after the fruitless search for a site elsewhere.

The following account is from the very early days of Jersey Zoo. Those times were rather chaotic – animals were often let out of their enclosures for a 'romp' and baby animals were hand-reared by Gerry's mother in the flat in the manor house where she lived with Gerry and Jacquie.

Many of Gerry's most endearing animal characters make their debuts in these pages: Trumpy, the Grey-winged Trumpeter from South America, and N'Pongo, the young gorilla, who plays so gently with the two-year-old daughter of the zoo superintendent.

A Zoo of My Own

To achieve a lifelong ambition before you are too senile to appreciate it is, I suppose, a rather rare thing, particularly when your ambition is to have your own Zoo. Ever since I can remember I have wanted a Zoo of my own, and it never seemed to me to be a very outrageous ambition, though the more staid of my friends obviously thought that I was mad to even contemplate such a scheme. But as I make a point of never listening to my friends' advice, I have eventually got what I wanted: a Zoo in the lovely setting of an old manor house, and a Zoo containing six hundred animals, most of which I have collected myself in out of the way parts of the world.

The first thing I found when the Zoo came into being was that, no matter how hard you tried to resist, the animals insinuated themselves into your life with such determination that you soon found you had little time for anything else. If you were not entertaining a gorilla in the spare room (because she had arrived before her cage was ready), you had a sick python in a box by the stove, or a basket full of baby squirrels which had been deserted by their mother, and which had to be bottle-fed at hourly intervals. However, when you have animals in your life like this you soon find out which of your friends really like you. A parcel of crocodiles arrives at the airport in midwinter and by the time you have rushed them back to the Zoo they are all so chilled that they are in imminent danger of dying. So you fill the bath with warm water and put them in it to revive. It takes a real friend to use your bathroom when eight crocodiles are glaring up balefully from the bath at them, and, moreover, not even to consider it unusual.

Even my mother, who lives with me, finds herself caught up among the animals. She adores any animal, of course, but particularly the smaller things, and has proved herself most valuable as foster mother to many of the young creatures we have acquired from time to time. At the moment she is acting as mother to an extremely rare little creature, an Emperor Tamarin, one of the Marmoset family which are the smallest of the monkey tribe. This diminutive little chap was in a very forlorn condition when we got him, and it was obvious that he would not thrive unless he was given a great deal of love and attention. So, inevitably, my mother was chosen to take on the task of nursing the tiny creature back to health and strength.

When he arrived he could fit comfortably into a tea cup, and his skinny little body combined with enormous white curling moustache which these Tamarins have on their upper lip gave one the impression that you had acquired not a monkey, but a very elderly Leprechaun. Within a fortnight my mother's careful treatment of him had worked wonders. He had put on weight, his coat was glossy, and his snow-white moustache so luxuriant and curly that it would have been the envy of any brigadier general. Moreover, from being a timid and retiring creature he had become very self-confident, even cocksure. He rules my mother with a rod of iron, and as soon as he is let out of his cage he takes over her room like a dictator. If she lies on the bed to rest he must either lie with her under the covers, or, if he does not feel like a siesta, then mother has to provide him with amusement by wiggling her toes beneath the bedclothes, so that he can stalk them and leap on them from a great height. He talks to her the whole time in a high-pitched twittering call that is extraordinarily bird-like, and, as my mother has pointed out, it is difficult to get forty winks when you have what appear to be twenty operatic canaries singing volubly into your ear. Every evening he crawls under mother's pillow and settles himself for the night, in the hopes that we will not notice his absence from his cage, and leave him there. When he is hauled out and put to bed properly his screams and twitters of indignation can be heard all over the house, and it is only when the front of his cage is covered that he reluctantly stops shouting and makes his way into his own bed, which consists of a piece of old blanket and an apron belonging to my mother.

The chief charm of having a comparatively small Zoo is that all your animals can get this sort of individual attention. They are, in fact, treated more as pets than as merely Zoo exhibits, and this, I am sure, has a tremendous psychological effect on the animals. Another important thing is to have a young and enthusiastic staff for the job of Zoo keepering is a twenty-four-hours-a-day job, and you have to have a real affection for and interest in your charges, or the animals suffer. Take, for example, Peter the Cheetah. He had been hand-reared by someone in Kenya, and had been kept round the house like a dog. So, when he came to us we knew that he would suffer if he was not given the same amount of affection he had been used to. So, Jeremy Mallinson, who was detailed to be Peter's keeper, was supplied with a large brush and comb and a gigantic rubber ball. Every day Jeremy goes into Peter's cage, to be greeted by such prolonged and vibrant purrs that it sounds like a dynamo, and Peter is given a good brush and comb. Then, for half an hour, they play football together. Not, I am afraid, regulation football, for Peter thinks nothing of suddenly wrapping himself round Jeremy's legs in a flying tackle and bringing him to the ground. But they both enjoy the game, and in consequence of this grooming, exercise and attention Peter has improved greatly in appearance, and he is, if anything, tamer than when he arrived.

Some of the tame animals, of course, we let out of their cages at certain times to have a romp around. There was Topsy the woolly monkey, for example, who used to be let out and roam the full length of the monkey house. But she eventually took to irritating the less fortunate inhabitants by hanging on the wire of their cages and making faces at them, so we had to put a stop to it. One creature that has never been in a cage is Trumpy, the Grey-winged Trumpeter from South America. Trumpy is our village idiot, as it were. In the cold weather his beat is in the warmth of the mammal house, but as soon as Spring arrives Trumpy comes out and paces sedately round the grounds, occasionally opening his wings wide, trumpeting and rushing up to some astonished visitor as though it was a life-long friend he had not seen for years. At one time he took to accompanying the last visitors out the main gate and down the road to the bus stop, and on many occasions slightly irritated holiday makers had to walk half a mile back to the Zoo with him, for he showed every sign of wanting to get on the bus with them. Trumpy has many endearing qualities, but the nicest is, I think, that he has appointed himself chief 'settler-in' for the Zoo. Whenever we have a new arrival he goes down and spends twenty-four hours standing outside or preferably inside the cage with them, until he feels they have got quite settled in.

When we first got our swans and put them out in the flooded water meadow where we keep them, Trumpy went down and spent twenty-four hours standing up to his ankles in water with them, and no amount of entreaties on our part would make him deviate from his duty. The swans seemed to like him, but it was a different thing when he went and flew into

Peter the Cheetah's cage, unbeknownst to us. Peter was obviously under the impression that Trumpy was a tasty morsel kindly provided by the authorities for his pleasure and he raced down on Trumpy like an express train. I arrived on the scene at this moment, and was sure that Trumpy's last hour had come. But luckily Trumpy seemed to realise that Peter was not going to be friendly and he hurled himself into the air and flapped over to the fence in the nick of time. Looking very ruffled, and grumbling to himself, he paced off sedately to another part of the Zoo where he knew he would be welcome.

Another creature that is frequently allowed out to play on the lawn is the most valuable animal we have got, N'pongo, our baby gorilla. N'pongo's favourite playmate is Caroline Smith, the Superintendent's two-year-old daughter, known to her friends as Moonbeam. Although the young ape is bigger than Moonbeam and tremendously powerful (it takes three adults to get her back into her cage if she doesn't want to go back) yet when playing with Moonbeam she is astonishingly gentle and tolerant. To watch them sharing a bag of sweets is a sight worth seeing. Both of them sit there, looks of extreme concentration on their faces, while Moonbeam carefully opens the bag and rations out the sweets into N'pongo's immense black paw. When the sweets have been equally divided then they will sometimes sit back-to-back, like a couple of bookends, while they eat, both of them occasionally spitting the semi-masticated sweets into their hands to have a close look at them, before popping them back into their mouths. After the sweets comes a game of tag, and here again N'pongo is most gentle. If she plays tag with me she is apt to suddenly seize my leg and swing on it, and if you are not prepared for three stone of gorilla using your leg as a sort of maypole you come crashing to the ground. Yet when playing with Moonbeam the

gorilla never does this, but contents herself with merely pluck-
ing the child's clothes with gentle hands. Both of them love to
be tickled, and they will roll about on the grass hysterically
when you do it, Moonbeam's shrill giggles contrasting
strangely with N'pongo's gruff, bass laughter.

N'pongo is, as I say, the most valuable animal we have, not
only in cash value, but because gorillas, like many forms of
wildlife all over the world, are in grave peril of being exterminated in the wild state. Already, in many places, wonderful
forms of animal life have become extinct through the interference of mankind, and today hundreds of species are in urgent
need of protection. Zoos can play their part in this work of
saving rare animals by building up breeding colonies of threatened creatures, so that, even if the animal becomes extinct in
the wild state, we have not lost it forever. It was with this in
mind that I started my Zoo, for here we intend (as funds
permit) to collect as many endangered creatures as possible
and breed them. N'pongo is first on this list. Unfortunately,
this is a costly business, and we have a collecting box on the
outside of the gorilla's cage in which we collect donations
towards the cost of a mate for N'pongo. Already, through the
sixpences and pennies and sometimes pound notes of visitors,
we have accumulated three hundred pounds towards the fifteen hundred we shall need to buy a mate; it is slow work but
we hope to get there in the end. We think that this business of
trying to preserve wildlife by breeding in captivity, as well as
protecting it in the wild state, is a very worthwhile ambition. I
am aiming to start a Trust soon, the funds of which will be
used for the purpose of acquiring and keeping these rare and
vanishing creatures and, we hope, preserving them for future
generations to enjoy.

Letter to J. F. Lipscomb

J.F. Lipscomb, Esq., O.B.E.,
Organising Secretary, Symposium: Zoos and Conservation,
Regent's Park,
London N.W.1.

20th June 1964

Dear Mr. Lipscomb,

I was interested to receive Paper No.6 on the Symposium and
to see that at the first session Dr. Lang is going to speak on
the breeding of endangered species in captivity. I realise that
many of the more enlightened zoos have been concerned
with this problem for some time, and the part that zoos have
to play is obviously of major importance in animal
conservation.

In view of this, I feel I ought to draw your attention to the
fact that I have recently formed The Jersey Wildlife Preservation Trust. The Trust has taken over the Zoo here as its
headquarters, and so in future our policy will be as follows:

1. To do whatever we can to assist in world conservation.
2. To try to build up breeding colonies of various threatened species, concentrating particularly on some of the
   smaller creatures (such as Solenodon) which tend to
   become partially or wholly neglected, as they are of
   little tourist value and are not sufficiently spectacular.

3. To replace the common animals now on display by the breeding colonies mentioned above and also by examples of any creatures which, though they may not now be in any danger, nevertheless have a good conservation story behind them, e.g., Père David's Deer, European Bison, Hawaiian Goose, Trumpeter Swan etc.

So it is hoped that eventually the Zoo here will be, I think, unique inasmuch as everything the public sees will be underlining the importance of conservation.

I believe we will be the first Zoo in the world to attempt to devote all our resources and energy towards conservation in this manner, and so I thought it might be of interest to you to know about the Trust. I enclose our first brochure. We are planning a more detailed, explanatory one which will be printed shortly and of which I will send you a copy should you be interested.

I am looking forward very much to meeting you at the Symposium, which I feel will be of tremendous interest and importance.

With kindest regards,
Yours sincerely,

Gerald Durrell

A Successful Marriage

The complexities of successful marriage among animals is shown by the difficulties we had with our gorilla group, for, in trying to establish these creatures we ran the gamut of practically everything that could happen. We acquired the female, N'Pongo, when she was an estimated two and a half years old. We then obtained Nandi, another female, slightly younger. N'Pongo, from the first, was a charming extrovert, with great gaiety of disposition and firm ideas about her own importance. Though she liked Nandi from the moment of introduction, N'Pongo made it quite clear that it was her zoo that they were living in, the staff were her friends and Nandi would do well to remember it. She was too charming and good-natured an ape to develop into a sadistic bully, as many animals would have done in the circumstances, and she treated Nandi with great affection but considerable firmness. Thus, for five years the relationship was one of mutual affection and regard, with N'Pongo in many ways taking the place of the male. The relationship, in fact, was one which, in a girls' school, might have been described as unhealthy.

It was at this point that we were having so much trouble getting a male. It began to look as though N'Pongo and Nandi would have to end their days as virgin spinsters, a thought that was naturally abhorrent to us. It was then that Ernst Lang offered us Jambo. This was an enormous piece of luck from many points of view. Lang had been the first person in Europe to breed and successfully rear a gorilla, the famous Goma, and since that remarkable breakthrough (for gorillas were one of those difficult beasts that it was said could not be bred in captivity), his gorilla family had gone from strength to strength. Jambo was one of the males born into the family. Not only was he zoo bred, but he himself was the father of a young male, the mother of which was his sister. This meant that Jambo was no callow teenager whose knowledge of sex was confined to perverted peeps at the health and strength magazines; he was a fertile male who knew how to mate.

This is very important, for there are many things in the apes' world that are learnt by example and successful copulation seems to be one of them. An ape reared without contact with a herd seems to be singularly inept and, in some cases, a totally unsuccessful lover, simply because he was never shown. Jambo had not only been shown by his enormous father, Achilla, but had proved that he had paid proper attention to the demonstration. His final qualification was that he was just the right age to become N'Pongo's and Nandi's husband. Lang had extolled his virtues in letters and, rather in the manner of the early royal marriages, photographs had been exchanged. We were told that Jambo was exceptionally powerful and exceedingly handsome, and with a rather humorous expression. We all thought he was perfect. Now we had to wait to see if the two females agreed.

Introducing animals is a heart-stopping business. Will they attack each other and, if so, will the hose pipes, the buckets of water, the pitchforks, be of the least avail? If not, will they simply ignore each other, or will they ignore each other to begin with and then attack each other later, when one has been lulled into a sense of false security? If they do ignore each other, does this mean that they might grow to like each other later on, or were all one's trouble and expense in vain? Anybody who cherishes the idea that all individuals of the species are bound to be alike in given circumstances, should have been there to watch the introduction of Jambo to N'Pongo and Nandi. It was a classic in every sense of the word.

We had confined the females in one of the three sections of the bedroom so that, through the barred divisions, they could look into the third bedroom into which we were going to release Jambo. Between the male and the females would lie a section of the bedrooms and two sets of bars. This would, we felt, act as a buffer-state, until we got some idea of all three participants' reactions to the whole idea. N'Pongo and Nandi could tell something curious was going on by all the untoward activity but they had no idea what, since Jambo was still invisible in his travelling crate.

The moment arrived, the slide on Jambo's crate was lifted, the door to the bedroom slid open and Jambo, massive and black as coal, reeking with the garlic-like smell of gorilla sweat, swaggered, hunching his shoulders like a professional heavyweight, into the cage. He gave one swift, all-embracing glance around him, saw the females, but made no sign. He squatted for a moment to gaze around him in a lordly fashion before starting a slow perambulation around the bedroom, examining every nook and cranny with interest, but still totally ignoring the two females. The effect of all this on the females was fascinating. Both of them, when they heard the slide, had come forward and peered, but when Jambo sauntered, dark and handsome, into their line of vision, the reaction of each one was totally unexpected by us.

We had thought that, if either of them displayed immediate interest, it would be the basically friendly, extrovert N'Pongo. Nandi always tended to be suspicious and kept herself to herself. But the moment Jambo strolled into view, N'Pongo took one good look at him and then turned and walked off, showing by the set of her broad back a measureless disdain. She expressed quite firmly a total lack of interest in the opposite sex and Jambo in particular. The effect on the anti-social Nandi was quite different and charmingly comic. She was a little way away from the bars, squatting on her haunches, when Jambo came into view. She took one look at the massive shape and reacted in much the same way as a teenage girl might if her favourite pop star suddenly walked into her bedroom, clad in nothing but a guitar. The expression on her face was one of incredulity and wonder; nothing in her previous life had prepared her for this miracle. No one had told her that such a thing as a handsome male gorilla existed. She took one look at Jambo and fell instantly and irrevocably in love.

I am sorry if this sounds unscientific and anthropomorphic, but in the dry and pedantic jargon of the biologist there is no way to describe it. She shuffled her way to the bars, never taking her eyes off this wonderful apparition, and clung on to them in a rather desperate sort of way, gazing wide-eyed and immobile at the apparently disinterested Jambo. She sat in a trance, drinking in his every movement. Once, during the course of investigations, he disappeared behind the wall for a few moments. Her distress was immediate; she ran to and fro, trying to see where he had gone. Eventually, when he did not reappear, she came to the conclusion that he had gone out through the slide into the outdoor area. Instantly she ran to her own slide, bent down and tried to peer under it. Fortunately for her peace of mind, Jambo reappeared, nonchalantly sucking a piece of orange and ignoring Nandi's display of uncontrolled passion. Relieved to see him again, she once more took up her station at the bars and gazed at him reverently and adoringly. N'Pongo, meanwhile, had eaten a few nuts, peered out of the window at us and finally lain down on her shelf, utterly ignoring the presence of a male in their midst.

When they were finally allowed in with each other, both females carried on in much the same way. It was obvious that N'Pongo, for so many years the queen of all she surveyed, viewed the newcomer with suspicion and jealousy but with a certain caution too. She decided to continue her policy of pretending that the eighteen-stone Jambo did not exist. Nandi, on the other hand, behaved, if possible, in an even more inane manner now that she could get close to the object of her passion. She would squat within a foot or so of him, gazing at him raptly, her eyes shining with affection. After a time, when Jambo lay in the sun and allowed her to groom him, her joy knew no bounds and she would lean up against his massive body, with a look of besotted pride on her face that was so human it was laughable. N'Pongo was somewhat distressed by this liaison, but she still maintained her domination over Nandi. However, there now developed an unfortunate association between N'Pongo and Jambo.

Jambo, for all his experience, was still very young and full of what can only be described as youthful high spirits and crude humour. He knew N'Pongo disliked him and this aroused in him a sort of devilment. He would practise all sorts of schoolboy pranks, which, as we know, can become very wearing to the nerves. He would jump out on her suddenly when she least expected it, or, sauntering past, would suddenly rush at her and pull her hair. Immediately N'Pongo would attack him and he would run off. This teasing would go on until N'Pongo was in a towering rage and would pursue him, screaming abuse, accompanied by Nandi who, rather half-heartedly, took her part. But it was obvious that Nandi would consider such attentions from Jambo as a pleasure and privilege and was somewhat puzzled by N'Pongo's reaction.

Jambo, of course, like all practical jokers, did not know

when to stop. He never actually hurt N'Pongo, except for a few minor bites and scratches (nothing by gorilla play standards), but as soon as he found that he could make her lose her temper, he teased her mercilessly. N'Pongo began to have the hang-dog air of the wife of a professional humorist and, what was worse, she started to lose condition. Reluctantly we had to separate her from Jambo, allowing them into the outer areas separately, and dividing Nandi's time between the two so that Jambo would not get bored and N'Pongo not become too jealous.

Then N'Pongo came into season and suddenly it was vouch-safed to her what a male gorilla, even an irritating practical joker male gorilla, was for. With complete shamelessness she would solicit him through the bedroom bars and, when allowed in with each other, copulation took place almost at once. During the whole time she was in season, N'Pongo tolerated Jambo. Although she did not display quite the hero-worship of Nandi, she nevertheless abandoned herself to the carnal delights in the most wholehearted fashion. Then, the moment she was out of season, she resumed her former relationship with Jambo. Once again they had to be separated. Though she became more tolerant of Jambo as the months passed, she still only really had time for him when she was in season. It would have made things much easier for us if she had lived in harmony with him, but we had to be thankful for small mercies. At least she had mated with him and that was the main thing. Nandi, too, had received his attention when in season and so now all we could do was wait and hope that both females would be fertile, give birth successfully and, most important, prove to be good mothers.

At long last, from the latest batch of urine samples that had been sent off to the laboratories, came back the exciting news that both females were pregnant. The first one to give birth was

Nandi. This, our first gorilla birth, was a never-to-be-forgotten occasion. Apart from the importance of the birth itself, gorillas have only been bred since the 1960s and only forty-seven of them have been reared successfully. We hoped that there were going to be no complications because it was Nandi's first baby. With the aid of a closed-circuit television we had installed in the den, a twenty-four-hour watch was possible and thanks to this we noticed that Nandi was starting her labour at eight o'clock one night. Operation Gorilla came into force at once.

Over the months, as Nandi and N'Pongo had grown more and more rotund, we had been making our preparations to try to cover all eventualities. We could not assume that both gorillas were going to be good mothers, nor could we assume that the births were going to be easy and normal; so everything, from the possibility of having to do a Caesarean section to taking the babies away and hand-rearing them, had to be taken into consideration and planned for.

The most likely event was that we would have to remove Nandi's infant and hand-rear it. This being so, a room in the Manor was prepared as a nursery. It had a built-in airing cupboard, wash basin and cupboard space, and in this room were installed our two Oxygenair baby incubators and, for use when the babies grew older, large wickerwork clothes' baskets to act as sleeping quarters and a playpen. The nursery was heated by a thermostatically controlled radiator and kept at between 70° and 75° F. As well as this, we installed a washing-machine for nappies and a tumbler clothes dryer. In addition, of course, we had to lay in a stock of oddments ranging from baby oil, baby lotion and nappies, to feeding-bottles, thermometers and plastic pants. In spite of the fact that the outlay had been considerable, we hoped we would not have to use any of it.

By the time Nandi started to strain at eight o'clock that

fateful night, we felt we had taken every precaution that was humanly possible. Now it was up to Nandi and we could only watch and be ready to help, should it be necessary.

It was a nerve-racking time. From the moment we noticed the first straining until the moment Nandi had the baby in her arms, took nine hours and twenty-four minutes – an unprecedented length of time according to the observations we had of gorilla births in other zoo collections. The baby was what is known as a vertex presentation – that is to say it was born face downwards instead of face upwards – and, as such, it inevitably produced an unnaturally prolonged labour. There was one point (when Nandi had already beaten the record for the longest labour so far observed) when we seriously and reluctantly started thinking in terms of a Caesarean section, but we eventually decided against it, as Nandi, although in pain and restive, was in good physical condition. We decided to wait, for a Caesarean section is not an operation you undertake unless you have to. Luckily Nandi gave birth before reaching the time limit we had set.

From the commencement of labour until the moment of birth, every move that Nandi made was recorded; a total of 260 observations, which make up one of the most comprehensive scientific coverages of a gorilla birth ever made. Nandi cleaned up the baby very well and then ate the placenta and membranes. She held the infant close to her body and with great tenderness, so we had high hopes that all was going to be well. But then we came up against the usual stumbling block. Nandi had no idea that the baby should feed. Four hours after birth, the baby, a male, tried to suckle, but was pulled off the nipple by Nandi. The maximum recorded time that a baby gorilla had been left with its mother before being removed for hand-rearing was thirty-two hours, but our baby was so strong and so eager to feed that we left him with Nandi for forty hours. Still she would not let the infant suckle. Reluctantly we loaded the capture-dart gun, tranquillized Nandi and removed the baby. This was taken up to the nursery (beautifully decorated with cut-out pictures of Walt Disney characters on the walls and ceiling, so that the babies' eyes would have something to focus on) and installed him in the incubator. The baby's first few feeds, which he took greedily, consisted of glucose and water; after that he was started on dextrose and rapidly gained weight. We christened him Assumbo after an area in the Cameroons, which is the most westerly part of Africa in which Lowland Gorillas are found. He proved to be an exceptionally good baby.

Three months later, it was N'Pongo's turn. Unfortunately, she gave no preliminary signs that she was going to commence labour and, as we had had several dates recorded as possible birth dates, we were taken by surprise. The first we knew of it was at eight o'clock in the morning, when our Curator of Mammals, Quentin Bloxam, came on duty and found N'Pongo sitting on her shelf, totally ignoring her baby, which was lying on the floor, waving its arms about and whimpering. N'Pongo had eaten the placenta, cleaned up the baby and then, feeling that that was the extent of her obligations to the future of the gorilla race, had placed it on the floor and left it to its own devices. Quentin opened the slide leading into the outside area and N'Pongo walked past the squealing infant without even a glance and went outside. It was obvious that, as far as she was concerned, it was now up to us. Quentin rescued the yelling baby and it joined Assumbo in the next-door incubator. It proved to be a male as well, so we christened it Mamfe, again after a place in the Cameroons which I had used as a base camp on my collecting trips in West Africa.

The two boys grew apace and eventually graduated from incubator to basket and playpen and (when they got too boisterous) to a cage in the Mammal House. Here, with access to sunshine and fresh air, they grew even quicker, beating up their toys and thumping their chests like adult gorillas in an effort to prove to us how powerful and savage they were, a boast belied by their enchanting looks and the humorous glint in their eyes.

They had hardly settled down in their new quarters when the nursery was filled again, for, once more, Nandi and N'Pongo, within a few weeks of each other, had their second infants. Once more, we had unfortunately to take them away. Nandi's second baby was a female, called Zaire, and was the cause of much rejoicing, for in gorilla births in captivity there has been, up to now, a preponderance of males. N'Pongo's second offspring was a male, Tatu, probably the handsomest baby we have yet had and the image of his father. As I write this, Nandi is pregnant for the third time and I have no doubt that N'Pongo will follow suit. If these two births are successful, it will mean that we have had six gorillas in three years, which cannot be considered bad going by any standards, when you remember that the first gorilla birth was recorded in 1956, just under seventeen years ago and that there have only been seventy-four successful births to date. It is to be hoped that we can keep at least a trio of these or subsequent youngsters, to form a potential breeding group for the future, when Jambo and N'Pongo and Nandi are past breeding age. The object of the exercise is to have our breeding groups self-sustaining, so that not only will it be unnecessary to catch gorillas in the wild again, but, from our breeding pool, we will be able to supply other zoos.

Return to the Wild

A good many years ago, when we had just started the Trust, I would try to point out to people the point and purpose of captive breeding. Their inevitable question was 'What have you put back?' as if the whole exercise consisted merely in breeding a few specimens, bundling them into crates, shipping them back to their country of origin and flinging them out into the nearest bit of forest. Nothing could be further from the truth.

The tricky thing about returning captive-bred animals to the wild is that it is a wholly new concept, a wholly new art if you like, and we are learning as we go. To begin with, no two species are alike in their demands, and the wants of each have to be learnt as a vital preliminary. Second, you cannot take an animal which may be the third or fourth generation born in captivity and simply push it back into the wild. Surrounded by food it would in all probability perish, for it would be used to having its fruit or whatever cut up and served in bowls. It would be the same as taking a millionaire of long standing out of the Ritz and making him sleep on a park bench covered with newspapers and forage for his food in dustbins.

A few years ago, we were ready to go ahead with a creature called the Jamaican hutia. This had all the hallmarks of success, but what happened shows how a project which on the surface seems simple and straightforward can develop unsuspected pitfalls if you are unwary.

Hutias are a group of rodents confined to the Caribbean Islands. There are different species in the Bahamas, Cuba and

Jamaica. The Jamaican species, locally called a 'coney', is a browny green animal about the size of a miniature poodle and looks not unlike an enlarged guinea pig. They are the only large indigenous surviving mammal found on the island, although at one time they were abundant and provided a major food source for the original inhabitants as well as for the indigenous Jamaican boa constrictor. However, excessive hunting with modern weapons and destruction of the forests in which they live put them in peril. The Trust received its first hutias in 1972 – two males and a female captured in the John Crow Mountains – through the good offices of a Trust member, and eight more were acquired in 1975. From these came the first captive birth ever recorded, and during the next 10 years 61 litters comprising 95 young were produced. Of these, acting on our principle of never having all your eggs in one basket, 19 were sent on breeding loan to six other collections in four different countries.

Back in 1972, just as our splendid new hutia accommodation was nearing completion, I got a telephone call from Fleur Cowles, one of our trustees. She told me that the Hollywood star, Jimmy Stewart, and his wife Gloria were going to visit her and that she was going to bring them over to Jersey. Always with an eye to the main chance, I asked if Mr Stewart would like to open our new hutia breeding unit to provide some publicity for the Trust. Back came the answer that he would be delighted.

On the appointed day I went down to the airport to meet them. Stewart was unassumingly himself, walking with a slight cowboy slouch, drawling sentences in his lovely husky voice. Gloria was a handsome woman, immaculately groomed as only a wealthy American can be, with immense charm but a slight glitter in her eyes, which told me she could easily resemble one of Mr Wodehouse's famous aunts if things did not turn out to her satisfaction. She was the sort of spirited person to whom maîtres d'hotel give instant allegiance and servility, in case worse than their wildest nightmares should ensue. As we waited outside the airport for John to bring the car round, talking about this and that, James Stewart suddenly disappeared. One minute he was there tall, gangling, a gentle smile on his face – the next he had softly and silently vanished like a puff of smoke. One would have thought it impossible for such a big man (in every sense of the word) to eclipse himself so deftly without anyone noticing.

'Where is Jimmy?' Gloria asked suddenly and accusingly, as if we were concealing him from her. We all looked around vacantly.

'Perhaps he has gone to the comfort station,' I said, using an American euphemism I adore.

'He did that on the plane,' said Gloria. 'Where on earth is he?'

Having eliminated the comfort station as a possible hiding place, I could not think for the life of me where he could have gone. Gloria's increasing agitation infected me with a sense of unease. Had he been kidnapped? I could see the world headlines in the illiterate press: 'James Stewart snatched at hutia party – famous actor becomes as extinct as the animals he went to visit.' This was not the sort of publicity I was seeking for the Trust.

At that moment, John rolled up in the car. 'Shall I go and tell Mr. Stewart the car's here?' he asked.

'Where is he?' everyone asked in unison.

'He's out there on the tarmac looking at a plane,' said John.

'Go and get him, please,' said Gloria. 'He can't keep his hands off planes.'

'How did he get out there?' I asked, for airport security is very tight in Jersey.

'Can you imagine anyone stopping him, seeing who he is?' asked John.

Presently, the truant loped back into our midst.

'Er . . . kinda nice little plane out there,' he explained. 'Yeah, sorta little job, very neat. Kinda cosy, you know. Neat. Hadn't seen one before.'

'Get into the car, Jimmy,' said Gloria, 'you're holding everyone up.'

'Yeah, yeah,' said Jimmy, either unrepentant or not listening. 'I'm glad I saw that. Kinda neat.'

After we had lunched he opened our hutia nursery with great charm, saying that he had always liked Hoot Ears ever since he first met them, which was about five minutes ago. This ordeal over, we took them out to dinner at a friend's house.

Over drinks in the conservatory and the excellent meal that followed it, Jimmy seemed preoccupied. I think he was suffering from jetlag, which has a stultifying effect on anyone. The meal over, we repaired to the drawing room where Jimmy carefully lowered his gangling shape into the bosom of an enormous sofa. His eyes wandered vaguely round the room and suddenly focused on something that interested him.

'Gee, it's a piana,' he said, his eyes fixed longingly on the baby grand that crouched in the corner.

'Jimmy, no,' said Gloria Stewart, warningly.

'Yes sir, a piana,' said Jimmy, with the delight of one making the discovery of the century, 'a kinda little baby piana.'

'Jimmy, you're not to,' said Gloria.

'A little toon . . .' said Stewart musingly, starting to unravel his length from the sofa, a fanatical gleam in his eye, 'a toon – what's that toon I like?'

'Please Jimmy, don't play the piano,' said Gloria desperately.

'Oh, I know . . . "Ragtime Cowboy Joe" . . .' said Jimmy approaching the instrument. 'Yes siree, "Ragtime Cowboy Joe".'

'Jimmy, I beseech you,' said Gloria, her voice breaking.

'Yes, a kinda nice, swinging toon, that.' Jimmy seated himself on the piano stool. He lifted the lid and the baby grand grinned at him like a crocodile

'Now – er – let's see – er, how did it go,' said Jimmy, plonking his long fingers on the keys. We were immediately apprised of two facts. The first was that Jimmy Stewart was tone deaf and the other that he could not play the piano. In addition, he had forgotten all the lyrics except the basic one of the title. In all the years I had watched his impeccable performances on the screen, I had never seen him do anything like this. He played all the wrong notes and sang out of tune, trying to make the two match. In his husky, croaking voice he sang the title of the song over and over again, going back to the beginning when he thought he had missed something out. It was like watching an armless man try to swim the English Channel and yet it was excruciatingly funny, but you did not dare laugh as he was taking such pride in his performance. In the end, he exterminated 'Ragtime Cowboy Joe' to his satisfaction and then turned to us, happy in his achievement.

'Would anyone like to hear some other toons?' he enquired generously. I was tempted to ask for the 'Star Spangled Banner', but it was not to be.

'Jimmy, we must go,' said Gloria.

And go they did.

To have been given a performance like this by the great James Stewart was an honour, but I was sure his wife did not agree.

When the numbers of Hoot Ears (as christened by Jimmy Stewart) we had bred were sufficiently high, we started thinking in terms of reintroduction. Our then Research Assistant, William Oliver, went out to Jamaica to fix up all the preliminaries, which included the selection of a suitable site (a place that seemed satisfactory from the hutias' point of view, particularly freedom from hunting pressure) and the involvement of Hope Zoo in Kingston in the venture. A total of forty-four of our Jersey-bred hutias were sent out in 1985–6, and settled in their family groups in specially built cages at the Hope Zoo. Meanwhile, an extensive vegetation survey was done on the chosen site to make sure that the hutias would lack for nothing in terms of foodstuffs. Then they were transferred to the release site, each family group into a temporary enclosure surrounding a specially constructed, semi-artificial rock warren or 'coney' hole. After a week or two, when the animals seemed to be used to their new situation, the fence was removed and the progress of each group was monitored for up to three months.

Early reports were most encouraging. Only three disappeared during this initial monitoring period, but the rest of them rapidly became self-sufficient and remained in good condition. Our hopes were high that the reintroduction was going to be a great success. However, when the site was reinvestigated later in the year only eight hutias could be located. These animals, which included two conceived and born on the site, were all in excellent condition. However, no others were found during a six-week search. In the following year only two animals were found, one a Jersey-bred specimen and the other thought to be wild born. Both were in good condition, but the whereabouts of the rest of the specimens was, and remains, a mystery. The animals that had been released had, early on, adapted to the wild excellently and behaved as normal wild hutias do. This site seemed eminently suitable with a plentiful food supply and freedom from hunting pressure. We had to conclude, therefore, that the disappearance was due to illness or to predation by feral dogs and cats. However, we haven't given up hope – literally – because we are now working with the Hope Zoo to establish a sufficiently large breeding colony there from which a second reintroduction, with the help of students from the University of the West Indies, will be attempted.

All the frustrations involved in releasing animals to the wild are more than made up for when you join forces with people and meet with success, as in the case of the golden lion tamarins. These enchanting creatures, smallest of the primates, along with their close relatives, the marmosets, live in the coastal rainforest of Brazil. Unfortunately, this special rainforest has been ruthlessly and thoughtlessly destroyed and all that is left are pockets of trees, some not even connected with one another, so that the animals of each of these pockets are isolated and cannot renew their species' genetic resources by mixing and mating with others of their kind, even if they are only a few miles away. At one time, the Atlantic coastal rainforest covered an area of 135,000 square miles. Now less than five per cent remains and this is being steadily whittled down by axe, fire and bulldozer. As this forest is stripped, it not only drives to extinction – or its brink – the tamarins, but the myriad other creatures and plants that go to make up this extraordinary ecosystem. When you fell a tropical tree you are doing the equivalent of destroying a huge city, because of the thousands of creatures that live in, on and around it.

The golden lion tamarin is probably one of the most beautiful of all mammals. A little bigger than a newly born kitten, it has incredibly long 'artistic' fingers and its long fur looks, quite literally, as if it is spun gold. This amazing glittering pelt stands away from its face in a sort of semi-recumbent mane which gives it a lion-like look. Like all the marmosets and tamarins, their movements are incredibly quick and sometimes they move with such speed it is impossible to follow the movement with your eye. They are omnivorous, the bulk of their food being fruit and insects, but they will eat tree frogs with relish and will even (it has recently been discovered) go into hollow trees in the daytime to hunt for roosting bats to add to their diet. Their vocalizations are very bird-like as they communicate in a series of trills, sharp squeaks and chatterings.

In addition to the destruction of the forest, these beautiful little animals had been popular with the pet trade and for bio-medical research, so by the late sixties and early seventies it was apparent that the species was in serious danger. It was estimated then that no more than 150 individuals were still living in the fragmented forest blocks which remained. In 1972 a conference was held, during which the plight of these animals was discussed and an attempt made to assess both wild and captive populations. It was obviously of the greatest importance that self-sustaining captive populations were established while, at the same time, trying to address the problem in the wild.

Between 1972 and 1980 very few zoos had golden lions and these were mostly American. These zoos carefully expanded their small populations, and the result was spectacular. The captive population sprang from 153 to 330 – about double the wild population – within five years. Fifty to sixty golden lions were being born every year and so there was now a sufficiently large and stable population to start thinking about putting some captive-bred specimens back into the wild. The success of this project was due to the formation of a consortium of zoos for the management of this species.

In 1978 we received our first pair of golden lions and also joined the consortium. The arrival of our golden lions caused quite a sensation. It is one thing to see a painting or colour photograph of a creature, quite another to see the animal in the flesh. These tiny primates, glittering like doubloons, raced about their cage at such speed they looked like ingots being thrown about. As they whisked about exploring their new domain, they kept up a chorus of chirrups, squeaks and chitters as if each were a miniature tour guide telling the other where it was and what to look at.

Finally, when they had settled down, they became the centre of attraction in our marmoset range for they were by far the most striking and attractive of this enchanting group of primates. Finally came the day when the female successfully gave birth to twins (the normal complement), two minuscule little gold nuggets which could each easily have fitted into a small coffee cup. At first, clinging to the dense fur of their parents and matching it so beautifully, they were extraordinarily difficult to see, for their little faces were smaller than a fifty-pence piece. As they grew older they grew bolder and would leave the security of their parent's body to explore the cage on their own, though always ready to fly back to the security of the parent's fur at any imagined danger. To see them in the sunshine chasing butterflies unwary enough to drift through the wire mesh was an entrancing sight. Not only was it an incredible, dainty ballet as they twisted and turned, leapt and scuttled after the pirouetting insects, but as the light caught them their coats sparkled in myriad colours from sandstone red to the colour of the palest wedding ring. For some reason my suggestion that the babies be christened Fort and Knox respectively met with such antagonism from all quarters that, outnumbered, I was forced to relinquish the idea. Meanwhile the plans for release into the wild of captive-bred lions were moving ahead. Naturally, a plan of this magnitude had to be approached with great caution and attention to detail. An ecological survey had to be done to assess the wild population of golden lions and, this done, to locate an area of forest uninhabited by a wild population but suitable for the release of the captive-bred specimens.

Meanwhile, fifteen animals from five US zoos were chosen and sent to the Rio Primate Centre for training. An animal which is perhaps the third generation born in captivity is used to set mealtimes and never has to go out and search for its food. Most important of all in the cushioned world of captivity, there are no predators in the shape of snakes and hawks, and even *Homo sapiens* is considered an obliging gift-giving friend. So the animals have to be introduced slowly to the stern realities of life in the forest if they are to survive. At one point it was discovered that they were alarmed and daunted by tree branches which bent. In the well-conducted zoos they came from the branches were rigidly nailed into place, so a branch which gave under your weight was an alarming experience until you learnt how to cope with it. They had to learn how to incorporate into their diets wild fruit they had never seen before and here it was discovered, fascinatingly enough, that the younger animals were quicker at learning this and were showing the older ones what to do.

The initial releases got off to a slow start, but as the animals and the people in charge of the project learnt more and more they were finally successful. One photograph shows a captive-bred specimen eating a frog, an item never included in her diet in Washington, and proof that the animals had settled down in their environment. The next phase involved releasing captive-bred animals with wild ones, and it was a great day when twins were produced by a female born in captivity but who had mated with a male born in the wild. By this time we had bred over twenty-five golden lions in Jersey and so were able to take part in the venture by donating five of our animals. These were released as a family group in a patch of forest with no wild tamarins present, and we're very proud to say that our group was the first in the project to produce offspring from parents which had both been born and raised in captivity. This is proof, if proof were needed, that if all the various disciplines involved work in harmony towards a common goal, captive breeding can and does work, and with it we should be able to pull back innumerable species from the brink of extinction.

I always remember having a delightful picnic lunch with Roger Payne and his family on my second visit to America. It is Roger, of course, who has done so much wonderful whale research and is responsible for those mournfully beautiful whale songs to which one listens enraptured, longing to know what these huge and extraordinary animals are saying to each other. However, during the course of the picnic, Roger asked me what the Trust was all about and I endeavoured to explain our aims and objectives.

Finally, Roger said, 'I think I see what you mean – you're breeding them to put back there, providing there is a there to put them back into.' Thus, in one pithy sentence, he highlighted one of captive breeding's great problems: call it the 'There Syndrome' for want of a better description.

The stark reminder by Roger Payne that an intact 'wild' was necessary for returning captive-bred animals 'to the wild' did not dent Gerry's conviction that breeding endangered species was a valid way to contribute to conservation. Apparently, HRH Princess Anne agreed with him, in spite of the gaffe Gerry thought he made on her first visit to Jersey Zoo. A few years later she again visited Jersey Zoo, this time to mark the double birthday of the zoo and the trust in 1984. There was much to celebrate, not least the formal opening of the 'International Training Centre' (now called Durrell Conservation Academy), which was so near and dear to his heart.

The Princess and the Zoo

By now, the early seventies, our breeding successes with rare animals were excellent, and the list of species in our care had grown considerably. This was mostly the result of my own collecting expeditions, but also of purchasing animals from other zoos or even dealers. At that time the commercial trade in rare animals was not illegal, as it is today, and purchase was often the only way to obtain specimens to set up a breeding group. I felt that a good home at the Jersey Zoo, where the animals would prosper and reproduce, was infinitely preferable to their languishing in dealers' shops or potty little menageries. (Today, of course, we and most other reputable zoos exchange or lend rare animals, with no money changing hands.) We still suffered from that chronic disease, lack of funds, but we were moving forward and our reputation was gradually increasing so that people outside the zoo world were beginning to understand what our motives were and not only to applaud our successes but to be generous in their contributions to our work.

It was at this time, just as I was taking off for my little house in the south of France to earn my living by writing a book, that I learnt that the island was going to be honoured by a visit from HRH Princess Anne. At everyone's insistence, I phoned up the powers-that-be who organize such events and asked innocently if they intended bringing the princess to the manor house to meet the animals. I was only enquiring, I said, because I had intended to take off for France but would, of course, delay my departure if Her Royal Highness intended to grace us with her presence. The powers were shocked. Show the princess the zoo? Never! Her schedule was far too tight. Besides, they had other much more stimulating treats for her to enjoy, like the new sewage works (I think it was) for example. Slightly miffed that we were considered of secondary interest to a sewage works, I reported back and our Council said that this was ridiculous. I must phone up again. So I did and said I hoped they were quite sure, as I was going to France and there I intended to remain until I had finished my book. No, came the reply. The princess's interests lay in sewage rather than the salvation of obscure forms of animal life. So I went to France.

I was just getting into my stride in Chapter Two when I got a frantic phone call from Jersey. The princess had asked to see the zoo. Would I please be present? No, I said, I would not. I had been told she would not visit the zoo. I had come to France and there I intended to remain, writing for my bread and butter. I had, of course, every intention of returning, but I felt piqued at their inefficiency and intended to let them stew in their own juice for a bit. There were more phone calls. Bribery, blackmail, flattery and cajolery had no effect. Finally, when it seemed that everyone was going to commit suicide en masse, I said I would condescend to return. Down in the south of France, I could hear the sigh of relief emanating from Jersey.

I had never been involved in such a visit before. My only contact with royalty had been peripheral, waving a small paper Union Jack on the outskirts of a crowd of some hundred thousand on an occasion in London in my youth. I had no idea of the complexity of it, the intensive searches by detectives of every nook and cranny (I asked if they wanted to search the gorillas, but they refused), everyone with stopwatches timing each step of the way. They had allotted twenty-five minutes for me to show the princess 700 animals spread out over twenty-odd acres and explain the functions of the Trust. I felt it would not do my peace of mind any good to enquire how much time they had allotted to the new sewage works.

It was obvious that the visit would have to be taken at a canter rather than a slow, civilized trot, and so it was essential to try to choose the animals in which the princess would be most interested and, moreover, to have them bunched together. The imminent approach of royalty has an odd effect on one, I discovered. What was I going to say to her? All of a sudden our achievements and our aspirations seemed as interesting as a vicar's sermon. The whole thing seemed a great mistake. I wished I was back in France, but I was stuck with it. Waiting for the car to arrive, I felt like someone going on stage for the first time, hands like windmill sails, feet like Thames barges filled with glue, and a vacancy of mind achieved only by having a thorough lobotomy. The moment she left the car and I bowed over her hand, all my whimsies were washed away. I was taking around a beautiful, elegant, highly intelligent woman who asked unexpected questions, who was interested. I wished the retinue of powers-that-be would go away as they shuffled and twittered nervously behind us and, more fervently, I wished the press would go away as they crouched, clicking like a field of mentally defective crickets in front of us. I think this was the combination that was my undoing, that made me commit the gaffe of all gaffes.

We were approaching a line of cages and in one of them, at that time, we had a magnificent male mandrill, whose name was Frisky. He was – and it is a term you can use only for a mandrill – in full bloom. The bridge of his nose, the nose itself and the lips were scarlet as any anointment by lipstick. On either side of his nose were bright, cornflower blue welts. His face, with these decorations, framed in gingery-green fur and a white beard, looked like some fierce Juju mask from an ancient tribe, whose culinary activities included gently turning their neighbours into pot roasts.

However, if Frisky's front end was impressive, as he grunted and showed his teeth at you, when he swung round he displayed a posterior which almost defied description. Thinly haired in greenish and white hair, he looked as though he had sat down on a newly painted and violently patriotic lavatory seat. The outer rim of his posterior was cornflower blue (as were his genitals) and the inner rim was a virulent sunset scarlet. I had noticed that the women I had taken around before had been more impressed by Frisky's rear elevation than the front and I had worked out a silly routine, which I now – idiotically – employed. As we approached the cage, Frisky grunted and then swung around to display his sunset rear.

'Wonderful animal, ma'am,' I said to the princess. 'Wouldn't you like to have a behind like that?'

Behind me, I could hear an insuck of breath and a few despairing squeals, as from dying field mice, which emanated from the entourage. I realized, with deep gloom, that I had said the wrong thing. The princess examined Frisky's anatomy closely.

'No,' she said, decisively, 'I don't think I would.'

We walked on.

After she had left, I had several large drinks to steady myself and then faced up to the fact that I had – still sticking to the animal motif – made a sow's ear out of a silk purse. I had intended to ask the princess if she would become our patron, but what chance now? What princess in her right mind would consider this when the leading figure in the organization had asked her if she would not consider exchanging her own adequate anatomy for that of a mandrill? One could not apologize, the deed was done.

Some weeks later, prodded by everybody, I wrote and asked the princess if she would become our patron. To my incredulity and delight she replied that she would. I am not sure how much he had to do with it, but I took Frisky a packet of Smarties – whose virulent colours so closely resembled his own – as a thank-you gift.

The final two pieces in this compilation are arguably the most important, each containing oft-quoted statements by Gerald Durrell. The first is the scientific rationale for nature conservation. Written more than fifty years ago, it is one of the first clarion calls for protecting wild areas and their fauna and flora. Although Gerry rarely used the term himself, he was talking about biodiversity: the great variety of ecosystems on Planet Earth and the animal and plant species that dwell in them and make them tick. He explains its infinite value to our own species and the peril the planet faces with its loss. His words are more relevant today than ever. The second piece succinctly encapsulates the first, but carries on with the spiritual rationale for nature conservation in an evocative prose poem.

Extinct and Vanishing Animals

*When man continues to destroy nature, he saws off the very branch on
which he sits since the rational protection of nature is at the
same time the protection of mankind.*

On the book shelves that line my office there are two squat, fat,
red books that glower at me continuously. They are the first
things that catch my eye in the morning and the last things that
catch my eye as I close the office door at night. They act as a
constant reminder. These are the Red Data Books produced by
the International Union for the Conservation of Nature. One
deals with mammals, the other with birds, and they list the
mammals and birds in the world today that are faced with
extinction – in most cases directly or indirectly through the
interference of mankind. As yet there are only these two volumes, but there are more to come, and they will make a
depressing line when they eventually arrive, for there is a further one on reptiles and amphibians, another on fishes, and yet
another on trees and plants and shrubs.

I was once interviewed by a reporter from some newspaper
or other, who said:

'Tell me, Mr Durrell, how many species of animals are actually endangered?'

I went to the bookshelf, I took down the two fat, red volumes, and I plonked them in his lap.

'I'm not sure,' I said. 'I haven't had the courage to count
them.'

He glanced down at the two volumes and then looked up at me with real horror on his face.

'Good God!' he said. 'You don't mean to say that all these are threatened?'

'Oh, those are only half of them,' I explained. 'Those only deal with the birds and the mammals.'

He was visibly shaken by this, because even today the majority of people do not realise the extent to which we are destroying the world we live in. We are like a set of idiot children, let loose with poison, saw, sickle, shotgun, and rifle, in a complex and beautiful garden that we are slowly but surely turning into a barren and infertile desert. It is quite possible that in the last few weeks or so, one mammal, one bird, one reptile, and one plant or tree, have become extinct. I hope not but I know for certain that in the same time one mammal, bird, reptile, and plant or tree, have been driven just that much nearer to oblivion.

The world is as delicate and as complicated as a spider's web, and like a spider's web, if you touch one thread, you send shudders running through all the other threads that make up the web. But we're not just touching the web, we're tearing great holes in it; we're waging a sort of biological war on the world around us. We are felling forests quite unnecessarily and creating dust bowls, and thereby even altering the climate. We are clogging our rivers with industrial filth, and we are now polluting the sea and the air.

When you start talking about conservation, people immediately leap to the conclusion that, as you are an ardent animal lover, what you mean is that you just want to protect the fluffy koala bear or something similar. But conservation doesn't mean this at all. Conservation means preserving the life of the whole world, be it trees or plants, be it even man himself. It is to be remembered that some tribes have been exterminated very successfully in the last few hundred years and that others are being harried to extinction. By our thoughtlessness, our greed and our stupidity we will have created, within the next fifty years or perhaps even less, a biological situation whereby we will find it difficult to live in the world at all. We are breeding like rats and this population explosion must be halted in some way. All religious factions, all political factions, the governments of the world, must face facts, for if we persist in ignoring them then, breeding like rats, we will have to die like them also.

Now, though my primary concern is with the conservation of animal life, I am fully aware that you must also conserve the places in which they live, for you can exterminate an animal just as successfully by destroying its environment as with gun or trap or poison. When asked, as I frequently am, why I should concern myself so deeply, I reply that I think the reason is that I have been a very lucky man and throughout my life the world has given me the most enormous pleasure. I feel indebted for it, and I would like to try and do something to repay the debt. People always look at you in a rather embarrassed sort of way when you talk like this, as though you had said something obscene, but I only wish that more people felt that they owed the world a debt and were prepared to do something about it.

Among the numerous letters I get every day there are always those from people who ask me about conservation. They ask whether it is really necessary. Well, as I have just explained, I think it is; I think it is one of the most necessary things in a world full of unnecessary activities, and conservationists are not just making a fuss about nothing. Then I get letters from people who have never, apparently, used their eyes in looking at the world around them. The only thing they understand is figures, because actual figures on paper mean something to them. To this type of person I give figures. And for this purpose the North American continent provides two very good examples of the wastefulness of man.

North America, when it was first discovered by the Europeans, contained two species of creature which were the largest conglomerations of animals that man has known on earth. One of these was the North American buffalo. At first it was killed in order to provide meat. Then it was killed as a deliberate act of policy, in order to try to starve the Native American to death, for it was one of the commodities that he could not do without. The buffalo meant everything to him – even the bones and the hide were of importance to his existence. The much-lauded 'Buffalo Bill' Cody once killed two hundred and fifty buffalo in one day. Passengers travelling in trains through buffalo country had to close the windows for the stench of rotting carcasses because by that time buffaloes were being killed merely for their tongues which were considered a delicacy, and the bodies were left where they fell. Mercifully, the buffalo was saved just in time, but even now we have only a minute remnant of the millions of animals that used to thunder magnificently over the North American prairies.

The second species was the Passenger pigeon, and it was probably the most numerous species of bird that has ever been or ever will be in existence in the world. Flocks of them estimated at two billion used to darken the skies. The weight of their numbers perching in trees could break off quite large branches. It was impossible, everyone thought, that the Passenger pigeon (so delicious to eat and so plentiful) could ever be exterminated. And so they killed and killed; they shot the parent birds, they robbed the nests of the eggs and young. In 1869, seven and a half million birds were captured in one spot.

In 1879 a billion birds were captured in the state of Michigan. This was because it was 'impossible' to exterminate the Passenger pigeon. It was too numerous. It bred too well.

The last Passenger pigeon in the world died in the Cincinnati zoo in 1914 . . .

Man is clever enough to obliterate a species but he has not, as yet, found a way of re-creating one that he has destroyed. This fact, however, doesn't seem to worry the majority of people. There are even some so-called zoological pundits who say that this is a natural part of evolution and that the animal would have become extinct anyway, with or without our help. I couldn't disagree more violently. To say that it is part of natural evolution is nonsense. It is just begging the question. It is like a man owning a blood bank and saying to somebody who is bleeding to death: 'Oh we've got plenty of blood, old boy, but we can't give you a transfusion because it's in the scheme of things that you should die now.'

'Ah, but,' people say, 'that's what happened in the old days; it doesn't happen now. You've got reserves and so forth where the animals are safe. We don't do that sort of thing nowadays.' To people who believe this I can only quote a few more up-to-date figures to make the picture a little clearer. Every year they 'harvest'– as they call it – between sixty and seventy thousand whales. Although scientists have warned that this exploitation will very shortly make several species of whale extinct and will probably put an end to the whaling industry once and for all, they still continue to do it. It seems that the motto of the whaling industry is: 'Get rich today, and to hell with tomorrow.'

There are many different ways in which an animal can be exterminated and not all of them are simply killing for the sake of clothing or food or because they are considered to be pests. The various species of rhinoceros that were found in the east have been hunted until their numbers are at such a low level that now most of them are only represented by a couple of hundred animals at the most, and the reason for this is the quite stupid belief that the horn, powdered and taken, would act as an aphrodisiac, making the old men virile and attractive to young girls – and this in one of the many parts of the world that is so heavily overpopulated that a contraceptive would be more appropriate than an aphrodisiac. Having exterminated practically all the rhinos that were found in India, Sumatra, and Java, they have now turned their attention to the African and, I presume, these will be the next on the list to go down the slippery slopes to extinction.

Let us take the case of the Pacific walrus. When the Inuit used them simply as a source of food they utilised the massive tusks to do the most intricate and beautiful carvings. When Inuit art was 'discovered' by the intelligentsia it became all the rage, and so now the walrus is hunted for its tusks alone and, in fact, is being massacred to such an extent that it will probably shortly be extinct. It is already on the danger list.

Let us take another example of the clever thinking of sections of mankind, who have no knowledge of nature. In Africa it was decided that the wild-living animals were hosts for the organism that causes Sleeping Sickness. So a brilliant decision was taken: in order to protect man and coddle his scrawny cattle (which were – and are – rapidly eating up all the undergrowth and turning vast areas into dust bowls) it was decided to kill off all the wild animals. Half a million zebras, antelopes, gazelles, and other animals were destroyed before it was discovered that all the smaller animals could also carry the disease. The extermination of this vast quantity of beautiful wildlife had therefore been utterly useless.

People get worked up when a couple of thousand human

beings per annum are killed on the roads of Great Britain. That is a tragedy of course – but few people know that two million wild birds are killed per annum on the roads, or that in a small area studied by a Danish scientist the number of road deaths were: hares 3,014; hedgehogs 5,377; rats 11,557; various small mammals 27,834; birds 111,728; amphibians 32,820. These, of course, are only figures for the main roads; if you included the figures for the side roads they would probably be trebled. Now, if human beings were knocked down to that extent in any country in the world there would be such a shriek of protest, such an outcry, such a lamentation, that any government in power would be forced to make us give up the motor car as a means of locomotion and go back to the horse and cart. Not that I'm against the motor car per se, but you do see my point?

What is not generally realised is that if you look at a map of the world and see the areas that have been set aside for reserves for wildlife, it makes an infinitesimal pinprick on the map; the rest is all a gigantic reserve for mankind. And even if you have reserves, you have to have adequate resources to run them properly. Most governments are reluctant to pay out money for the preservation of habitat or fauna (unless there is some great public outcry and the animal in question happens to be particularly attractive), and many others do not have the necessary resources.

Do not think, for one moment, that I am painting too gloomy a picture. I could go on reeling out these breathtaking statistics and it would only go to prove that, of all the creatures that have ever lived on earth – whether the giant carnivorous reptiles of past ages or the creatures of today – the most rapacious, thoughtless, and blood-thirsty predator is man. And, moreover, he is doing himself irreparable harm by behaving like this. It is suicide; an extraordinary form of Roman death whereby, in bleeding the world white, you kill yourself.

We can, perhaps, forgive our ancestors their sins, saying, 'They knew not what they did,' but can we – in this technological age that we are so proud of – forgive ourselves for the things we are doing now, and continue to do in the face of opposition from all thinking people whether they be professional zoologists, ecologists, conservationists, or merely thoughtful and perceptive human beings? We have now landed on the moon, and that is a remarkable achievement. But have we gone there just for a few extra minerals, or is the moon to be a great white stepping stone to other planets, some of which may well harbour their own forms of life? If we are going to go from planet to planet creating the same mess that we have made on our own, then I think it would be a happier thing if the vast sums of money that were spent on space projects were used to try and cure some of the ills that we have inflicted on earth.

The problem of trying to preserve wildlife and habitat (both for our own sakes and for the sake of those who will follow us) is a gigantic one, and complicated indeed. There are a great number of countries in the world which, as I have said, give 'paper protection' only to an animal, because the government concerned will pass a law to protect a certain creature but will not allow sufficient funds available so that the reserves – even when they are created – are properly controlled and adequately run. In one country I visited I asked what reserves they had, and the man in charge of fauna conservation unrolled an enormous wall map which was covered with green blotches. These, he explained to me proudly, were all reserves.

Had they, I inquired in a casual sort of way, been investigated by zoologists or ecologists or biologists, who could tell whether they were, in fact, the most important areas that could be turned into reserves? Oh no, he said, they couldn't afford to do that. Then had investigations been done on these areas, those great green blobs, to find out whether there were, in fact, any animals in them and whether they were suitable as reserves? No, he said, that hadn't been done either, because they lacked the resources to employ the proper people . . . Were they, I asked, patrolled in any way? No, he said, they hadn't got the money to have guards or wardens . . . So there was this very fine map, covered in green blotches, which meant nothing at all.

This, as I say, is a common complaint in nearly every country in the world that has any sort of regulation for the preservation of habitat and fauna, and, of course, there are many other countries which have no legislation at all. This is widely recognized by conservationists and they are doing their best to put the matter right, but it is a slow process. Before we reach the day when the conservation and protection laws are implemented I'm afraid many species will have vanished for ever from the face of the earth.

In most literate countries there are a vast number of clubs, study groups, and societies, be they for the ornithologist or for the general naturalist, all trying desperately to do what they can to save their local fauna. On a wider scale you have organisations like the International Union for the Conservation of Nature, the World Wildlife Fund, and so on. In many instances, I'm delighted to say, they have been successful. They have saved, for example, an enormous area of Spain, the Guadalquivir of 625,000 acres. In Australia they rediscovered the Noisy Scrub Bird which had been thought to be extinct. Unfortunately its nesting ground happened to be on a site which had been scheduled for a large new township. Fifteen years ago this would have been considered a most inconsiderate thing for the bird to do and no doubt the township would have been built there, but today the whole thing was replanned in order that the Noisy Scrub Bird should be left in peace and have its own reserve. These are the bright spots; but there are too few bright spots and too many dark ones.

Now, while pressing for conservation of animals in the wild state, there is something else we can do, and that is precisely why I formed my Trust. Many species have been saved from extinction by being taken into zoological gardens or parks and bred under controlled conditions. This, of course, is a last ditch stand, but at least it prevents the species from being completely wiped out and one hopes that, at some future date, the conservation rules and regulations will be enforced in their country of origin so that, having saved a nucleus breeding stock, it will be possible to release them once again to their native area. The list of animals that have been saved in this way is a long and impressive one. There is, for example, the Père David's deer which became extinct in China during the Boxer rebellion. Fortunately, the then Duke of Bedford collected together all the Père David's deer he could find in the zoological gardens of Europe and released them on his estate at Woburn where they flourished and bred. Now the herd has reached large enough proportions for pairs of this rare deer to be sent to zoos all round the world, and recently they have even been sent back to their place of origin in China. If the Chinese succeed in breeding them – and there is no reason why they shouldn't – they could set aside an area, a reserve, properly patrolled and run, and once more there would be Père David's deer in their natural habitat. The Hawaiian goose is another example. This beautiful bird was almost extinct but, due to the sensible attitude of the Hawaiian authorities and the far-sightedness of Peter Scott, it has been saved from certain extinction. There is quite a list of creatures that have been helped in this way, such as the European bison, the North American buffalo, the Saiga antelope, Przewalski's wild horse, and so on, but there are many more that desperately need such help.

The Trust I have created is trying to fulfil exactly this function. I realise that it is merely a cog in the complicated picture of protection today, but we hope that it is an important cog in its own way. It has not been created just to keep the animals in captivity. I look upon it as a reservoir – a kind of stationary ark – in which I hope that we can continue to keep and breed some of the species most urgently in need of protection. Then, at some future date, we can reintroduce them into their original homes. I would gladly see the Trust dissolved tomorrow were there no more need for it. But at present I'm afraid there is a very great need and I wish I could see similar Trusts springing up all over the world.

I have devoted my life to this work and I have spent a considerable amount of my own money on it, so therefore I do not feel embarrassed at asking you, dear reader, if you will help. If you have read this book and enjoyed it; if any of my books have given you pleasure; may I point out that they could never have been written if it had not been for the wildlife of the world? Yet all over the world many of these same animals are in a desperate plight and unless they are helped they will vanish. I am trying to do what I can, but I cannot do it without your assistance, so would you please join the Trust, and try and get as many as possible of your friends – or, for that matter, enemies – to join as well?

Finally, may I just say that if you don't want to join my Trust, then I beg of you to join some sort of organisation that is doing something to try and halt the rape of the world. Do anything you can: worry your local MP – or whatever the equivalent is in your country – into a nervous decline should you think there is going to be some unnecessary, ill-planned encroachment on a valuable piece of habitat, or that some plant or bird or animal is in danger and not receiving sufficient protection. Write indignant letters. It is only by lifting up your voices that the powers that be will be forced to listen. It is worked on the principle that if you shout loud enough and long enough, somebody is bound to hear.

Remember that the animals and plants have no MP they can write to; they can't perform sit-down strikes or, indeed, strikes of any sort; they have nobody to speak for them except us, the human beings who share the world with them but do not own it.

Her Royal Highness The Princess Royal buried a time capsule below the Princess Royal Pavilion at Jersey Zoo on the trust's twenty-fifth anniversary in 1988. It contains the following letter by Gerald Durrell.

Time Capsule

To Whom it May Concern
Many of us, though not all, recognise the following things:

1. All political and religious differences that at present slow us down, entangle and strangle progress in the world will have to be solved in a civilised manner
2. All other life forms have as much right to exist as we have and that indeed without the bulk of them we would perish
3. Overpopulation is a menace that must be addressed by all countries; if it is allowed to continue it is a Gadarene syndrome which will cause nothing but doom
4. Ecosystems are intricate and vulnerable; once misused, disfigured or greedily exploited they will vanish to our detriment. Used wisely they provide boundless treasure. Used unwisely they create misery, starvation and death to the human race and to a myriad other lifeforms
5. It is stupid to destroy things such as the rainforests, especially because in these great webs of life may be embedded secrets of incalculable value to the human race
6. The world to us is what the Garden of Eden was supposed to be to Adam and Eve. Adam and Eve were banished, but we are banishing ourselves from Eden.

The difference is that Adam and Eve had somewhere else to go. We have nowhere else to go.

We hope that by the time you read this we will have at least partially curtailed our reckless greed and stupidity. If we have not, at least some of us have tried . . .

We hope that there will be fireflies and glow-worms at night to guide you and butterflies in hedges and forests to greet you.

We hope that your dawns will have an orchestra of birdsong and that the sound of their wings and the opalescence of their colouring will dazzle you.

We hope that there will still be the extraordinary varieties of creatures sharing the land of the planet with you to enchant you and enrich your lives as they have done for us.

We hope that you will be grateful for having been born into such a magical world.

Gerald Durrell

Message from Durrell Wildlife Conservation Trust

Gerald Durrell's childhood efforts at zoo-keeping, which so bemused his long-suffering family, were the beginning of a lifelong dedication to saving endangered species and preserving the rich diversity of life on our planet.

This crusade to save species from extinction did not end with his death in 1995. His work goes on through the untiring efforts of Durrell Wildlife Conservation Trust, the charity he established more than sixty years ago. In those six decades the trust has ensured the recovery of dozens of species, begun rewilding gravely threatened habitats in ten different countries, trained thousands of conservation practitioners from around the world and inspired people with a love of nature.

Over the years many readers of Gerald Durrell's books have been so motivated by his experiences and vision that they have wanted to continue the story for themselves by supporting the work of his trust. We hope that you will feel the same. Through his books and life, Gerald Durrell set us all a challenge. 'Animals are the great voteless and voiceless majority,' he wrote, 'who can only survive with our help.'

In 2025 Gerald Durrell would have been one hundred years old. Please celebrate the centenary of this great man by joining us in our efforts to save species from extinction.

For further information or to make a donation, please visit our website:
www.durrell.org
or email us at:
supportercare@durrell.org

With thanks in advance for your interest and support,
TEAM DURRELL

Acknowledgements

Gerald Durrell was a prolific author best known for his auto-biographical accounts, but he also wrote short stories, novels, poems and film scripts, some published, some not. After much groundwork and discussion, however, I made the difficult decision not to embrace the full variety of his work in one book. I felt that the book celebrating Gerry's centenary should lead the reader through his extraordinary life as it unfolded on its mission to save species from extinction.

The process of reading through practically the entire *oeuvre* of Gerald Durrell and choosing what to include and what to omit was a monumental task, begun last year by the intrepid literary agent for the estate of Gerald Durrell. This is Norah Perkins, of Curtis Brown, who spent many hours poring over books and manuscripts and made numerous visits to the Gerald Durrell Archive at Jersey Zoo and the Jersey Archive in St Helier. Norah's assistant, Lily Kovacs, skilfully managed the logistics and never complained about typing up Gerry's voluminous words from handwritten scraps of paper and obscure magazines. Norah and I were greatly aided by the sharp eyes and memory of Catherine Kirby, the archivist for the estate, who ferreted out with ease the many pieces we dimly remembered. Thanks also go to staff at the Jersey Archive, who patiently retrieved documents deposited there some years ago.

In the latter stages of putting the book together, Norah spent countless hours on video calls with me in my home in Corfu. For your time, patience and good humour, Norah, I thank you!

Acknowledgements

For the editorial stage I would like to extend my gratitude to Greg Clowes, commissioning editor at Penguin, and Sam Wells, copy-editor, both of whom patiently bore with my questions as they tidied the manuscript.

I have interspersed some of the chapters with short, and I hope helpful, remarks, but Gerry speaks for himself throughout the book. I hope you will take delight in Gerry's inimitable view of the natural world, which shows just how precious it is and so worth fighting for.

Lee Durrell
Corfu, August 2024

Sources

'How to Give Birth to an Autobiography.'

Part One

A Silver Spoon in His Mouth', 'Mother's Delusions of Grandeur', 'Like Being Born for the First Time' and 'Surrounded by Miracles' are from Gerald Durrell's unfinished memoirs in his archive. 'The Strawberry-Pink Villa', 'Tribute to My Mother', 'The World in a Wall' and 'A Treasure of Spiders' are from *My Family and Other Animals*, 1956. 'An Omnipotent, Benign and Humorous Greek God' is a previously uncollected piece from the Gerald Durrell Archive. 'Island Education' was broadcast on the BBC World Service, 1952.

Part Two

'New and Rediscovered Animals' was first published as an introduction to *The Lost Ark: New and Rediscovered Animals of the 20th Century* by Karl Shuker, 1993. 'Rainforests' was first published as a foreword to *The Enchanted Canopy* by Andrew Mitchell, 1986. 'Ground Nut Chop' was first published in *Tsunami* magazine, Jersey, 30 January 1992. 'The Hunt for the Hairy Frog' was broadcast for BBC Radio, 1951–2. 'Brow-leaf Toads' is from *The Bafut Beagles*, 1954. 'A Charm All of Its Own' was first published in *Geographical* magazine, 1957. 'The Magical Creek Lands' is from *Encounters with Animals*, 1958. 'The Kitten' and 'Vanished Peoples of Patagonia' are from *The Whispering Land*, 1961. 'Jabirus and Jaguars' was first published in the *Sunday Times*, 1989. 'Operation Takahe' is from *Two in the Bush*, 1966. 'Australian Friends' and 'Great Barrier Reef' are from Gerry's unpublished notes for a book on Australia. 'Dragons and Giants from the Sea' was first published in the *Sunday Telegraph*. 'The Enchanted World' is from *Golden Bats and Pink Pigeons*, 1977. 'Miraculous Madagascar' was first published in the *Daily Telegraph*, c. 1986. 'Whiffling through Its Tulgey Wood' is from *The Aye-Aye and I*, 1992.

Part Three
The first publications of 'The Abominable Snowman' (1952) and 'Little Brown Jobs' (1960s) are unknown. 'A Tortoise Called Melville' was first published in the *Sunday Telegraph*, 1988. 'The Art of Birdwatching' was first published as an introduction to a new Penguin edition of Viscount Grey's *Charm of Birds*, c. 1981. 'Dogs in My Life' was first published in *Apex* magazine, 1989. 'An Explorer in Lilliput' was first published as the introduction to an edition of *The Insect World of J. Henri Fabre*, 1991. 'Panda Politics' was first published in the *Sunday Times*, 1992.

Part Four
'First Job' is from *Fillets of Plaice*, 1971. 'Student Keeper' was first published as the introduction to a book on Whipsnade Zoo, 1990. 'A Zoo in My Luggage' is from *A Zoo in My Luggage*, 1960. 'A Zoo that is More than a Zoo' and 'A Successful Marriage' are from *The Stationary Ark*, 1976. 'A Zoo of My Own' was first published in *Weekend*, early 1960s. 'Letter to J. F. Lipscomb' is a previously uncollected piece from the Gerald Durrell Archive. 'Return to the Wild' and 'The Princess and the Zoo' are from *The Ark's Anniversary*, 1990. 'Extinct and Vanishing Animals' is from *Catch Me a Colobus*, 1972.

List of Illustrations

1. Gerald as a child. © Estate of Gerald Durrell, photographer unknown.
2. The bungalow in India where Gerald was born. From a booklet published by Tata Iron and Steel Co in 1926. Photographer unknown.
3. Gerald gazes at Mouse Island, Corfu. © Estate of Gerald Durrell, photographer unknown.
4. The Durrell family in Corfu. © Estate of Gerald Durrell, photographer unknown.
5. Gerald with his beloved dog, Roger. © Estate of Gerald Durrell, photographer unknown.
6. Louisa Durrell. © Estate of Gerald Durrell, photographer unknown.
7. Lawrence and Nancy Durrell. © Estate of Gerald Durrell, photographer unknown.
8. Gerald's tutor and friend, Theodore Stephanides. © Estate of Gerald Durrell, photographer unknown.
9. Gerald greets Theodore on set of *This is Your Life*. Possible press photo from the Thames Television show *This is Your Life*, photographer unknown.
10. First page of *Man of Animals*. © Lee Durrell / Estate of Gerald Durrell.
11. Cover of first typescript of *My Family and Other Animals*. © Lee Durrell / Estate of Gerald Durrell.
12. Leslie, Louisa and Gerald Durrell. © Estate of Gerald Durrell, photographer unknown.
13. Gerald feeding a giraffe. © Estate of Gerald Durrell, photographer unknown.
14. Gerald on first expedition to Cameroon. © Estate of Gerald Durrell, photographer unknown.
15. Gerald with angwantibo. Photographer unknown.
16. Gerald with hairy frog. © Estate of Gerald Durrell, photographer unknown.
17. Gerald with young giant anteater. © Estate of Gerald Durrell, photographer unknown.
18. Flyer for Gerald's lecture at the Royal Festival Hall. © Lee Durrell / Estate of Gerald Durrell.

19. Gerald, his wife Jacquie and baby chimp Chumley. © Estate of Gerald Durrell, photographer unknown.
20. Gerald with tapir. First published in *La Nacion*, 1959. Photographer unknown.
21. Poster for Jersey Zoo. © Lee Durrell / Estate of Gerald Durrell.
22. Gerald with Trumpy. © Durrell Wildlife Conservation Trust, photographer unknown.
23. Whiskers. © Durrell Wildlife Conservation Trust, photographer unknown.
24. Louisa playing ball with Chumley. © Loomis Dean / The LIFE Picture Collection / Shutterstock.
25. Jacquie, Gerald, Christopher Parsons and Keeper plan the expedition to Australia. Photographer unknown.
26. Gerald with a kaka. Photographer unknown.
27. Gerald with dead wedge-tailed eagles. Photographer unknown.
28. Gerald with N'Pongo. © Durrell Wildlife Conservation Trust, photographer unknown.
29. Jambo. © Phillip Coffey / Durrell Wildlife Conservation Trust.
30. Assumbo. © Phillip Coffey / Durrell Wildlife Conservation Trust.
31. Gerald with fiancé Lee and ring-tailed lemurs. © Phillip Coffey / Durrell Wildlife Conservation Trust.
32. Lee and Gerald with fossil egg of the elephant bird. © John Hartley.
33. Gerald with aye-aye. © Quentin Bloxam / Durrell Wildlife Conservation Trust.
34. Gerald and HRH Princess Anne opening the International Training Centre. © *Jersey Evening Post*, photographer unknown.
35. Gerald and Lee with students at the International Training Centre. © Phillip Coffey / Durrell Wildlife Conservation Trust.
36. Golden lion tamarins. © Phillip Coffey / Durrell Wildlife Conservation Trust.
37. Mission stone at the entrance to Jersey Zoo. © Lee Durrell.
38. Statue of Gerald Durrell by John Doubleday. © Colin Stevenson.
39. Gerald feeding a Mauritius kestrel. © John Hartley / Durrell Wildlife Conservation Trust.